LATIN AMERICAN JOURNALISM

COMMUNICATION
TEXTBOOK SERIES
Jennings Bryant—Editor

Journalism
Maxwell McCombs—Advisor

LATIN AMERICAN JOURNALISM

Michael B. Salwen
Bruce Garrison
University of Miami

LEA LAWRENCE ERLBAUM ASSOCIATES, PUBLISHERS
1991   Hillsdale, New Jersey   Hove and London

Lawrence Erlbaum Associates, Inc., Publishers
365 Broadway
Hillsdale, New Jersey 07642

Library of Congress Cataloging-in-Publication Data

Salwen, Michael Brian, 1954-   .
    Latin American journalism / Michael B. Salwen, Bruce Garrison.
        p.   cm.
    Includes bibliographical references and index.
    ISBN 0-8058-0767-5 (c). — ISBN 0-8058-0768-3 (p)
    1. Journalism—Latin America.   2. Press—Latin America.
I. Garrison, Bruce, 1950-   . II. Title.
PN4930.S24   1991
079'.8--dc20   91-13964
                                                            CIP

Printed in the United States of America
10 9 8 7 6 5 4 3 2 1

Contents

Preface

Only a few years ago, not many people would have predicted the political, economic, and social changes in the Soviet Union and in Eastern Europe. But when democratic reform came to these nations, the world took notice. Since the beginning of the 1980s, Latin America experienced similar changes. Far less attention has been taken of the changes in Latin America than those in the Soviet Union and Eastern Europe. It seems that only when some natural or man-made disaster takes place south of the border, does the world take notice of events in that region. And then only for a short while.

This book was written as a tribute to earlier books about the development and status of Latin American news organizations and the practice of journalism in Latin America and the Caribbean. Two of those books had a major impact on the authors. Marvin Alisky's *Latin American Media: Guidance and Censorship* (1981) and Robert N. Pierce's *Keeping the Flame* (1979) each have served readers well since they were issued more than a decade ago. But events have changed drastically in the region since then, demanding a re-examination of the practice of journalism. Events changed rapidly even as we completed this book.

From our perhaps narrow vantage point in Miami, we kept track of events, interviewing numerous media professionals from the region as they passed through our town. We hope to provide a fair and complete overview of the subject through our travel to Latin America, through interviews with key publishers and broadcasters, and through our review of the ever-growing base of literature on Latin American mass communication. Our intent was to offer an overview of Latin American news media through analysis and interpretation of the major topics that concerned Latin American news media at the beginning of the 1990s.

ACKNOWLEDGMENTS

To write a book such as this one, the assistance of many busy people is required. Thus, there are dozens of Latin American scholars and professional journalists who are owed much by the authors for their interest and generous gifts of time leading toward production of this work. Our sincere thanks go to them.

Special thanks to:

Dean Edward Pfister for his assistance in providing the support of the School of Communication at the University of Miami, Coral Gables.

Dr. Gonzalo Soruco, assistant professor of advertising and public relations, University of Miami, for reviewing the entire manuscript, for various translations, for his research on licensing and *colégio* laws, and for his excellent advice.

Dr. John C. Merrill, professor of journalism, Louisiana State University, for his thorough comments on professionalism and for his review of the manuscript. It was Dr. Merrill's encouragement that led to this project in the first place. His invitation to work on the second edition of *Global Journalism* led to this project.

Dr. Julio Munoz, assistant executive director of the Inter American Press Association, for assisting in research for the book and for his background information. He was also helpful in providing the resources of IAPA to the authors. We deeply appreciate his assistance in critiquing much of the manuscript during editing stages of production.

William Williamson, executive director of the Inter American Press Association, for assisting in research by making the resources of the IAPA available to the authors.

Dr. Robert Buckman, assistant professor at the University of Southwestern Louisiana, Lafayette, for his comments on portions of the manuscript.

Joel Solomon, Latin America specialist for the Committee to Protect Journalists, New York, for his research assistance in determining the extent of recent serious violence against journalists in Latin America.

Pieter Van Bennekom, senior vice president for International Operations, United Press International, for his extensive discussion and background information on UPI's operations in Latin America. We also appreciate his willingness to review and critique portions of the manuscript.

Dr. Erwin Thomas, assistant professor at Norfolk State University, and M. Kent Sidel, associate professor at the University of South Carolina, for their comments on the chapter dealing with the New World Information Order.

Dr. Mary Gardner, professor at Michigan State University, for comments on the section dealing with *colégio* laws.

Dr. Frances Matera, assistant professor at Arizona State University, for comments on the section dealing with advertising and public relations.

Susan Clark, administrative assistant in Corporate Communications, Associated Press, New York, for her background research on AP's operations in Latin America.

Linda Hossie, Latin America correspondent in Mexico City for *The Globe and Mail* in Toronto, for her comments on the Mexican news media. We also thank A. Roy Megarry, publisher, for his assistance and support.

Manuel Jimenez, late publisher of *La Nacion*, in San Jose, Costa Rica, for his extensive comments on the news media in Latin America.

Dr. Horacio Aguirre, director, and Alejandro Aguirre, sub-director, *Diario Las Americas*, Miami, for their research travel support and for their background information.

Randy Stano, director of News-Editorial Art, *The Miami Herald*, for providing vital graphics assistance and advice.

Sara Maria Castany, editor of *Cosmopolitan en Espanol*, Miami, for her comments in reviewing portions of the manuscript.

Brothers Goar and Abel Mestre, for their extensive discussion and background information on the early days of broadcasting in Latin America, particularly in pre-Castro Cuba.

Knight-Ridder/Tribune News Graphics Network for permission to reprint its graphic on the Chamorro family of Nicaragua.

Telemundo and Univision television networks for providing background materials for the chapter on broadcasting.

The Miami Herald and Knight-Ridder, Inc., for permitting access to its computerized library database, "Vu-Text." This courtesy made research easier and it certainly was a major time-saver.

The Miami Herald for its permission to use graphics in this book.

Dr. Kyu Ho Youm, Arizona State University, and Prof. Alan Prince, for their comments and review of portions of the manuscript.

Sherrie Lisitski, graduate assistant and masters student in the School of Communication at the University of Miami, for her tireless library research assistance.

Joanne C. Acosta, broadcast journalism student at the University of Miami, for her editorial assistance.

And Okhee Lee-Salwen, Zoya Garrison, and Mishi for giving up family time for the work on this project.

Michael B. Salwen
Bruce Garrison
Coral Gables, Florida

Foreword

John C. Merrill
Emeritus Professor of Journalism,
University of Missouri

As media-related and journalism books become more common and more numerous, they have a way of shedding the superficiality of a broad global concern and tending toward localization and specificity. It is not strange, therefore, that here we have another regional treatment of mass media dimensions and issues. *Latin American Journalism*, coming on a crest of a wave of regional and national media literature, has arrived at a very propitious time. Students of the press south of the United States should find on the following pages timely, and given prognosticative, insights.

Latin America's own *glasnost* and *perestroika* developed all through the 1980s, but were under-reported in the United States where all eyes were on the Soviet Union and the Eastern Bloc countries. Significant changes were shaking the media worlds of Latin America, and it is our good fortune that Professors Salwen and Garrison were awake to these changes, were recording them, and on the following pages have shared many of them with us.

As one who has endeavored to deal with the media globally, I know the tremendous difficulty in such a pan-national and multinational journalistic treatment such as the authors have here provided. Latin America is a large and complex area, with varied traditions and cultures—and this book goes a long way in explaining this in the context of mass communication. The task that the authors set for themselves has been formidable, but they have met the challenge well as they provide a broad spectrum of information and analysis of Latin American journalism.

One interesting and significant point that the discerning reader will find all through this book is that Latin American journalism is quite different from the journalism of most of the so-called Third (or developing) World. And one reason for this is the literary and analytical power brought by Latin American journalists to their craft. Probably this cultivated, articulate, sophisticated, and humanistic journalistic strain has come to Latin America from the Hispanic culture that dominates its journalism and literature.

At any rate, Latin American journalism has a certain European cast about it and a certain level of intricacy that belies the general physical poverty in which it exists. The diversity and general high quality of media and their content throughout the region is really quite remarkable. And the authors, in this wide-ranging book, document this situation in country after country.

It is also noteworthy and laudable that on the following pages the reader finds such a wealth and variety of information. The book shines a light, however short its focus, on many problems and issues related to Latin American journalism. For instance, we get a look at media history, government and press relationships, the practice of journalism and growth of professionalization, the issues surrounding the New World Information and Communication Order (NWICO), the news agencies and flow of news in the region, and the social impact of the media. And, in addition, considerable emphasis is given to the economic problems that tend to confound journalism education, ethical development, and press freedom.

In addition to the problems and issues just mentioned, the authors have also managed to provide descriptive data about newspapers, magazines and books, broadcasting, public relations, and advertising. This in itself is quite an accomplishment!

In spite of their upbeat and optimistic forecast for Latin American journalism, the authors are realistic. Although they see the media picture in Latin America improving, they make it quite clear that such a picture is far from utopian. Serious weaknesses exist, many of them stemming from a corrupt political tradition and from a weak and tottering economic situation. And the old *troika* of power, politics, and pragmatism that has dominated Latin America at least since its European beginnings, is still potent in its journalism.

This book is a welcome addition to the literature of global journalism, and should be greeted enthusiastically by all those who teach and study in the area of international communication—and even by those who recognize the power of journalism in the shaping of relations and images among nations.

A New Decade

As the 1990s began, Latin American and Caribbean nations witnessed a frenzy of free national elections. Fifteen nations in the region held national elections during 1989 and 11 more scheduled or promised national elections for 1990 (see Fig. 1.1). In Chile, long regarded as one of the region's last bastions of 1970s-style military dictatorships, Christian Democrat Patricio Aylwin received 55% of the vote among three major candidates during a December 1989 election. He was sworn in 3 months later in front of 80,000 Chileans in the national stadium that served as a center for torture and detention during the rule of the former dictatorship.

When Aylwin took office, Cuba and Haiti were the only nations in the region without elected leaders. Cuban leader Fidel Castro was promising to stand firm against the democratic changes sweeping the region and much of the Communist world. Haiti's military dictator was forced to flee the island the day before Aylwin was sworn into power. Haiti's new provisional government, the fifth since former President Jean-Claude Duvalier fled the country 4 years earlier, promised free elections within a matter of months.

Latin America's electoral binge began during the early 1980s and intensified as the decade drew to a close. It was clear that a new decade was dawning in the region and all political institutions would be affected by these changes, including the press. For instance, 2 months after taking office, President Aylwin of Chile signed a bill repealing some 30 regulations that the previous military government used to silence the press. Although much of the world focused its attention on the rapid pace of democratic reforms in the Soviet Union and Eastern Europe during the late 1980s and early 1990s, Latin America's political reforms were largely overlooked.

FIG. 1.1.   From the *Miami Herald* graphics department.

During the 1970s, press–government relations in Latin America seemed de-ceptively simple. Although simple "press theories" such as that of the libertarian-authoritarian continuum have received a number of criticisms over the years, press–government relationships in Latin American nations during the 1970s ap-peared to fit the "authoritarian" model surprisingly well. Most of the region's governments in the major nations were military dictatorships. The leaders of these autocratic governments were simplistically portrayed as "bad guys," whereas members of the press were portrayed as "good guys." The press was often justly portrayed as a primary source of defiant opposition to dictatorial governments. In many cases, news organizations were also collaborators with the dictatorial governments. Latin American press scholar Robert N. Pierce (1979) described the press–government situation in these brutal governments:

> Throughout their two centuries of independence, most citizens in the area have not acquired the psychological rhythm of other Western nations which develops from regular elections every four or six years, resulting in a peaceful transfer of power. . . . Thus the most typical time for a Latin American government to change hands is when the public or one of its subdivisions, such as the military, can no longer endure it. The boiling point is brought about not only by the government's actions but also by the way its critics—particularly those in the mass media—perceive those actions. (p. 211)

Given the large number of military dictatorships in the region during the 1970s, and their often crude and blatant methods for dealing with a critical press, scholars of Latin American journalism concentrated their attention on the relationship between governments and the press (Alisky, 1981; Pierce, 1979). This seemed a logical approach. In his classic work on Latin American news media, Alisky (1981) was able to identify only three nations in the region that truly permitted press freedom—Venezuela, Colombia, and Costa Rica. The rest had governments that either practiced censorship of the news media or strong "media guidance." With the trend toward increased democratization during the 1980s, the role of the press in Latin American societies became more complex than the relations between governments and the press. Other institutions, including the church and the business sector, and their relations with the press had to be considered.

Latin America's transition to democracy does not mean that government-press relations will no longer be an issue. It remains an issue in all democratic societies. But democracy means that differences between governments and their news media will probably be settled in public within legally prescribed frameworks. Forces from the political right as well as left within Latin America that once exercised the political power to silence a critical press are not happy with the transition.

A recent case of a Uruguayan police inspector attacked in the editorial pages of a leading newspaper illustrates how the old autocratic forces feel threatened by the new democracy. The daily *La República* accused the police inspector in the capital of Montevideo of engaging in smuggling. In an earlier era this would have been considered *lèse majesté,* an attack on a sovereign, and the police would have closed down the newspaper and tossed the editor in jail. In this case, however, the inspector—a member of the old school of honor and tradition—challenged the editor to a duel. The editor, Federico Fassano, agreed to the duel. The government sanctioned the duel, despite a public outcry. As it was, the duel was cancelled on a technicality because the inspector violated the "code" of dueling prohibiting public statements about the squabble (Anon., February 23, 1990).

Democracy will not solve all the problems faced by Latin America's press. Costa

Rica is an established Latin American democracy with fully functioning press freedom and an independent media. In a recent article on the media in Costa Rica,
Andrew Reding (1986) indicated that the independent press poses a problem for
Costa Rica's peace and stability. In Costa Rica, as in much of Latin America,
the large mainstream media are often comprised of members from conservative
families espousing traditional, conservative views that are often out of line with
public opinion. In theory, this should not be a problem if the "marketplace of
ideas" is large enough to permit a wide array of opinions to be disseminated.
In practice, however, financial constraints in small nations such as Costa Rica
often limit the size of the mass media marketplace.

Reding (1986) noted that four of the five privately owned television stations
in Costa Rica are operated by conservative management, while the fifth station
broadcasts sports news. Meanwhile, few Costa Ricans watch the state channel,
primarily devoted to education. During the height of the Nicaraguan conflict between the Sandinista government and the contra rebels, the private stations regularly warned viewers about the *sandinocomunista* threat. The stations often called
on the government to establish an army to deal with foreign threats. Costa Rica
is at peace and does not have a standing army.

THE IMPROVED ATMOSPHERE

Most observers, including the most skeptical, concede that by the end of the 1980s
government–press relations throughout the region were remarkably better than
during the previous decade. Even the Inter American Press Association (IAPA)
concedes vast improvements (Muñoz, personal interview, 1990). As the hemisphere's media "watchdog" association, IAPA comes to the defense of privately
owned media in press–government disputes.

The IAPA, which is comprised largely of media owners and top-level management, adheres to a philosophy of press–government separation. It rails against
every government intervention against the press. It earned its reputation as a
defender of press freedom in the hemisphere, particularly during the 1950s and
1960s when it fiercely fought government-enacted press restrictions by the likes
of Peron in Argentina, Batista (and later Castro) in Cuba, and Trujillo in the
Dominican Republic.

In IAPA's January 1990 *IAPA News* (the organization's monthly newsletter),
it reported the results of a survey of members. The IAPA's members are mostly
management-level journalists and publishers in Latin American nations. The IAPA
conducts such surveys on regular bases and the results reflect the opinions of
media owners in their respective nations. The survey reported on such categories of press restrictions as restraints on newspaper circulation, prerequisites
to the practice of journalism, closure of publications, censorship, and legislative
restrictions.

In striking contrast to previous IAPA surveys a decade earlier, most respondents reported few restrictions in their nations. What few restrictions were reported were "indirect" restrictions on press freedom, such as right-to-reply laws, university degree requirements to practice journalism, and taxes on newsprint and other supplies. The categories representing blatantly repressive measures to restrict the press were noticeably absent of checkmarks. These blatant restrictions include prior censorship of the press, jailing of journalists, and the detention of journalists without due legal process.

Earlier analyses of Latin American journalism took a nation-by-nation approach, devoting chapters or sections to individual countries or groups of countries. Typically, at the conclusion of these chapters or sections, some attempt would be made to find commonalities in Latin American journalism. This is a logical approach that allows for in-depth elaboration of journalistic practices within individual nations. We intentionally avoided this approach, however. Instead, we examined the practice of journalism in Latin America by devoting each chapter to various issues facing the Latin American press. We also devoted chapters to various media (i.e., newspapers, broadcast media, magazines, and so forth) in Latin America. In this way we tried to highlight commonalities among various nations *within* the chapters.

The attempt to examine an entire region is not without difficulties. It is almost a cliché to say that every nation is unique from other nations in some way. In international communication, in particular, some researchers get deeply involved in studying the news media in certain nations. This sort of research is invaluable for an in-depth understanding of media operations within particular nations. This approach, however, lacks generalizations about media operations beyond these nations. Each approach has its strengths and weaknesses. We opted for making broad generalizations about the entire region over in-depth investigations of individual countries.

Admittedly, lumping the Caribbean with the rest of Latin America did pose some difficulties. We chose this route anyway because of geographical proximity and the general tendency to treat all the nations in the Western hemisphere south of the United States as a single region. Some nations in the region, such as English-speaking Belize and Dutch-speaking Suriname, are not part of Latin America. And cultural and linguistic differences among nations in the region might at first blush suggest more differences among nations in the region than commonalities (Hagstrom, 1990). Throughout our examination of Latin American journalism, however, we were impressed by the similarities among nations in the region more than differences.

As an example of cultural similarities among Latin American nations, in chapter 8 on broadcasting we discuss the exploits of Goar Mestre, the "father of Latin American broadcasting." Mestre apparently tapped into some shared cultural values in the region when he successfully established television systems in several Latin American nations during the early days of television. Mestre, a U.S.-

educated Cuban broadcast magnate brought television to Cuba in 1951. He and his brother Abel built CMQ into the largest television system in Latin America.

Goar Mestre fled the island in March 1960 after the Castro government put intense political pressure on his CMQ radio and television networks. Mestre's media holdings were expropriated by the government in September 1960, six months after he fled. After fleeing Cuba, Mestre duplicated his successes in establishing broadcast media organizations elsewhere throughout Latin America. With the financial resources from large U.S. media organizations such as CBS and Time-Life Inc., Mestre established successful television systems in different Latin American nations, ranging from Peru to Venezuela to Argentina by building on what he viewed as shared cultural values in all these nations.

"I don't think that, in general, television differs in Argentina from television in the United States," Mestre told journalism scholar David Manning White (1969) during an interview in Argentina. "People, when they come home from work, basically want to laugh. They want to forget their problems" (p. 25). When we interviewed Mestre (personal interview, May 10, 1990) for this book at his Key Biscayne, Florida, residence 21 years later, he still maintained his view that people all over want the same thing from television.

DOING AWAY WITH STEREOTYPES

One stereotype of Latin America that fortunately is now largely a remnant of the past is that of *caudillo* (strongman) dictatorships, usually from the military sector. Another stereotype is that of the poor nations. Although Latin America still has its share of poverty, and the unequal distribution of wealth continues, there is also a growing middle class.

Latin America's combination of wealthy businessmen and a growing middle class means that conditions exist for a thriving news media. There are private individuals with the resources to create and maintain mass news media, and there is a need and public demand for news media. In this regard, Latin American news media cannot be viewed as similar to the news media in what is globally referred to as the "Third World." For instance, Mexico alone has more new newspapers than all of Africa. And U.S. journalists traveling to Latin America are frequently awed by the technological sophistication of Latin American newspapers and magazines (Salwen, Garrison, & Buckman, 1991).

Latin American nations were among the first in the developing world to adopt television during the 1950s. In most cases, the medium was introduced to the region by private entrepreneurs. For instance, Cuba had an advanced television system that almost covered the entire island with locally produced live programming during the early 1950s (Dizard, 1966). Given this early start in television, it should come as no surprise that some of the largest broadcast networks in the world are located in Latin America. In recent years, Latin American mass media organizations have reversed the tide of the "one-way flow" of information primarily from the industrialized nations to developing nations and have successfully penetrated the U.S. market by exploiting the large Spanish-speaking U.S. market. Some would go so far as to describe the large Latin American media organizations as examples of "reverse media imperialism."

NEW PROBLEMS FOR THE REGION

The 1980s was sometimes optimistically referred to as Latin America's decade of democracy, as military dictatorships throughout the region fell and were replaced by democratically elected governments. Democracy came to the region as a result of the public's dissatisfaction with military dictatorships.

Democracy, however, did not solve all of Latin America's ills. As the 1980s drew to a close, the region's concern turned to economic problems. Some of the larger nations were experiencing triple-digit inflation rates each month. Economic conditions were so harsh that, despite the "democratic miracle," some observers pessimistically referred to the 1980s as Latin America's "lost decade" (Salwen et al., 1991, p. 267).

To deal with public dissatisfaction, many democratically elected Latin American governments took out foreign loans while already deep in debt, kept public salaries high, and subsidized goods and services to satisfy the public and buy time and support for their fledgling democracies. Their efforts to satisfy the public through these means often aggravated the debt problems accrued under former military regimes. As the decade ended, some Latin American governments decided to institute tough and unpopular austerity measures that threatened to lower standards of living and heighten social unrest. These tough measures held the potential for the loss of public support for democratic leaders and, in the worst scenario, the return of dictatorships. Many of the national elections throughout the region during the 1980s focused on economic issues. Only in Nicaragua, where incumbent Sandinista President Daniel Ortega was running against Violeta Chamorro, publisher of the nation's opposition newspaper *La Prensa,* was political ideology an issue.

Although issues dealing with human rights and personal freedoms—including freedom of speech and press—were still on Latin America's political agenda during the 1980s, they were not as important as the region's economic problems. During 1989, a nonpartisan panel commissioned to investigate political conditions in Latin America warned of the possible dire consequences of the region's debt problems:

> The Latin American debt crisis may soon touch off a political crisis. As governments lose credibility and authority, the appeal of extremist solutions is rising and it becomes harder to institute the economic measures needed for recovery and growth.

Latin America may be condemned to a long period of economic hardship and political turbulence, which may force civilian authorities to yield to military rule in some place. (Sciolino, 1989, p. A3)

The 1980s drew to a close with some ominous signs. In February 1989, riots erupted in Venezuela. The riots, which resulted from reduced government subsidies on petroleum and transportation aimed at curbing the nation's $30 billion debt, left more than 300 dead. Three months later in Argentina, with inflation running at over 1,000% per year, mobs broke into food stores taking whatever they could carry. The Argentine riots resulted in 2,000 arrests and at least 11 deaths. At the time of the food riots, Argentina had not made any payments on its $60 billion foreign debt in more than 1 year. In Brazil, "inflation police" vigorously watched prices in stores to ensure that businesses adhered to national price guideline measures. Demonstrations and strikes, spurred by austerity measures, also broke out in Brazil, Bolivia, the Dominican Republic, Guatemala, Uruguay, and elsewhere in the region.

Former Argentine President Raúl Alfonsín (1983–1989), widely hailed as one of Latin America's "new breed" of leaders committed to liberal values, democracy, and human rights, illustrates Latin Americans' widespread disappointment with economic conditions in much of the region (Salwen, Garrison & Buckman, 1991). Despite his liberal values, Alfonsín could not deal with Argentina's economic crisis, and so he was forced to leave his office before his term expired.

Alfonsín was elected president after 7 years of dictatorship. He successfully returned Argentina to democracy. Nevertheless, he was decisively defeated during a 1989 re-election bid by Peronist Party opponent Carlos Menem, who had little political experience at the national level and exhibited little commitment to human rights and democracy. To his credit, as the 1990s began, Menem has continued many of Alfonsín's democratic policies.

Although charges of press censorship existed under both Alfonsín and Menem, they were fewer in number and severity than in the past. During 1989, the Association of Newspaper Editors of Argentina (ADEPA) declared that press freedom existed in Argentina. However, ADEPA went on to denounce incidents of censorship. For instance, it denounced the house arrest of Raul L. D'Altri, editor of *La Arena,* for his refusal to identify an unnamed source. It also denounced a government prohibition against an advertisement by former President Jorge Videla (Anon., February 1990).

The military dictatorship that preceded Alfonsín was perhaps the most brutal in the region. It launched a "dirty little war" against its opponents—real and imagined—that resulted in widespread torture against civilians and at least 8,900 deaths, including almost 100 journalists. Human rights organizations put the estimate much higher. Many of those killed were buried in unmarked graves, or their bodies were dumped by helicopters in the South Atlantic.

Under the Argentine dictatorship, the ever-present dangers of confiscation of equipment and physical violence against journalists sufficed to silence most press criticism. The government enacted security laws prohibiting newspapers from publishing names of *desaparecidos* (the disappeared ones) and the locations of detention centers (de Onis, 1976). Two Buenos Aires newspapers, the English-language *Herald* and *La Opinion,* did not heed the bans. The editor of the *Herald* was forced to flee the nation in 1979. The editor of *La Opinion* was arrested by the police in 1977 and tortured for allegedly supporting left-wing terrorists because he published the names of those who disappeared while in the custody of the government. The arrest and torture of Jacobo Timerman, the editor of *La Opinion,* received worldwide publicity, and eventually the government was forced to exile the Jewish editor to Israel.

Not until Argentina's disastrous military defeat to Great Britain over disputed islands 300 miles off Argentina's southeast coast in 1982 (which the British call the Falkland Islands and the Argentines call the Malvinas Islands), did the dictatorship collapse. The Argentine government's total control over the news media, among the most developed media systems in the region, kept even the most educated segments of the Argentine public uninformed about the possibility of an Argentine victory over the British (Fox, 1984).

Despite Alfonsín's success in returning Argentina to democracy, he left office in disgrace. Hyperinflation, which surpassed 100% a month when he left office, was the cause of his problems. Under pressure, Alfonsín was forced to resign his office in July, 5 months before his term expired. The day he left his offices in the Argentine equivalent of the White House, he was met by a jeering crowd. One local newspaper claimed that demonstrators cast "gross epithets that questioned the honorability of the chief executive's mother" (Golden, 1989b, p. 1).

THE DECLINE OF MILITARY DICTATORSHIPS

Latin America's decade of democracy rings of déjà vu. After World War II, many Latin American nations experimented with democracy. By 1959, only four military governments held power in the region. But the inability of democratic leaders to maintain social stability resulted in a series of military coups during the 1960s. By 1970, military governments were in power throughout Latin America: Argentina, Brazil, Bolivia, El Salvador, Guatemala, Honduras, Panama, Paraguay, and Peru. With occasional exceptions, such as Peru in 1968, the military governments rolled back reforms achieved under democratic leaders (Burns, 1986).

The military leaders who emerged in Latin America during the 1970s usually sided with conservative forces. It would be a mistake, however, to regard Latin America's strongman military leaders as adherents to political ideologies. With some exceptions, they simply sought social stability and continued system maintenance, which they viewed as desirable ends in themselves. Military dictators usually regarded conservative forces as best equipped to achieve these goals. But

Latin America's military leaders were prepared to support almost anyone who could bring stability.

Brazil was such a case. In 1945, the military ousted a conservative government in favor of a liberal reformist government. In 1964, the military ousted the liberal government and replaced it with a conservative government when the liberal government could not maintain stability. The dictatorship that ruled until 1985 was anything but a proponent of *laissez-faire* ideology, favoring what has been called "state-directed capitalism" to make the economy prosper (Dassin, 1982). It eliminated protectionist policies, curbed equitable distribution of wealth, and lured foreign investors with promises of low wages. The military achieved economic stability by instituting repressive measures. During this time, Brazil enjoyed extraordinary economic development, the growth of an urban-industrial labor force, and a leading role in the international marketplace.

Among the industries that Brazil's military leaders targeted for expansion was telecommunications, to be used as a propaganda tool to publicize the military's economic accomplishments. The military helped build TV Globo, a private, commercial enterprise, into the largest Brazilian network, and the fourth largest television network in the world. TV Globo became "the television version of state-directed capitalism" (Guimaraes & Amaral, 1988, p. 127).

With the fall of military dictatorships in the region, the boot-in-the-groin technique of press control lost much of its appeal. Even Paraguay witnessed a coup that ousted long-time dictator Alfredo Stroessner in 1989. The new government immediately instituted press freedom, allowing banned radio stations and newspapers to re-open. In Chile, strongman Gen. Augusto Pinochet reluctantly liberalized his regime somewhat. By 1989, a number of formerly closed publications in Chile re-appeared, including left-wing newspapers such as the Communist Party organ *El Siglo*. By 1990, a democratically elected president took office, although Pinochet did not cede all his power.

In Haiti, the situation looked less optimistic. When Haiti's President-for-Life Jean-Claude Duvalier was forced into exile after a popular uprising in February 1986, there was optimism that the Caribbean island would become a democracy. A failed November 1987 election marked by violence and election fraud squashed any hope of a smooth transition to democracy.

In January 1990, Haitian President Prosper Avril declared a "state of siege," jailing opposition leaders and clamping down on the news media as the nation prepared for an October election. Many former Duvalier backers joined forces with the Avril government while opposition leaders were deported or jailed. A number of outside observers expressed doubts that a fair election could be held in such conditions. By March, Avril was ousted from power during a military coup and replaced by a provisional president.

Panama witnessed a military strongman ousted from power in 1989. Gen. Manuel Antonio Noriega, who was toppled during a December 20 U.S. military invasion, silenced virtually all criticism of his regime at the time of his ouster.

Prior to Noriega's crackdown on the press, the press was highly critical of Noriega's rule and sometimes downright mean, referring to the acne-scarred leader as "Pineapple Face." The Noriega government responded with a law making it illegal to poke fun at people's physical defects in the press.

A free press began to emerge in Panama even while Noriega was in asylum in the Vatican Embassy in Panama City. After Noriega surrendered to U.S. forces and was extradited to Miami to stand trial for drug smuggling, several exiled leaders returned. Among them was the publisher of Panama City's *La Prensa,* Roberto Eisenmann Jr., whose paper was shut down in June 1987 and re-opened again for 5 weeks in January and February 1988 before being closed in a general crackdown against the press. *La Prensa* was founded in 1980 as an opposition newspaper by a group of conservative businessmen and modeled after opposition newspapers with the same name in Nicaragua and Argentina.

Noriega supporters had used brutal methods to silence *La Prensa* before shutting down the paper. These included confiscating files, pouring acid into computers, threatening and intimidating reporters, and even stealing coins from the soda machines (Balmaseda, 1989; Buckman, 1990c). In addition to *La Prensa,* the daily *El Panamá-América,* confiscated and closed since 1968, returned to the newsstands. *La Prensa*'s circulation just after the invasion neared 100,000, and *Panamá-Americá* sold 30,000. The tabloid *Crítica Libre,* part of the *Panama-América* publishing house, sold 50,000 copies a day.

Freedom of the press just after the U.S. invasion consisted largely of denouncing Noriega. This was easy and safe to do with Noriega out of power. In addition, denouncing Noriega was immensely popular and sold papers. Whether the press would criticize the new government of Guillermo Endara, and whether the new government would tolerate criticism, was another matter. For his part, Endara encouraged the press to point out his mistakes. The new government enjoyed a honeymoon period with the press immediately after the invasion, so there was little press criticism of the government anyway. Before the new year began, Panama witnessed the first pro-Noriega paper, *Primera Plana.* The paper was headed by the former director of state-run radio under Noriega (Oppenheimer, 1990a).

Freedom of the press in post-Noriega Panama also included press criticisms against fellow members of the press. Panama's oldest daily, the 137-year-old *La Estrella,* was viewed as sympathetic to Noriega during Noriega's rule and to the dictator Omar Torrijos before him. Just weeks before the invasion, Noriega had nominated *La Estrella* publisher Tomás "Fito" Altamirano Duque as the first Panamanian administrator of the Panama Canal. With Noriega gone, *La Estrella* quickly changed sides and took a position as violently anti-Noriega as any of Panama City's dailies. Because of its close association with Noriega, however, circulation was reported at less than 20,000 after the invasion. *El Siglo,* a leading tabloid, reminded readers that *La Estrella* was once close to Noriega. It published a list of prominent Noriega supporters that included *La Estrella*'s publisher, Tomás "Fito" Altamirano Duque. *La Estrella* responded to this attack by republishing a glowing birthday greeting to Noriega that appeared in *El Siglo* 5 years earlier (Otis, 1990).

One of the last Latin American nations to practice boot-in-the-groin press control methods was the former Dutch colony of Suriname. The nation's military dictatorship that ruled the nation of 400,000 people from 1980 to 1988 practiced strict press censorship and sometimes used brutal methods to control the press (Terrell, 1990). In late 1988, Suriname's voters overwhelmingly rejected the continuation of the military regime. Only three of the 51 persons elected to the National Assembly were from the ruling military government. A 1990 report by the U.S. Department of State on worldwide human rights practices claimed that the Surinamese news media "robustly exercised their right to criticize government policies. Opposing political views faced little or no restriction in gaining a forum, particularly in the print media" (Anon., 1990, February, p. 740).

Latin American governments, more so than their Third World counterparts in Africa and Asia, seem embarrassed by the classical notion of "authoritarian" control over the press. The notion of privately operated, independent mass media is well established in Latin America. Privately run media are the norm in Latin America, even if private media sometimes exist side by side with state-owned media (Fox, 1988b). Some observers have argued that although Latin American societies attach social importance to freedom of the press through privately operated media, along with this freedom comes obligations and duties. For instance, the press in Latin American society is expected to respect authority and engage in careful self-censorship (Wiarda, 1980).

IN THE CHAPTERS AHEAD

The 1990s is an important decade for Latin America. Latin Americans have opted for democracy. By opting for democracy, Latin American governments have also opted for press freedom. Indeed, the concepts of democracy and press freedom are inseparable. Every theory of democracy sees an important role for press freedom in a democratic society. This book examines Latin American media, and news media in particular, during its new era of democracy.

We decided to study the practice of journalism in Latin America by examining both substantive issues and the workings of various media. Each chapter concludes with a "Spotlight" of a brief case analysis and discussion to illustrate points raised in the chapter.

Chapter 2 deals with government–press relations. As is immediately apparent, the boot-in-the-groin method is given short shrift in this chapter. It is mentioned largely for historical perspective. Government restraints on the press described in this chapter are of a much more subtle character. This chapter also discusses the potentially beneficial aspects of government intervention in the press and the often overlooked influence of the press on the government. Chapter 2 concludes with a discussion of the IAPA's activities.

Chapter 3 focuses on the contemporary practice of journalism in Latin America. Although the chapter addresses government–press relations, the focus is on how the press interacts with nongovernmental groups or institutions, such as the business sector and terrorist groups. The chapter concludes with a discussion of Colombian journalists' recent attempts to deal with rampant terrorism aimed against the nation's journalists.

Chapter 4 analyzes the practice of journalism in Latin America from the perspective of the nebulous New World Information and Communication Order (NWICO). The NWICO represents a number of ideas and complaints from developing nations. These ideas and complaints have been expressed over the years in a series of United Nations' resolutions in that organization's Educational, Scientific and Cultural Organization (UNESCO). We wrestled with whether to include this chapter because the raging "debates" between the developing and developed nations over the NWICO during the 1970s have died down and compromise appears to be the general trend today. Many would even argue that the NWICO has become passe. Whatever worldwide changes may be affecting the political characteristics of the NWICO, we treated the NWICO as a guiding perspective for understanding Latin American nations' complaints about "cultural imperialism." To that extent we found the perspective useful. The chapter examines the influence of Western nations, particularly the United States, on Latin American journalism. It also examines Latin America's experiments with new roles for the press in society. Chapter 4 concludes with Guyana's attempts to implement national media policies that reflect the intent of the NWICO.

Chapter 5 examines the role of regional, national, and international news agencies in Latin America. It deals with how media and governments attempt to manage news flow in their regions by dealing with foreign news agencies and by establishing regional and national agencies. Chapter 5 concludes with a case study of the operations of United Press International (UPI), the self-described "General Motors of Latin America."

Chapter 6 discusses the current state of the newspaper industry in Latin America and the role of newspapers in Latin American societies. It also describes the operations of the region's newspaper industry. Finally, the chapter provides an overview of the most influential newspapers in the region. Although this method of presenting the "most prestigious" newspapers in the region has received some criticism because of its arbitrary nature, we felt that this method offers a useful "tour" for readers through the many newspapers in the region. And despite the arbitrary nature of naming the most prestigious newspapers in the region, we were heartened by the wide agreement of what constitutes the most prestigious newspapers in Latin America. Chapter 6 concludes with a discussion on Nicaragua's *La Prensa* and its long-running dispute with the Sandinista government before the election of Violeta Chamorro in 1990.

Chapter 7 examines the magazine and book industries in Latin America. The chapter discusses the leading magazine publishers and the major types of magazines in Latin America. Further, the chapter outlines the leading book publishing countries. Chapter 7 concludes with a case study of the Chilean political commentary magazine, *Análisis*.

Chapter 8 reports on the state of broadcasting in Latin America. Attention is given to the rapid development and growth of broadcasting. The influence of two large television networks, Mexico's Televisa and Brazil's TV Globo, receive substantial attention. Because broadcasting is not primarily a news medium, a good deal of this chapter veers from the focus on journalism. However, as an example of how the commercial broadcast media can contribute to the public's knowledge of political affairs. Chapter 8 concludes with a discussion of how TV Globo, Brazil's leading broadcast network, contributed to the democratization of Brazil during the waning days of its most recent military dictatorship.

Chapter 9 examines the role and influence of advertising and public relations in Latin America. Advertising's development as a uniquely North American practice is discussed. Attention is given to the role of U.S. public relations firms working on behalf of Latin American governments and leaders. Chapter 9 concludes with a discussion about how national governments attempt to manipulate their national and international images by contracting with U.S. public relations agencies.

Chapter 10 summarizes the issues facing contemporary media in Latin America. The chapter also offers an agenda for research directions.

Chapter 2

Press and Government Relations

Latin America has a long history of private ownership of mass media. Most Latin American governments adhere to the concept of an independent press free of governmental restraint. Nevertheless, even democratic Latin American nations intervene in press affairs in ways that might involve subtle controls over the press. It has been claimed that Mexico has practically institutionalized the practice of compromising the news media through offering indirect bribes, putting journalists on government payrolls, maintaining control over newsprint, mandating a portion of airtime from broadcast media, and using the government's considerable control over the economic sector to withhold national advertising from critical media. As the 1990s began, major economic and political changes in Mexico aimed at divesting the government's unprofitable industries promised less government interference in press affairs. As a result of the increased number of terrorism incidents against the press, particularly in Colombia and Peru, these nations have implemented anti-terrorism laws that could conceivably be used by governments to restrict the press. Dangers to journalists from drug-related terrorist organizations and from faltering economies have done more to silence the press in most Latin American nations than the actions of governments.

Relations between governments and the news media are usually spelled out in national constitutions. Latin American nations, like all nations in the world, constitutionally guarantee press freedom. Not surprisingly, many of these nations place caveats on these constitutionally guaranteed freedoms, often within the very sentences and paragraphs that grant these freedoms. A few Latin American nations guarantee press freedom in simple and even sweeping terms. For instance, Article 14 of the Argentine constitution guarantees the right to publish ideas by the press without censorship.

By contrast, a number of complex constitutional guarantees in Latin America put limits on press freedom. For instance, the Ecuadorian Constitution maintains that "insults, calumny and all immoral expressions" are restricted. The Dominican Republic's Constitution states that "all subversive propaganda is prohibited . . . but this shall not limit the right of analysis or criticism of legal principles." Brazil, which has a multi-ethnic society, warns that "prejudice of race or class shall not be tolerated" (Paraschos, 1989).

In most cases, the constitutional guarantees of press freedom are sufficiently ambiguous to allow for numerous interpretations. Table 2.1 presents a list of sections from national constitutions in Latin America that promise press freedom. The most important questions involving press freedom concern the role of the press relative to the government. Should there be total government control and ownership of mass media? Private mass media ownership with governmental regulatory controls? Totally private ownership with no regulation? In the case of Cuba, the constitution directly addresses these questions and asserts that the mass media are the property of the state. In most cases, Latin American nations have opted for private mass media ownership with various degrees of government intervention.

During the 1980s, democratically elected governments have been unambiguous in their commitment—if not practice—to freedom of the press. The boot-in-the-groin military dictatorships and their blatant forms of press control so common in the region a decade earlier, were viewed as an embarrassment and tragedy by the new democracies. This meant that more acceptable government–press policies had to be formulated within legally specified frameworks.

Even within legal frameworks, however, legal traditions exist in Latin America that do not always put the press in a favorable situation relative to government. In the United States, for instance, libel laws have developed under conditions that favor the press. Although U.S. law is based on British tradition, which is not always favorable to the press, libel laws started developing in the United States along a different path more favorable to the press during the early days of the American republic. In the United States, libel laws have developed to a point where elected political officials often have difficulty suing the press for libel because public knowledge about the activities of political officials is considered to be of valid public interest and a cornerstone of a functioning democracy. Therefore, the press is given great leeway in reporting public officials' activities under the so-called "actual malice" rule (Youm, in press-a).

In addition, American courts were more liberal than their British counterparts in extending the "fair report privilege." The privilege under British law permitted the press to report parliamentary and judicial proceedings without fear of libel as long as the information was correct. American courts extended the defense to include some "nongovernmental" proceedings such as political campaign speeches and church board meetings. As a result, it became exceedingly difficult for public officials in the United States to sue the press for libel when the infor-

TABLE 2.1
Grants of Press Freedom in Latin American Constitutions

ARGENTINA

"All inhabitants of the nation enjoy the following rights, in accordance with the laws that regulate their exercise, namely: working in and practicing any lawful industry; of navigating and trading; of petitioning the authorities; of entering, remaining in, travelling through, and leaving Argentine territory; of publishing their ideas through the press without previous censorship . . ." (Article 14).

BOLIVIA

"Every person has the following fundamental rights, in accordance with the laws which regulate their exercise: . . . b) To freely express his ideas and opinions, by any means of dissemination" (Article 7, section b).

COLOMBIA

"The press is free in time of peace, but liable under the law, for attacks on personal honor, the social order, or the public tranquility.

"No newspaper publishing enterprise may, without permission of the government, receive a subsidy from other governments or from foreign companies" (Article 42).

COSTA RICA

"Everyone may communicate his thoughts by word of mouth or in writing and publish them without previous censorship; but they still shall be responsible for abuses committed in the exercise of this right, in such cases and in the manner established by law" (Article 29).

CUBA

"Citizens have freedom of speech and of the press in keeping with the objectives of a socialist society. Material conditions for the exercise of that right are provided by the fact that the press, radio, television, movies and other organs of the mass media are the state or social property and can never be private property. This assures their use as the exclusive service of the working people and in the interest of society" (Article 52).

THE DOMINICAN REPUBLIC

"Everyone may, without prior censorship, freely express his thoughts in writing or by any other means of expression, graphic or oral. Whenever the thought expressed threatens the dignity and morals of persons, the public order, or the good customs of society, penalties prescribed by law shall be imposed.

"All subversive propaganda is prohibited, whether anonymous or by any other means of expression, for the purpose of inciting disobedience of the law, but this shall not limit the right of analysis or criticism of legal principles" (Article 8, section 6).

GUATEMALA

"The expression of thought through any mass medium without censorship or prior restraint is free. This constitutional right cannot be restrained by law or any governmental provision. Whoever enjoying this freedom that shall fail to respect private lives or morals will be held responsible in accordance with the law. Whoever may feel aggrieved has the right to publish his defense, clarifications, and rectifications.

"Those publications which contain denunciations, criticisms, or censure against officials or public employees for actions affected in the performance of their duties do not constitute a crime or misdemeanor" (Article 35).

(Continued)

TABLE 2.1

(Continued)

HAITI

"Journalists shall freely exercise their profession within the framework of the law. Such exercise may not be subject to any authorization or censorship, except in cases of war" (Article 28-1).

"Journalists may not be compelled to reveal their sources. However, it is their duty to verify the authenticity and accuracy of information. It is also their obligation to respect the ethics of their profession" (Article 28-2).

HONDURAS

"Printing shops, radio broadcasting, television stations, and other means of broadcast and dissemination of information, as well as their machinery and equipment, may not be seized or confiscated nor may their work be closed down or interrupted by reason of an offense or misdemeanor relating to the dissemination of thoughts and ideas, without prejudice to the liabilities incurred by these reasons in accordance with the law" (Article 73).

MEXICO

"Freedom of writing and publishing writings on any subject is inviolable. No law or authority may establish censorship, require bonds from authors or printers, or restrict the freedom of printing, which shall be limited only by the respect due to the privacy, morals, and public peace. Under no circumstances may a printing press be sequestered as the instrument of the offense" (Article 7).

NICARAGUA

"Nicaraguans have the right to freely express their beliefs in public or private, individually or collectively, in oral, written, or any other form" (Article 30).

PARAGUAY

"Journalism in any of its forms may be practiced freely. Press organs lacking responsible direction shall not be permitted, nor shall the publication of immoral subject matter be permitted" (Article 73).

PERU

"Every person has the right . . . . (T)o the freedoms of information, opinion, expression, and diffusion of thought through words, writings, or visual means, by any mass medium, without previous authorization, censure, or impediment of any kind of subject to sanctions under the law.

"Crimes committed through books, the press, and other mass media are detailed in the Criminal Code and are adjudicated in ordinary courts.

"Also considered a crime is any measure that suspends or shuts down any organ of expression or hinders its free circulation" (Article 2, section 4).

VENEZUELA

"Everyone has the right to express his thoughts by the spoken word or in writing and to make use of any means of dissemination, without prior censorship; but statements which contain offenses are subject to punishment according to law.

"Anonymity is permitted. Likewise, propaganda for war, that which offends public morals, and that for the purpose of inciting disobedience of the laws shall not be permitted, but this shall not repress analysis or criticism of legal principles" (Article 66).

Source: Blaustein (1989).

mation pertained to the officials' duties, even in cases where the information was incorrect (Youm, in press-a).

In the English-speaking Caribbean, the colonial heritage has passed down old British libel laws (White, 1976). Oliver Clarke (personal interview, January 13, 1990), the chairman of the board of the Jamaica *Daily Gleaner*, claimed that as a result of Jamaica's tradition with British libel laws, which do not distinguish between political officials and private figures, *The Gleaner* faces about 35 libel suits at any given time. Almost all the suits come from politicians. The *Gleaner*, Clarke said, eventually wins almost all the cases. But that isn't the point, he added. Clarke claimed the suits are not launched by politicians to be won but to intimidate the paper into self-censorship.

Although a large newspaper such as the *Gleaner* may be able to withstand these "irritants," as Clarke described the suits, many smaller newspapers cannot. One scholar of Caribbean press law asserted that Caribbean nations' stringent libel laws result in excessive self-censorship:

> People in this (Caribbean) region have been taught by history to be wary of verbal commitments to greater responsibility, and collective and individual integrity in government. Although the press, mainly but not solely out of fear of actions for defamation never did much to bring this to popular awareness, whatever little was done, was often greeted by unfavorable governmental reaction. Governments only tolerate constructive criticism and criticism of the government is not constructive by the very fact of being criticism of the government. (White, 1976, p. 31)

This lack of legal distinction between public officials and private figures is illustrated in the former British colony Guyana. The *Catholic Standard*, an independent weekly newspaper critical of the government, was hit by four libel suits in a 2-week period during 1982. One was brought by then president Forbes Burnham. That suit was dropped when Burnham died in 1985. Another suit was dropped after the plaintiff left Guyana. The two other suits, which the *Standard* eventually lost, were brought by Hugh Desmond Hoyte, the head of the Ministry of Economic Planning and Finance. In 1985, Hoyte succeeded Burnham as president (Fraze, 1988).

In one suit, the *Standard* published a press release from a political party opposed to Hoyte. The release accused Hoyte of misleading the U.N. Development Program in a funding request. In the second suit, the *Standard* published the allegations of an insurance firm alleging that the government was "strangling" the private sector by pressuring Guyanese insurance companies to repatriate foreign investors who had lost their assets in Guyana. The story claimed that the government was trying to qualm the fears of foreign investors so that Guyana would receive loans from the World Bank and International Monetary Fund. Hoyte was not mentioned by name in the story. He claimed, however, that he was libeled because as head of the Ministry of Economic Planning and Development he was ultimately responsible for national economic policies.

In February 1988, Guyana's highest court, the Court of Appeal, ruled in Hoyte's favor in both suits. Hoyte was awarded a total $10,500 (U.S.) for damages in both cases, including another $5,000 in legal fees. In Guyana, the award was large enough to intimidate the press to refrain from criticizing public officials. The independent *Standard,* a frequent critic of the government (for further discussion, see the "Spotlight" section in chapter 4), is raising private donations to pay the suit.

In addition to the influence of British libel law in English-speaking Caribbean, the Spanish legal tradition of most nations on the South American continent is also not favorable to the press in libel cases. Spanish legal tradition is not based on the assumption that public officials should be accountable to the public. The Spanish tradition of libel is based on the maxim of *lèse majesté*, the assumption that the ruler and his or her officials can do no wrong. As a result, the offense of libel against political officials fell under so-called *desacato* (disrespect) laws, considered a criminal offense. In theory, truth is not considered a defense in *desacato* laws.

Derivatives of *desacato* laws were used by military regimes, such as that of the first government of Argentine dictator Juan Domingo Peron (1946–1955, 1973–1974) to silence a critical press (Deutsch, 1957). Although Latin American nations during the 1980s attempted to restructure their laws to grant more press freedom in line with emerging democracies, long-held legal traditions do not give way easily.

MEXICO'S SUBTLE PRESS CONTROLS

Although various forms of subtle government intervention and potential control of the press exist throughout Latin America, the situation in Mexico deserves special attention. Mexico is frequently used to illustrate how a government has legally institutionalized management of the news media through a web of subtle interventions. With its one-party democracy, the Institutional Revolutionary Party (PRI), Mexico transcends such simple press classifications as "libertarian" and "authoritarian" (Stein, 1986b; Wiarda, 1988–1989).

Alisky (1981) has classified Mexico as a nation with neither "media freedom" nor "censorship," but strict "media guidance." The fact that a single party has been in continuous power since 1929 has allowed the government to formulate and institutionalize methods to deal with the press (Cole, 1975; Knudson, 1969). As the 1990s began, however, Mexico was witnessing a remarkable transition toward privatization of the economic sector. Although this transition was never specifically directed toward the press, it could, nevertheless, radically change government–press relations in Mexico and alter the long-held perception of Mexico as the model of institutionalized press control.

As a result of the Mexican government's intervention in press affairs, many critics have claimed that the Mexican press has been compromised and corrupted. These critics assert that the Mexican press has become so compromised that it is not necessary for the government to enforce existing laws that can be used to control the press. For instance, Article 7 of the Mexican Constitution, which creates the Printing Law (*Ley de Imprenta*), makes the press subject to prosecution for violations of people's privacy and violations of obscenity standards. But as Miguel Angel Granados Chapa, deputy director of Mexico City's prestigious *La Jornada,* states:

> There has not been a single case in which (the Printing Law) has been applied, due perhaps to the particular relationship which exists between the government and the press, a relationship based on an understanding which makes its application unnecessary. It is not even used in cases of obscene publications. (Boyle, 1988, p. 98)

As an observer of the Mexican press scene recently wrote: "The predominant opinion among Mexican journalists is that most newspapers in Mexico either reflect vested interests or are directly controlled by vested interests" (Jackson, 1989b, p. 14). A leading Latin American press scholar claimed that the Mexican press is so tainted that the press and journalists "are held in widespread disdain by all citizens at all levels" (Pierce, 1979, p. 97). Typical of these criticisms, John Merrill, Carter R. Bryan, and Marvin Alisky (1972) described Mexican journalists as obsequious to the government:

> Throughout Mexico it has become difficult in recent years to find criticism of public officials in daily newspapers, except for a few scandal sheets where partisan polemics border on defamation. . . . In general, Mexican mass media traditionally do not criticize the President of the Republic directly, but do sometimes criticize his cabinet ministers. (p. 198)

These unflattering portrayals of the Mexican press, although based in truth, are unfortunate because there are many honest journalists and fine news organizations in Mexico. Latin American and Western journalists familiar with the Latin American press say several publications, such as *El Norte* of Monterrey, *La Jornada* of Mexico City, and the weekly news magazine *Proceso,* are deserving of special praise. A small Tijuana newspaper called *Zeta* has recently received some attention for its investigative stories about government corruption (Murray, 1989). Newspapers in Tijuana, possibly because of their proximity to the United States, are more bold than their Mexico City counterparts in criticizing the government and engaging in hard-hitting investigative journalism (Hartung, 1985; Murray, 1989). Until top editors of Mexico City's *Excelsior* were purged in 1976, in what many Mexican journalists are convinced was a government-engineered overhaul of the critical daily, *Excelsior* was considered among the best newspapers in the hemisphere (Vargas, 1976).

According to Linda Hossie (personal communication, February 15, 1990), the

Toronto *Globe and Mail*'s correspondent in Mexico City, the corruption that plagues the Mexican press is no different than the corruption that pervades all Mexican institutions. The corruption, she claimed, stems from flaws in the Mexican political system and the fact that one party has stayed in power so long. Hossie added that the Mexican government's attempts to manipulate press coverage are not limited to its dealings with the Mexican press. The government also selectively disseminates and withholds news from foreign correspondents.

A large-scale content analysis of editorials and columns in six leading mass circulation Mexican newspapers representing a diversity of political views suggests that the Mexican press may not be fully deserving of its image as a subservient press. According to Prof. Louise Montgomery's (1985) study, the Mexican newspapers that she analyzed from 1951 to 1980 criticized cabinet ministers and, occasionally, the president. However, criticism of the president was usually reported in oblique fashion.

According to Alisky (1981), the Mexican government's institutionalized control over the press stems from a number of government activities in the nation's economic sector. He claimed that the source of intervention in the economic sector dates back to the "Revolution," which Alisky stressed is always spelled with a capital "R." The underlying philosophy of the Revolution, which started in 1910 with the overthrow of dictator Porfirio Diaz, encourages government to protect the public from economic exploitation by the rich. Alisky (1979) noted three important ways the federal government controls the press in Mexico:

1. import regulations for new equipment for printing and broadcasting,
2. import regulations on parts for equipment, and
3. taxes and rebates on the manufacture of equipment.

Until recently, the government's control of the flow of newsprint, as well as other important needs such as ink, chemicals, and so forth, have been viewed as the government's major method of press control. Still another means of government influence over the press has been through government investment in private corporations. Government purchase of large blocks of stock in privately owned corporations can lead to outright control of media companies by the government. The situation in Mexico is currently changing as the government seeks to privatize the economy, making many of the generalizations about Mexican control over the press obsolete.

Although the Mexican government wields control over the press through a variety of methods, the government's control over newsprint has been singled out for special attention. The government's newsprint business, *Productora e Importadora de Papel*, SA (PIPSA), was created in 1935 to make newsprint available at a competitive price. The Mexican government monopoly includes the import, distribution, sale, and manufacture of newsprint. On occasions, past Mexican governments have used PIPSA to assert their control over print media. For decades, critics charged that PIPSA represented a subtle but potent method of government control over the press by tightening the supply of newsprint to newspapers that challenge authority. During the 1970s, when dictatorships were common throughout Latin America, government control of newsprint was one of the most common methods for silencing the press (Brown, 1974).

For instance, in 1974, Monterrey's independent *El Norte* saw its newsprint supply cut by 83% when the then president of Mexico was angered by the newspaper's reporting and editorials. Alejandro Junco de la Vega, publisher of *El Norte,* claimed that the government turned on and off the control of newsprint to reward its friends in the press and punish its enemies:

> It would have been unreasonable at the height of the Watergate scandal for Katharine Graham (chief executive officer The Washington Post Company) to be obligated to purchase newsprint from Richard Nixon. We Mexican publishers have been doing the equivalent of that for a long time. (Junco de la Vega, 1989, p. 6)

PIPSA highlights the difficulty in maintaining the proper relationship between government involvement and press independence. In 1989, Mexican President Carlos Salinas de Gortari announced plans to privatize PIPSA and open the nation to easily available paper imports. He made the dramatic announcement before assembled journalists from the hemisphere at the 45th annual IAPA General Assembly meeting in Monterrey. Salinas also promised greater press freedom and to investigate allegations of government death squads aimed at journalists. The announcement to privatize PIPSA and open up Mexico to the importation of newsprint was part of Salinas' larger economic plans to unsaddle the government of numerous money-losing industries. Salinas' economic and social policies have been described as ushering in a period of Mexican-style *perestroika,* or "*salinastoika.*" They were praised by the IAPA and other world press organizations.

When Salinas announced his intent to privatize PIPSA, he said: "I await the response of publishers and journalists on this (PIPSA's) destiny" (Anon., October 8–12, 1989, p. vii). Ironically, Mexican publishers and journalists did not greet Salinas' announcement to privatize PIPSA with unanimous approval. A week after the announcement the Mexican Publishers' Association called on the government to keep PIPSA in the government sector. Many publishers and news media managers had grown comfortable accepting the financial rewards that had accompanied this government intervention of the press. The publishers feared losing the financial advantages of a state-run newsprint business and seemed willing to trade off the potential of government control for economic benefits. PIPSA has been known to permit newspapers unlimited financial credit, which allows unprofitable newspapers to avoid paying their bills, or to pay discounted debts (Rohter, 1989b).

Part of the reason for the Mexican Publishers' Association objection to the privatization of PIPSA was that there was no recent evidence to suggest that the government used PIPSA to limit press freedom. The organization further argued that by providing publishers with newsprint at a reasonable price the government serves as a guardian of press freedom rather than as a hindrance to press freedom. The organization warned that eliminating the government monopoly on newsprint could result in a *de facto* private monopoly that could harm small, independent publishers.

Newsprint regulation, however, is not always used by Latin American governments to punish critical media voices. Argentina, which many believe has the highest import tax on newsprint in the world, uses newsprint revenue to gain revenue in a nation where income tax abuse is widespread (Ruth, 1985). In 1986, the Argentine government agreed to sharply cut the tax on imported newsprint from 48% to 28% (Stein, 1986a).

The Mexican government intervenes in the broadcast media by means of regulations that far surpass the Federal Communications Commission's regulations of the broadcast media in the United States (de Noriega & Leach, 1981). The Mexican government mandates that, as a public service, a portion of the airtime be devoted to government-sponsored programs without charge. There are two categories of free time that must be given to the government (Alisky, 1981; Pierce, 1979). The first, referred to as "official time," consists of 30 minutes each day for public service announcements and government advertising. If the government passes its 30-minute limit, it pays the stations for the extra time. Another category of free time is "fiscal time," which consists of time given by the broadcasters to the government in exchange of taxable revenue.

Although several observers have complained that these restrictions can be used to manipulate the broadcast media, government intervention in the broadcast media may in fact result in increased media profits through increased government advertising. In addition, little evidence exists to suggest that government advertising has resulted in restrictions against the broadcast media. No Mexican broadcaster has seen his or her license permanently revoked since 1934, although there have been several brief suspensions for violations of broadcast regulations (Alisky, 1988).

Finally, Mexico's leading television network, Televisa, possesses economic and political power that may permit it to overcome government pressure. Televisa's strong financial position as the pre-eminent television organization, and one of the strongest private industries in the entire nation, makes it difficult for the government to manipulate Televisa. Although there have been instances in which Televisa's coverage has brought the government's wrath upon it, Televisa has generally been sympathetic with the ruling party's politics (Mahan, 1987). In the area of political coverage, the ruling party has traditionally received the lion's share of Mexico's broadcast news coverage.

Things may be changing for the better. Government opponents appeared to receive more broadcast coverage during the 1988 presidential election than in past elections. Even during this election, however, the government demanded that a journalist at Televisa, which operates four of the government's eight television channels, be dismissed after he ran footage of imprisoned members of the oil workers' union who criticized the government. He was immediately fired. The footage, which had been filmed several years earlier, showed a union boss bragging of his close connections to leaders in the ruling party (Asman, 1988).

AUTOCENSURA: PRESSURE TO SELF-CENSOR

The overt violence, subtle pressures, and even nonviolent threats against the press often lead to self-censorship, or *autocensura*, as it is known in democratic Venezuela and Colombia and elsewhere in the region, where the practice is thought to be common (Knudson, 1989; Servant & Vissuzaine, 1985). To some observers, *autocensura* illustrates the worst form of press censorship because governments that succeed in pressuring media to apply their own censorship may not experience the public and world condemnations that come to governments that overtly censor the press. Cases such as the coverage of the divorce of Venezuelan President Jaime Lusinchi in 1988 illustrate the point.

Venezuela is usually—and rightly—regarded as one of the most democratic nations in Latin America. Two days before the nation celebrated 30 consecutive years of democracy in 1988, the nation's journalists publicized the practice of pressuring journalists to censor their own work. More than 2,000 print and broadcast journalists marched in the streets of Caracas to protest. Their complaints were aimed at President Lusinchi, who came to power 4 years earlier. They accused Lusinchi of pressuring the news media to give him and his administration favorable coverage (Anon., February 1988).

The first attempts of government pressure on the Venezuelan press came in October 1984, when Lusinchi suspended radio broadcasts produced by the Venezuelan Chamber of Radio Broadcasters. The broadcasts claimed that Lusinchi was aggregating his power through unorthodox means. In 1986, the editor of *El Diario de Caracas* was jailed twice for criticizing Lusinchi's handling of the nation's debt problem as well as a series of articles on governmental corruption. The editor was released after his second arrest only after he and several critical columnists agreed to resign and the newspaper halt its critical coverage of governmental corruption. In January 1987, the editor of a small weekly in the southeast section of the nation was sentenced to 5 years in prison for running stories about government corruption. The sentence was later reduced to 3 years. He was jailed for violation of a law aimed against ''vagrants and hoodlums'' (Bamrud, 1988).

The government's pressure on the press over President Lusinchi's divorce proceeding caused the greatest anger, however. This pressure was responsible for the nationwide protest by journalists. Although rumors and stories about the divorce and affair were widespread, the news media were pressured to refrain from publishing news about both events (Knudson, 1989).

Lusinchi filed for divorce and had a relationship with his secretary. A number of political observers claimed that the secretary used her power to influence political issues. Heavy pressure was put on the press to refrain from mentioning anything about the affair and the filing for divorce. In November 1987, the secretary held a press conference in which all the leading news media attended. Only one daily, however, *El Nacional,* carried extensive reports of the conference.

A month later, Lusinchi's wife publicly spoke to members of Congress to give her side of the growing scandal. Once again, *El Nacional* was the only newspaper to report the event. *El Nacional* also reported that the government had police agents at Congress taking photographs of the journalists in attendance. When *El Nacional* published the First Lady's account before Congress, the government withdrew all its advertising from *El Nacional* for 3 months. The government pressured media not to report the scandal, and reportedly even asked a television station to fire a reporter for making jokes about the divorce (Bamrud, 1988).

Self-censorship in most Latin American nations results from fears—whether real or imagined—of government reprisals against the press. In Mexico, where political leaders and government officials often enjoy a cozy arrangement, self-censorship frequently results from publishers' attempts to ingratiate government officials to curry their favor. Many publishers with political ambitions may try to avoid offending government officials they may need favors from in the future (Camp, 1985; Ronfeldt & Tuohy, 1969).

GOOD AND BAD OF GOVERNMENT INTERVENTION

Latin American governments generally reject the authoritarian tradition of harsh government interference in press affairs to silence a critical press. However, this does not mean that they embrace all aspects of the libertarian concept that calls for no government interference in press affairs. Nor do they accept the libertarian proposition that all government intervention in press affairs must lead to negative consequences.

Robert Picard, a journalism scholar at California State University, Fullerton, has observed a trend toward increasing "positive" state economic "intervention" in press policies among even western nations. For instance, Scandinavian nations, regarded as paragons of political freedom, practice a substantial degree of government intervention in news media activities (Picard, 1988b). As Picard (1988a) wrote:

> In itself, state intervention in press economics is neither good nor bad. In practice, however, it may or may not be a threat to the editorial or financial integrity of the press. In some cases it can be used to promote diversity and integrity and other social goods. (p. 36)

Although examples of negative state intervention in Latin American news media matters are well-known, the literature gives less attention to some of the positive aspects of intervention. Picard (1988a) catalogued a number of government economic interventions in privately owned Latin American newspapers. Among some of the positive interventions Picard noted in various Latin American nations are:

1. Special tax waivers to newspapers that other industries don't receive.
2. Special postal and telecommunication rates.
3. Government advertising that, in some cases, is the prime economic support for newspapers.
4. Laws limiting the number of newspapers a single entity may own, limitations on cross-media ownership and foreign ownership for the stated purpose of promoting media diversity and local media voices.
5. Government loans to newspapers have created new newspapers and helped existing newspapers modernize their facilities.
6. Government investment in newspapers, which has kept some newspapers in existence that otherwise may have gone out of business.

Leo Bogart (1990) reviewed how Latin American news media cope with the harsh economic conditions of the 1980s and 1990s. He noted that many Latin American governments have given a "helping hand" to newspapers during these hard times. In particular, Venezuela permits the press to maintain a two-tier exchange rate to help newspapers purchase newsprint. Recently, the Venezuelan government announced a plan whereby some government services to the media, such as electricity and telephone, could be exchanged for advertising on behalf of government-owned industries instead of cash.

Those uncomfortable with Latin American governments' intervention in the newspaper industry, Picard (1988a) observed, seem less perturbed by foreign government involvement, mostly U.S. government involvement. In 1985, the United States provided *La Prensa* of Nicaragua with $100,000 to purchase vital supplies to continue its fight against the Sandinista government then in power. During the last days of the Allende government in Chile, the U.S. Central Intelligence Agency allegedly provided the opposition newspaper *El Mercurio* with close to $2 million.

INFLUENCE OF NEWS MEDIA ON GOVERNMENT

In discussions of press–government relationships, it is common to speak of the influence of governments on the news media. But the influence can run both ways. Some Latin American media have developed into potent economic forces in their nations, wielding considerable economic and political power.

In most Latin American countries, the best way to characterize the interaction between the privately owned media and governments is that of a love–hate relationship. Although the media are often portrayed as critics or watchdogs of governments, they are also economic enterprises with vested interests in the economic and political systems in which they function.

A case in point is Mexico. The government pays close attention to the business community, including the news media, which may insist on removal of certain cabinet-level officials (Camp, 1989). The business community may communicate directly with the government or make its positions known through the mass media.

ECONOMIC CONDITIONS AND THE PRESS

Economic pressures on the press are among the most common methods used by governments to keep the press under control. During the 1970s, several Caribbean nations, including Antigua and Grenada, instituted a number of restrictive press laws that applied economic pressures against the press (White, 1976). Such laws typically require those starting a newspaper to keep large amounts of money on deposit. Ostensibly, the purpose of the law is to demonstrate that an owner of a newspaper has the economic capability to maintain a media organization. In practice, however, such a law insures that those who start newspapers will have to risk financial loss and therefore may avoid being critical of government.

During the 1980s, the region's dire economic situation served to silence news media as effectively as the dictatorships of an earlier era. IAPA President Manuel J. Jimenez, publisher of *La Nación* in San Jose, Costa Rica, said in an address before the International Federation of Newspaper Publishers in New Orleans in 1989, that the pessimism over the economic problems in the region has led media people to overlook the region's political achievements:

> In the past, a report from Argentina would have centered on freedom of the press. The fact that today the practice of journalism in Argentina entails no particular physical risk, despite the phenomenal economic hazards, is an indication that the country is politically healthy. For the time being, at least, democracy is standing up to the economic shocks that Argentina is experiencing. (Jimenez, 1989, p. 3)

As Jimenez noted, it wasn't necessary for Argentina to have a dictatorship to witness widespread newspaper closings during the rule of President Raúl Alfonsín (1983–1989). With the return to democracy throughout the region, combined with economic crises, many newspapers and magazines closed as a result of the economic conditions. In June 1989, *El Heraldo* of Buenos Aires, established only 10 months earlier and managed by the prestigious English-language Buenos Aires *Herald,* shut down. The banner headline of *El Heraldo*'s final edition told the story: "HYPERINFLATION SWALLOWED EL HERALDO" (McCullough, 1989). According to the story, *El Heraldo* had to increase its newsstand price threefold from April to May 1989 in order to recoup costs for ink, newsprint, photo/graphics supplies, and other materials, which increased 430% during the same period.

Every publication in Argentina was experiencing similar difficulties. During the weeks prior to the closing of *El Heraldo,* Argentina witnessed the closing of the weekly *El Ciudadano,* the weekly news magazines *El Periodista,* and *Siete Dias.* The Argentine Newspapers Association issued a warning that the trend of folding newspapers and news magazines posed a threat to the nation's fragile democracy (McCullough, 1989).

THE INCLINATION TO CONTROL THE PRESS

One must wonder why some press scholars make such an issue about laws that may help or hinder the practice of journalism. After all, any nation that wishes to do so has the power to force its press to report or not report certain news, or report the news in a way that does not offend authority. This is especially the case if the nation is willing to withstand international censure, as many nations have.

The fact that Costa Rica, one of the region's most stable democracies, has enforced what some regard as restrictive laws against the press—one called a *colégio* law is discussed at length in the next chapter—troubles press advocates more for the precedent it sets rather than any likelihood that the Costa Rican government will use the law to manipulate the press.

Louisiana State University Prof. John C. Merrill (1987) has claimed that some nations have a greater tendency or "inclination" to control the press than other nations. He interviewed government press/information officials in New York and Washington, DC, from 58 nations representing six geographic regions, to measure their inclinations to control the press. The officials were identified and quoted as representing the official views of their governments.

Merrill saw inclination to control the press as a construct comprised of six factors related to the control of journalists:

1. in-country licensing,
2. international licensing,
3. identification or accreditation cards,
4. university education requirements,
5. in-country codes of ethics, and
6. international codes of ethics.

From these factors he created a "control inclination index." Overall, Merrill reported that Latin American nations were rated among the most likely nations in the world to control the press, second only to Middle Eastern nations. Cuba, Peru, Paraguay, Panama, and Bolivia were among 19 countries classified with "strict control" of the press.

Perhaps more telling than these numbers, however, were selected texts of the interviews with the officials. The representative from then authoritarian Chile, who was at the time serving as the press attache at the United Nations, defended the regulation of journalism in his nation through college training and membership in the *Colégio de Periodistas* (College of Journalists). However, the Chilean spokesman added:

> I am not in favor of international licensing of journalists. The reason is that socialist countries favor it and want to rule and control every step of the news. . . . I am against the control of journalists by any sort of government, especially socialist ones who are pushing for some sort of international licensing of journalists. (Merrill, 1987, p. 241)

A spokesman from Cuba, the government's press officer at its United Nations Mission, found himself in agreement with the Chilean spokesman regarding the internal licensing of journalists through a *colégio,* in Cuba's case the *Unión de Periodistas.* The Cuban spokesman also went a step further and supported the international licensing of journalists: "In a real sense Cuban journalists are licensed; this is the way it should be, for unless journalists accept standards and basic policy in line with the Revolution, they should not be journalists" (p. 241).

All Latin American spokesmen interviewed by Merrill believed there should be some degree of control over the press by governments. But several also conceded possible dangers in controlling the press. The spokesman for Mexico, the minister for press and public affairs in Mexico's Embassy in Washington, DC, accepted the notion of "licensing" broadcast journalists, but not print journalists. He contended that the reason for his distinction between print and broadcast journalism is that broadcasting "is more pervasive in society; reaching greater segments of the people, and therefore must be more responsible; therefore there is a need for more control" (p. 242).

*   *   *

SPOTLIGHT

IAPA: Watchdog Press Association for the Americas

Although all the major media watchdog organizations speak out against press abuses in Latin America, the 1,300-member Inter American Press Association (IAPA), headquartered in Miami, focuses specifically on speech and press freedom issues in the Western hemisphere, particularly in the Caribbean and South and Central America.

IAPA members are mainly newspaper editors and publishers, with a few magazine executives and scholars also involved. Although there is a growing number of members from U.S. and Canadian news media organizations, the majority of members come from Latin America. The IAPA's active members represent 34 countries in the hemisphere, including U.S. territories. Members identified as coming from Cuba bear an asterisk after their names denoting that they are "members in exile."

As with all media watchdog organizations, IAPA has no real "power" other than its ability to publicize the plight of journalists and speak as a single voice representing its members. After a media organization in Latin America suffers under a despotic regime, IAPA members launch "blitzes" of telegrams and faxes to the offending government. Members also publicize the abuse in their media (Harvey, 1959).

In 1943, the second National and Pan American Congress in Havana established the organization under its current name—Sociedad Interamericana de Prensa. Cuban liberals exercised control over the executive committee of the Pan American Congress and, from 1943 to 1949, convinced the Cuban government to subsidize the organization's secretariat in Havana. During a New York meeting in 1950, the organization was restructured and the bylaws revised (Carty, 1976). Instead of representing countries, as previously done, member journalists attended representing their media organizations.

Although IAPA may not be very visible in the industry or public at large in the United States, it is widely recognized in important circles throughout Latin America because its membership is dominated by some of the continent's most influential journalists, who are often also leading businessmen and occasionally political party leaders in their countries as well.

The IAPA's defense of beleaguered journalists dates back to 1953, when Demétrio Canelas, publisher and editor of *Los Tiempos* in Cochabamba, Bolivia, was sentenced to death for refusing to succumb to government demands to cease its editorial attacks on the government (Gardner, 1965; Shanks, 1988). Canelas said of the IAPA help he received: "I owe not only my freedom but my life to the Inter American Press Association" (Gardner, 1965, p. 547).

Within the next few years, IAPA came to the defense of a number of other Latin American journalists such as Pedro Joaquin Chamorro in Nicaragua and Germán Ornes in the Dominican Republic and won similar praise (Gardner, 1965). Probably the greatest praise came from Argentine dictator Juan Domingo Peron, who had a 437-page book published denouncing the IAPA. The book accused the IAPA of coming to the aid of "imperialistic interests of Wall Street" and "attacking national sovereignty with its aggressions, its excesses, its frauds and lies." The IAPA took it as a compliment that a Latin American dictator would find it worth attacking the IAPA by name (Gardner, 1965). During the 1960s, the IAPA continued to rail against press abuses in dictatorial nations in Cuba, Haiti, Paraguay, Honduras, and Guatemala.

In 1952, IAPA joined forces with its broadcast counterpart in Latin America, the Inter-American Association of Broadcasters (IAAB; the organization has since changed its name to the International Broadcasting Association). As a result of the "Panama Agreement" in 1952, the IAPA and the IAAB agreed that any act of suppression against a newspaper or broadcast station in the hemisphere would be considered an act of suppression against all newspapers and broadcast stations in the hemisphere (Harvey, 1959).

IAPA convenes twice a year, alternating between North and South America, to discuss current issues, including government relations with the press. The major committee of the organization, the Freedom of the Press and Information Committee, dominates meetings with member reports of government and press relations, violent incidents, and other attempts to suppress news organizations of the past 6 months.

High on the IAPA agenda has been its opposition against what it views as obligatory licensing of journalists in several countries in the form of *colégio* laws, which mandate journalists to be members of legally recognized organizations called *colégios* to practice their trade (Velverde, 1989). It also has fought efforts by governments to restrict imported newsprint and other supplies and limit imported equipment.

Pierce (1979) described the IAPA, as well as several other press organizations, as taking "a rather uncomplicated view of press freedom" in which

> the enemy is always the government, private investors are the only rightful owners, commerce is the best calling of the media, society can exert demands on them (the press) only through the marketplace, and any legal norms beyond the most basic defamation and pornography laws are unacceptable. (p. 218)

A number of critics see this "simplicity" borne out in IAPA reports that often describe the state of press freedom in various nations with the bold pronouncement that "There is freedom of the press in . . ." or "There is not freedom of the press in . . ." (Pierce, 1979, p. 218). Other critics see the IAPA as associated with conservative forces (Brown, 1962). This conservative bias at least resulted in the expulsion of *The New York Times* journalist Herbert Matthews from the IAPA's board of directors during the mid 1960s for his pro-Castro views (Knudson, 1978).

Generally speaking, IAPA sees little or no role for even benign state intervention in press policies. To this end, IAPA's policies and concerns are at odds with another leading Latin American journalism association, the Latin American Federation of Journalists (FELAP), founded in 1976. The left-leaning organization comprised of journalists in the region strongly advocates NWICO order polices as a way of improving the lot of Latin American journalists and freeing Latin American media from dependence on the developed nations (Anon., May 17, 1989).

Although the IAPA is usually associated with conservative views, it condemns abuses by governments of both the political left and right (Hochberger, 1957). It has also frequently leveled criticisms against the United States and Canada. According to Julio Muñoz (personal interview, January 26, 1990), the director of the IAPA's technical institute, the guiding philosophy behind the IAPA is that news media organizations should maintain independence from governments.

Occasional missions to meet with governmental leaders take place under extraordinary circumstances. When the news organizations of a country have been physically damaged by government or private groups, or when news organizations have been restricted in their reporting and publishing or closed by government decree, these missions of a handful of IAPA leaders will take place. The missions usually bring pressure on governments by directly meeting with officials. Sometimes, governments that believe they have made significant human rights improvements have invited representative of the IAPA to see the improvements first-hand. The organization also pressures governments by sending telex and facsimile messages to national presidents, urging them to rescind decisions that have closed publications or otherwise made news reporting difficult for national media.

Leftist critics of the organization claim that the IAPA represents the business interests of its members. They also claim that although the IAPA criticizes government attempts to curb freedom everywhere, including the United States, it tends to be harsher on communist and left-wing nations than on right-wing nations.

The IAPA's technical institute established in 1957, is responsible for continuing education of members through frequent production and technical and management training seminars throughout Latin America. According to Muñoz (personal interview, January 26, 1990), the purpose of the center is to help Latin American media be financially strong as the best means of maintaining autonomy from governments. In addition, IAPA provides an independent circulation auditing service, a series of annual international reporting and photography awards, and scholarships for journalists from Latin America to study in the United States.

With the transition to democracy throughout most of Latin America during the 1980s, Muñoz (personal interview, January 26, 1990) viewed the IAPA's role shifting from supporting independent media in their fights against governments to dealing with other nongovernment related problems in the region. He said he sees the rise of narco-terrorism as one of the major threats to Latin American journalists. Muñoz noted that the nations where Latin American journalists are in greatest physical danger are the same nations where the drug trade is thriving.

The Practice of Journalism

Various social, political, and economic forces may enhance or inhibit the routine work of journalists in Latin America. This chapter examines how advertisers, political and economic conditions, and extra- and quasi-governmental organizations such as terrorist organizations and hit squads may put pressures on the news media to influence media content. This chapter also examines the professional orientations of journalists in the region. Latin American journalists have long been characterized as very political. Both government and political party involvement—often through financial support or outright ownership—in the press is a major characteristic in the practice of journalism. Journalism education in Latin America continues to improve. Relying on the North American model developed earlier in the century, many Latin American journalists today have the opportunity for college-level education in journalism. This chapter focuses on new efforts and systems for improving the performance of journalists through formalized education and training. *Colégio* laws are the major legal forces that control qualifications of journalists to practice in many countries in the region. Perhaps most significant, however, in influencing the daily work of journalists in some Latin American nations is violence and threats of violence from terrorist organizations. The extensive nature of violent acts in countries such as Colombia and Peru have had a chilling effect on news reporting. Journalists continue to be murdered and kidnapped for unfavorable stories or for positions involving political and social issues of the day.

The daily practice of journalism in Latin America involves a number of complex interrelationships among journalists, media organizations, and various sectors of society. Perhaps the most important sector with which journalists must deal is the government. The subject of press–government relations is of such central importance that the previous chapter was devoted to that topic. In addition to the press' relationships with governments, journalists must also interact with the public and advertisers.

Although press–government relations became more favorable for journalists during the 1980s over the previous decade, journalists are experiencing intimidation and physical danger from extra- and quasi-governmental terrorists. A number of other factors dealing with the professional training of journalists, the function of journalism in society, journalists' self-perceptions of their jobs, and day-to-day news gathering activities all influence the practice of journalism. During the 1960s, several systematic studies of Latin American journalists suggested that journalists were frustrated by their inabilities to practice journalism, contribute to society, and make a decent living. These studies presaged journalists' acceptance of *colégio* laws, recognized laws that set standards for entry into the field of journalism.

MEDIA-ADVERTISER PRESSURES

In every free market society, there is a concern that advertisers may use their power to withhold advertising revenue to influence news coverage. The power of advertisers on the press in a society depends on the competition among media organizations for advertising revenue. For instance, in the United States, with the increasing trend of one-newspaper cities in large metropolitan markets, the power of advertisers to influence the editorial content of newspapers may be decreasing because advertisers in one-newspaper communities upset with editorial content cannot simply take their business elsewhere and other news media such as television do not always substitute for newspapers. It is a fact that constantly needs to be restated that advertisers do not advertise in the mass media simply to help the press. The primary motivation of advertisers is to increase sales. In addition, the United States has a large number of advertisers, ensuring that in most cases no single advertiser can wield inordinate control over the press.

In some Latin American nations such as Guatemala, El Salvador, and Honduras, where wealth is highly concentrated, the mass media are dependent on a relatively small number of industries for their revenue. The scramble for advertising revenue among Guatemalan newspapers from a relatively small, wealthy business elite who maintain tight control over the business sector sometimes serves to keep Guatemalan journalists in check (Goldman, 1988).

Goldman, who unsystematically examined the content of leading newspapers in El Salvador, Guatemala, and Honduras, argued that the economic situation of dependency on a limited number of advertisers effectively keeps newspapers from reporting stories that might offend big business. If the newspapers dare to challenge the interests of the wealthy elite, they face the possibility of seeing their advertising revenue disappear. This was the case in the late 1970s when Guatemala's then leading daily, *El Gráfico,* reported that the country's most successful fried chicken franchise was secretly owned by then-Nicaraguan dictator Anastasio Somoza. The story so upset the business community that leading advertisers withdrew their advertising, turning the usually bulging daily into a flimsy newspaper with as few as four pages per issue. It took a long time before advertising returned to *El Gráfico,* and the newspaper was far more reluctant to run such critical stories in the future (Goldman, 1988).

Newspapers in Guatemala, Honduras, and El Salvador frequently serve the interests of the relatively small number of economically prosperous readers by reporting many light feature stories of what is essentially the lifestyles of the nations' richest and best-known families. As Goldman wrote about the conservative editorial policies of El Salvador's leading dailies, *La Prensa Gráfica* and *El Diario de Hoy*: "The reason for such unanimity (in conservative views in the media) isn't hard to fathom: you have to be rich to own a newspaper, and on the right politically to survive the experience. Papers in El Salvador don't have to be censored: poverty and deadly fear do the job" (p. 60).

In other societies, such as Mexico, the central control of industries by the state and the fierce competition among newspapers in Mexico City combine to give advertisers and the state a great deal of control over the media. The competition for advertising revenue by the Mexican media has forced newspapers to adopt practices that sometimes compromise their credibility and has earned the Mexican press opprobrium.

Mexican newspapers sell news space that is presented as stories and often appear no different from other stories. These packaged public relations releases, known as *gacetillas,* often consist of favorable stories about certain politicians and government agencies. They are openly sold by some newspapers, with their going rates quoted in rate books. Sometimes the *gacetillas* are prominently displayed on front pages. The better papers set off these stories by printing them in different typeface. They may even identify them as paid insertions (Bailey, 1988; Pierce, 1979).

The Mexican government also purchases conventional advertising in the print and broadcast media. Because the Mexican state is integrated into the economy, the distinction between press–government relationships and press–advertiser relationships in Mexico is often blurred. The government owns a national airline, a national bank, a chain of movie theaters, and runs a national lottery. As it was mentioned in the previous chapter, this situation is currently changing as the Mexican government seeks to divest itself of money-losing industries.

In addition, Mexican politicians and political agencies seek to co-opt low-paid journalists. In 1986, the typical starting salary for a journalist in Mexico City was about $120 (U.S.) a month. Journalists in the provinces earned even less. To supplement their incomes, it is not unusual, and perhaps even expected, that they accept *embutes,* a noun derived from a verb meaning to gorge oneself. Often, these are not outright bribes, but expenses for travel or extra work meant to influence favorable coverage from journalists. Journalists may receive *embutes* from news sources for such activities as writing or picking up public relations releases or covering news conferences (Pierce, 1979). In some cases, journalists are often also expected to solicit advertising from the sources they cover and receive commissions for bringing in advertising to their employers (Alter, Contreras, & Kreimerman, 1986).

Journalists assigned to cover leading politicians can expect to supplement their incomes. During the 1982 presidential campaign, journalists assigned to cover President Miguel de la Madrid received $75 a day from the candidate's staff to cover "expenses." Some reporters who traveled overseas to cover Madrid's trips went on spending sprees, knowing they would be waived through customs without paying duties upon their return (Alter et al., 1986). A few leading Mexican newspapers have attempted to maintain high standards in Mexico's corruptive environment. *El Norte* of Monterrey claims to be a new breed of Mexican newspaper. It pays its reporters higher salaries; in return it expects that its reporters will not accept *embutes*.

PROFESSIONALISM OF JOURNALISTS

In a society where everyone naturally expects journalists to accept indirect bribes and be easily compromised, there is reason to suspect that journalists may not be committed to their profession. Even the honest journalists may become frustrated by perceptions that they are dishonest. Journalists' perceptions of their professional roles and functions influence how they practice their craft. Journalists in different societies may see their roles ranging from that of servants of power and authority, independent information transmitters, social gadflies, watchdogs over political power, soldiers for national development, political analysts, and so forth (Jeffres, 1986).

The adjective "professional" should not be confused with the noun "profession." To do a professional job is to do a job that meets high standards. In this regard, even a grave digger may perform a professional job. But experts agree that a profession must meet certain criteria. Although they do not agree just what these criteria are, five common criteria are: (a) systematic theory, (b) authority, (c) community sanction, (d) ethical codes, and (e) a culture (Greenwood, 1957).

In the United States, there is some debate as to whether journalism is a profession, and even whether it is desirable for U.S. journalism to aspire to become a profession. Certainly U.S. journalism is not a "true" or "undisputed" profession such as law or medicine, in which there are certain barriers to entry. No one in the United States may legally practice law or medicine without meeting certain legally established standards. However, there are no legal barriers to entry against the practice of journalism in the United States. As a matter of practice, however, journalism degrees are fast becoming the accepted standard for attaining jobs with news media organizations in the United States (Garrison & Salwen, 1989).

Louisiana State University Professor John C. Merrill (personal communication, December, 1989) leads the clarion call against U.S. journalism seeking to aspire to become a profession, claiming that it would be harmful to pluralism, journalistic autonomy, and press freedom. Merrill wrote:

> People like me, we see journalism as a profession as harmful to pluralism, to press freedom, to the whole concept of openness; we see certain types of people being frozen out of journalism—eccentrics, etc. We see professionalism of this type a danger to a free and open press where everyone can practice regardless of education, political views, etc.

Although Merrill is not as bothered by the word "professional" as an adjective as "profession" as a noun, he worries about the connotations of the word. The quest of Latin American journalists to attain "professionalization," he claimed,

> implies, I think, that there is the attempt being made to achieve some kind of status for journalism in Latin America that it doesn't now have. . . . It probably means that journalism is considered weak or inefficient in some way; therefore it needs to be professionalized.

Mexican communication scholar Fernando Reyes Matta (1977, 1979a, 1979b) is also critical of the trend toward "professionalism" in Latin American journalism, but for reasons quite different from Merrill's. Reyes Matta viewed the trend of professionalism as a distinctly Western and particularly U.S.-style of professionalism that involves such practices as objectivity and neutrality. In his view, the Latin American "tradition" of news involves political interpretation.

Journalistic organizations helped launch journalism programs in universities throughout the region just after World War II, ostensibly as a means of promoting "professionalism" in journalism. But what was originally meant to increase journalistic professionalism evolved into a drive to turn journalism into a true profession. Over the years, the universities and journalistic organizations were able to convince many Latin American governments to *legally require* practicing journalists to obtain degrees and belong to recognized organizations in order to practice journalism. This arrangement suited the journalists because it provided a means of restricting entry into the field—a method that kept journalists' skills in demand and salaries high. It also suited the universities, providing them with students and closer relations between universities and news media industries (Gardner, 1985).

The legally recognized professional journalism organizations, known as *colégios,* worked to improve the economic lot of journalists. A *colégio* is not a union, *per se,* although it works to enhance the economic benefits of its members. A *colégio* sets and enforces standards for entry into the "profession" of journalism, and in this way is closer to a bar association membership required to practice law than a union that simply looks out for its members' interests.

The issue of *colégios* has developed into a heated hemispheric debate. Many U.S. journalists view *colégios* as *de facto* licensing of the press, and a means by which governments may control the press. But, as we will see later in this section, the reasons for *colégio* laws are complex. Many were established without government initiatives, but there are active attempts by Latin American journalists themselves to pressure governments to adopt *colégio* laws. Thus, U.S. journalistic organizations that believe they are coming to the defense of their brethren in Latin America by attacking the legitimacy of *colégios* find themselves in opposition with rank-and-file journalists. Empirical research conducted in the 1960s on Latin American journalists' perceptions of their professional values and aspirations presaged their willingness to accept legislation making journalism a true profession through *colégios*.

RESEARCH ON JOURNALISTIC PROFESSIONALISM

International communication scholars have long been concerned about how journalists in developing nations view their societal roles. Sydney Head (1963), a scholar of international communication, maintained that in order for journalists in developing nations to be professionals, they must think of themselves as performing a service to the public rather than as servants of the state.

During the 1960s, a number of U.S. researchers systematically studied journalists' perceptions of their professional roles. This research began when Jack M. McLeod and Searle Hawley (1964) developed an index to measure journalists' "professional orientations." After their groundbreaking survey-based study of journalists in Milwaukee, several other studies attempted to investigate whether the concept of journalistic professionalism had cross-cultural validity. Some of the earliest empirical attempts to investigate the cross-cultural validity of journalistic professionalism occurred in Latin America.

Menanteau-Horta (1967) sampled 235 Chilean communicators, including 128 newspaper people. He reported that Chilean journalists showed strong "professional identification" despite working long hours for low pay requiring them to hold extra jobs.

Day (1968) replicated Menanteau-Horta's findings with a purposive sample of 94 journalists in the capital cities of Argentina, Bolivia, and Mexico. Day, like Menanteau-Horta, also reported that journalists have strong professional aspirations. However, Day went a step beyond mere self-evaluations and aspirations and looked at actual practice. He reported that despite their professional aspirations, Latin American journalists were realists willing to compromise their ethics for economic gain or survival. Most respondents to Day's study said they had to take on outside employment, half of them in other news media jobs. Nearly 25% of the journalists sampled by Day took on outside public relations work that raised serious conflict-of-interest questions. Fully 50% of the Argentine journalists said they had to take on outside work in public relations to supplement their incomes.

Studies by McLeod and Rush (1969a, 1969b) highlighted the perceived lack of respect that Latin American journalists felt they experienced during the 1960s. McLeod and Rush administered a modified version of their professionalism scale to 46 veteran Latin American journalists attending an advanced journalism program in Ecuador. They compared the results of this select group of Latin American journalists with responses from U.S. journalists. In some ways, McLeod and Rush (1969a) reported, Latin American journalists were "surprisingly more professional than the United States journalists" (p. 589).

The major difference between the U.S. and Latin American journalists, according to McLeod and Rush, seemed to be that Latin American journalists were far more interested in attaining respect and prestige than their U.S. counterparts. There were also some sharp differences between the U.S. and Latin American journalists when McLeod and Rush asked the journalists to evaluate their perceived abilities to attain their professional goals. In this regard, the Latin American journalists were more dissatisfied than their U.S. counterparts.

The Latin American journalists in the McLeod and Rush study evaluated training and professional organizations as more important than their U.S. counterparts. On a number of questions, they expressed a far greater willingness to establish professional organizations that would set barriers to entry to practice the profession that would, in effect, make journalism a "true profession." Given their financial situations and perceived lack of respect, they displayed little fear of the dangers of losing their "autonomy," which U.S. journalists and some scholars such as Merrill see as critical to the field of journalism.

Overall, these early empirical studies of journalistic professionalism in Latin America by Menanteau-Horta, Day, and McLeod and Rush reported that Latin American journalists during the 1960s expressed high professional aspirations. They viewed themselves as playing potentially important roles in their societies. But the journalists raised serious doubts that they could practice their lofty values in societies where they believed that these roles were not valued.

Scholarly interest in journalistic professionalism, and especially professionalism among Latin American journalism, waned in later years. During the late 1980s, however, several studies once again addressed journalistic professionalism in Latin America when the debate over the value of *colégios* to promote journalistic professionalism emerged (Logan & Kerns, 1985; Ruofolo, 1987; Salwen & Garrison, 1989).

Ruofolo surveyed 108 Latin American journalists working for elite newspapers (in Brazil, Colombia, and Costa Rica). Overall, Ruofolo reported modest levels of professionalism. His study, however, highlighted the fact that journalists in different Latin American nations may have different levels of professionalism. Ruofolo reported that Brazilian journalists had relatively high professional orientations compared to Colombian and Costa Rican journalists. The Brazilian journalists also held a high regard for objectivity and a low regard for personal prestige. Colombian journalists, however, had low professional orientations.

Studies on journalists' evaluations of what constitutes newsworthiness, called *media gatekeeping,* also relate to professionalism because they shed light on professional values and judgments. Comparative studies of the news values of media gatekeepers in developed and developing nations suggest similarities as well as differences (Chaudhary, 1974; Mowlana, 1975). Despite Western journalists' allegations that the Third World's interest in promoting "developmental journalism" means that journalists in developing nations should become "soldiers of development" and report "good news" about their governments, a few empirical studies suggest otherwise. Both Western and Third World journalists view government interference in the press as a serious impediment to the practice of journalism (Ghorpade, 1984; Salwen & Garrison, 1989).

Salwen and Garrison specifically compared the news values of a small sample of Latin American journalists with U.S. journalists. They reported that both groups of journalists regarded "freedom of the press," in the form of government threats to the press, as serious problems facing journalists. Both groups also valued the importance of an independent press. However, Latin American journalists saw fewer dangers in the press actively seeking to promote the social, economic, and political "development" of their societies so long as there was no government interference. The U.S. journalists, by contrast, were far less comfortable with an active role for the press even for ostensibly beneficial purposes. The authors suggested that the term *development* apparently had negative connotations to the U.S. journalists.

Similarly, Logan and Kerns (1985) studied 36 Caribbean journalists attending visual communications workshops in the West Indies to examine the extent to which they embraced Western journalistic values. Based on the journalists' rankings of statements, more than half the respondents were strong proponents of Western press freedom with an independent, critical press.

THE POLITICAL PRESS

Latin American news media have frequently been associated with partisan political views. As a leading Latin American press scholar observed:

> In the context of history, political criticism is the most natural function of journalism in Latin America. . . . Traditionally the press has been operated by men schooled not in objective rigors of the scientific method, which is the philosophical parent of the news concept. Rather, they have been taught to value the classical Greek and Latin rhetoric and argumentation, which led to political criticism and thus editorials. (Pierce, 1979, p. 211)

There is some debate as to whether the partisan press is a positive phenomenon. Mexican press scholar Fernando Reyes Matta (1979b), who favors a "political-interpretive approach" to news reporting, asserted that the original Latin American concept of news involves "interpreting events and presenting opinion" (p. 164). Some of the early writings about Latin America's partisan political press, however, viewed the political nature of the press as a defect. Gerald (1931), for instance, maintained that the "iron-clad alliance to party, creed, and purpose adds vilification to the South American press and hinders progress" (p. 223).

Since the end of World War II, there has been a slow but growing trend in Latin America to develop less partisan newspapers. Even in war-torn Nicaragua, where each newspaper was viewed as pro- or anti-Sandinista until the 1990 election defeating the Sandinistas, the weekly *La Crónica* tried to establish itself as a centrist newspaper. Danton Jobim was editor-in-chief of Rio de Janeiro's *Diario Carioca* and dean of journalism at the University of Brazil during the 1950s. Writing at a time of transition from a political to neutral press (Jobim, 1954), he observed that Latin American journalists were personally torn between the Latin American model of "political journalism" and the U.S. model of "neutral journalism":

> North Americans readily recognize the truth—that producing a daily newspaper in this age is a business. European and Latin American journalism does not like to be called a business. Latin newspapermen like to speak of their profession as if it were a priesthood, even if in their hearts they know this is not precisely so. . . . This mentality is a survival from the epoch when journalism of opinion or doctrine ruled supreme. . . . Although the U.S. formula, "objectivity and accuracy," has made great progress in our press, the Latin paper, discreetly or openly, always emphasizes politics. (p. 63)

The newspapers in the large so-called "ABC nations"—Argentina, Brazil, and Chile—have led the way in adopting more modern styles of journalism, and have generally earned kudos as "prestige" newspapers from their U.S. counterparts for their efforts (Eulau, 1942). Many media practitioners in the United States look askance at Latin America's partisan press. Some U.S. practitioners would like to see the Latin American press become more "professional," meaning it should subscribe to notions such as "fairness," "detachment," "balance," "objectivity," and so forth.

John Lent, journalism professor at Temple University, described an account of newspaper coverage in St. Kitts in the Leeward Islands that many Western journalists would no doubt describe as "unprofessional" because of the partisan political nature of the reportage. In 1982, the *St. Kitts Democrat*, a partisan tabloid associated with a political party, ran a photograph of former Premier Lee Moore sprawled out drunk on the ground. The caption described Moore as so "knocked out with liquor that he vomited like a whale, urinated like a dog, exposed himself like a jackass and wallowed in his muck like a pig." The paper also ran a response from Moore that was equally amusing: "Let us start from the assumption that I was drunk. . . . Who money I drunk wid? Is my money. So why I have to explain to anybody if I drunk?" (Lent, 1987, p. 249). The coverage in St. Kitts certainly was not professional by the standards of Western journalism, but it was an example of a free press where different ideas could and were being disseminated.

Partisan, investigative journalism in Antigua has resulted in the exposure of national scandals. The weekly *Outlet,* the party organ of the leftist Antigua-Caribbean Liberation Movement (ACLM), exposed the Antiguan government's role in shipping Israeli weapons to Colombia's Medellin drug cartel during 1989. The newspaper is a fierce opponent of Prime Minister Vere C. Bird, and announced Bird's connection in the scandal with headlines such as VERE BIRD CAUGHT LIKE A RAT IN A TRAP (Bohning, 1990).

The debate over the value of a partisan versus neutral press in Latin America continues today. Recently, some newspapers and news magazines have appeared in Latin America that have gained attention as a "new breed" of news media, not associated with partisan political views. Santiago's *La Epoca,* a morning tabloid founded in 1987, claims to be such a newspaper. Publisher Emilio Filippi supports a Chilean transition to democracy and is therefore automatically labeled as part of the political opposition. But Filippi claims that although his publication is political, it is not partisan and obedient to any political party, group, or cause. In an interview with the *Los Angeles Times* news service, Filippi said, "Our job is more important than that of a political party. We offer access to ideas of all kinds: left, right, and center, resisting identification with any of them. This kind of newspaper is essential for Chile if democracy is to return" (Montalbano, 1987, p. 21).

The debate over the value of a political versus neutral press takes on increased importance in Latin America as Latin American media adopt new, sophisticated practices of reporting. In particular, a growing trend toward "precision journalism," as public opinion polling for the news media is sometimes called, raises questions as to whether polls are used to measure or to influence public opinion. This same debate exists in the United States and other industrialized nations. In the industrialized nations, however, the media usually hire independent survey firms with established reputations to avoid conflicts of interest. Although many Latin American media organizations also hire independent polling organizations, many continue to conduct polls of questionable validity that may be intentionally designed to yield certain outcomes (Mitchell, 1965).

The 1990 presidential election in Nicaragua between Sandinista incumbent Daniel Ortega and opposition candidate Violeta Chamorro was marked by a "war of polls." A spate of polls released before the election presented vastly different results and started a heated political debate over the polls' accuracy. Xavier Chamorro, the editor of the pro-Sandinista newspaper *El Nuevo Diario,* summed the situation up when he said, "You tell me what you want a poll to say, and I'll get it for you" (Marquis & McReynolds, 1990).

Both Ortega's and Chamorro's supporters understood that pre-election polling in Nicaragua was more than just a means to satiate audience interest in the excitement of the election. Pre-election polls were viewed as indicators of the honesty of the election. If the polls and election did not correspond, the election polls were just as likely to be believed as the final vote (Bollinger, 1990).

Even if the Nicaraguan polls were conducted with no attempt to shape their outcomes, questions were raised as to whether the rural populace could be accurately represented. There were also questions whether Nicaraguans, unfamiliar with polling techniques, would try to determine the pollsters' political positions and then tell the interviewers what they wanted to hear. The pre-election polling was marked by charges of shoddy research methods that included poor sample designs and misleading questions (Barnes, 1990).

There were charges of questionable and politically motivated opinion polling elsewhere in Latin America during 1989, including Brazil, Chile, and El Salvador. The growing trend toward the increased use of precision journalism in Latin America is the natural result of democratization and direct elections. Many Spanish-language television stations in the United States, which have sponsored polls in Latin America to appeal to their audiences, have contributed to an increased interest in public opinion polling in Latin America. Official tallies in Latin America can take days. As a result, news media coverage of exit polls is continuous for many days. Even English-language U.S. news media with large Hispanic audiences, such as the *Los Angeles Times,* have commissioned polls in the region (Anon., June 1986).

JOURNALISM EDUCATION

Until the middle of the 20th century, journalism education was viewed as a uniquely American (U.S.) practice. Latin American journalists had backgrounds in literature, politics, and other fields. Writing in 1931, when there was not a single journalism school in all of Latin America, Gerard reported that many Latin American journalists spent from $50 to $100 (U.S.) each to enroll in mail-order "quack" journalism correspondence courses from sellers in the United States. For their money, the journalists received out-of-date instructions and poorly prepared materials on North American journalism methods.

It is difficult to get a precise measure of the number and scope of training programs for journalists in Latin America. But in recent years, the number of programs in the region has been increasing astronomically. In 1954, UNESCO identified 650 journalism training programs in the world, all but 100 of them in the United States (Cooper, 1987). Journalism education in Latin America is currently experiencing rapid growth. In 1950, there were only seven journalism programs in Latin America. By 1978, there were almost 100. By 1985, there were almost 200 (Rota, 1985).

Despite the growth of Latin American journalism programs, many Latin Americans continue to learn about journalistic practices abroad, particularly in the

United States, Europe, and the Soviet Union. The U.S. journalism education model has historically been dominant. Cooper (1987) identified the U.S. model as consisting of three components: (a) journalism skills training, (b) liberal arts courses, and (c) conceptual courses dealing with mass media, such as journalism history and law.

Cooper (1987) surveyed 35 professional journalism programs in developing nations, including 11 Latin American and Caribbean nations, to determine the structure of their curricula. Based on the curricula and course descriptions, he concluded that the U.S. model was dominant. Overall, the responding journalism programs from the Latin American nations did not differ much from other ñing nations. Nine of the 11 Latin American programs included all three components of the U.S. journalism education model.

In addition, some Latin American programs included a fourth component not usually reflected in U.S. journalism education curricula, that of developmental journalism. Although U.S. programs may teach students "about" developmental journalism in international journalism courses, they do not teach students "how" to practice developmental journalism, as some Latin American programs do (Cooper, 1987). Cooper reported that the program at the University of Valle in Colombia went further than to just include a developmental journalism component in its curriculum—it offered a degree sequence in developmental journalism.

The Caribbean Institute of Mass Communication at the University of the West Indies in Jamaica is typical of this shift toward including developmental journalism in Latin American journalism curricula. The program, as it was founded in 1974 with the help of U.S. and British staffers, initially followed the U.S. model. It integrated a developmental philosophy into the curriculum over the years. This shift in the curriculum was met with unease by the U.S. and English staffers (Cuthbert, 1985).

Even with the growth of indigenous journalism training in Latin America, many newspaper managers in the region claim that journalists are receiving insufficient training. Although U.S. journalists have many of the same complaints about journalism education in their own country, they continue to hire journalism graduates. Oliver Clarke (personal interview, January 13, 1990), chairman of the board of the Jamaica *Daily Gleaner,* the leading privately owned daily newspaper in the Caribbean, claimed that journalism students who apply to the *Daily Gleaner* are so inadequately prepared that the paper trains its journalists on the job.

For a long time, the Soviet Union has trained foreign students from Latin America and elsewhere in the Third World in the Marxist model of journalism. Despite recent changes in policies of new media openness in the Soviet Union, Latin American press scholar Marvin Alisky (1989) reviewed Soviet journalism training, including training sequence at the Latin American Institute in Moscow, part of the prestigious Soviet Academia of Sciences. He reported that *glasnost* has had little influence on Soviet journalism education. The Institute was founded in 1961, shortly after Fidel Castro came to power in Cuba. Alisky reported that most of the texts adhered to conservative, hard-line Marxist theory. Alisky suggested, however, that the situation may change in the coming years.

Journalism programs in Latin America were originally associated with the humanities. With the support of professional journalistic organizations, they expanded to incorporate professional training (Fernandez, 1966). Michigan State University Professor Mary Gardner (1980) noted this trend was precisely the opposite of that in the United States, where journalism schools initially stressed professional skills and later included theory and research components. She claimed that the dangers of practicing journalism in the region at least partially accounted for this trend:

> Research is not only viewed as more prestigious than the accurate reporting of news, but also as a safer and more stable occupation. Researchers, after all, generally can select the topic of their work with greater discretion than journalists. It is no small caution that journalists tend to be among the first jailed or to be killed when they report dissent. (pp. 11–12)

The first journalism program in the region, established in Argentina's Universidad de la Plata, was created by the *Círculo de Periodistas* (the Circle of Journalists) in April 1934. A month later, another program was developed in Buenos Aires (Knudson, 1987b). These were followed by programs in Brazil in 1935 and Mexico in 1936. It took several years for even some of the larger Latin American nations to establish programs. Peru did not institute a program until 1945, followed by programs in Chile and Venezuela in 1947.

The first journalism program in Central America was established in Guatemala's Universidad de San Carlos in 1952. It was attached to the humanities faculty (Knudson, 1987b). In the Caribbean, the First National Congress of Journalists helped establish a professional journalism program in Havana, Cuba. The program was managed by experienced journalists and limited to 50 students each year. The Cuban program sought to ''professionalize'' journalism by establishing a journalism guild, the *Colégio de los Periodistas* (Guild of Journalists), which required successful completion of the program to practice journalism (Knudson, 1987b).

During the late 1950s, the United Nations Educational, Scientific, and Cultural Organization (UNESCO), an organization within the U.N. that has advocated restructuring what it views as the unbalanced ''world communication order,'' discussed the creation of regional centers for journalism education in Latin America (Faherty, 1965). As a result, UNESCO founded the International Center of Advanced Studies in Communication for Latin America (CIESPAL) in Quito, Ecuador. CIESPAL has been a major success. It trains journalists throughout Latin America. The support of *El Comercio,* a leading daily in Quito, and the Ecuadorian government also were central in the establishment of CIESPAL. One of the major founders of CIESPAL was Dr. Raymond B. Nixon, professor at the University of Minnesota and editor of *Journalism Quarterly* at that time. Scholars and media practitioners from the United States, Europe, and Latin America have lectured at CIESPAL (Alisky, 1981; Day, 1966).

CIESPAL included a scientific aspect to the study of journalism. The fact that CIESPAL's founders referred to the program as a School of Mass Communication Science instead of a School of Journalism was meant to stress the scientific foundation of journalism (Day, 1966; Fernandez, 1966; Nixon, 1970). Before CIESPAL, most communication research in Latin America came from a variety of disciplines and often approached communication tangentially within the larger frameworks of sociology, psychology, anthropology, and other disciplines (de Melo, 1988). CIESPAL has also become a communication research center in Latin America, publishing the respected journal *Chasqui.*

In addition to *Chasqui,* a number of other communication periodicals have found a niche in Latin America. Many of them appear on irregular publication cycles and have uncertain futures. Most of them are narrowly focused on communication problems and issues within specific nations. A few, however, stand out as publications dealing with communication issues in the region (Jones, 1989).

In the 1960s, much of the communication research in Latin America had been described as "diffusionist," based on U.S. communication researcher Everette Rogers' model of using mass media to disseminate information about modernization. During the 1960s and 1970s, much of the research in Latin America took on a decidedly political tone as researchers from the political left influenced the research climate. These researchers focused on the expansion of multinational industries, including multinational communication industries, into Latin America and the subsequent negative effects on indigenous cultures (de Melo, 1988). The increasing politicization of communication research and education in Latin America has been a step forward or backward, depending on various observers (de Melo, 1988; Rota, 1985).

A recent multimethod study of the intellectual influence of U.S. and Latin American media scholars in Latin America reported that since the creation of CIESPAL, Latin American scholars began developing their own research tradition based on the European "critical" model (Chaffee, Gomez-Palacio, & Rogers, 1990). After surveying U.S. scholars who published on Latin America, the researchers warned that U.S. researchers may not be aware of the changing research trends in Latin America.

Lozana and Rota (1990) also noted this trend toward a developing Latin American research tradition in communication. They interviewed leading Latin American communication scholars in order to describe aspects of this emerging tradition. In general, the scholars whom they interviewed suggested that Latin American communication research involves advocating social justice. Typical of their findings was a quote by Omar Oliveira, professor at Universidade Federal de Minas Gerais in Belo Horizonte, Brazil:

While in the U.S. it is quite easy to find scholars who devote their entire academic support to the political determinations of the Department of State, in Latin America it is hard to find researchers who are not working against the system, both theoretically and practically. They are in general motivated by a deep concern with political change. (cited in Lozano & Rota, 1990, p. 6)

Chaffee et al. (1990), in their multimethod study of the intellectual influences of research in Latin America, reported that the intellectual influence of one scholar on Latin American scholars, Armand Mattelart, stood out among the rest. Chaffee, Gomez-Palacio, and Rogers combined mail and personal surveys and analyzed leading Latin American communication journal citations to measure the influence of leading Latin American scholars. Both the survey of the Latin American scholars and the journal citations indicated the influence of Mattelart. As Chaffee, Gomez-Palacio, and Rogers classified the various researchers under various categories of their research (e.g., empirical, media imperialism, and so forth), Mattelart's contribution was considered so important that he was classified as a category by himself.

The finding of Mattelart as the most influential scholar in Latin America was curious because Mattelart is a Belgian scholar who taught in Chile from 1962 to 1973. Since the 1973 military coup that brought Gen. Augusto Pinochet to power in 1973, Mattelart has primarily lived and worked in Europe. The finding of his influence also highlights the dominance of critical theory in Latin American research. Meanwhile, Chaffee, Gomez-Palacio, and Rogers reported that among the U.S. researchers, empirical researchers were named as making the most significant contributions to Latin American research.

COLÉGIO LAWS

Latin American universities have played a central role in promoting *colégio* laws and the establishment of *colégio* organizations. *Colégios* claim to work to uphold professional journalistic standards by such means as promoting education, upholding ethical standards, and organizing professional meetings. *Colégios* have a good deal in common with guilds and unions. But they are more than unions, and in fact co-exist with unions in many nations. Their efforts to set legally established national standards for entry to the *colégio* and to mandate employers to hire *colégio* members, however, make *colégios* closer to bar associations than to guilds or unions.

It is widely agreed that the roots of *colégio* laws in Latin America stem from the poor economic lot of Latin American journalists. Latin American journalists have traditionally been underpaid, overworked, and received little job security. As the early empirical studies on journalistic professionalism in Latin America demonstrated, many Latin American journalists have found it necessary to hold two jobs. The second jobs have frequently been with the journalists' respective governments, raising conflict-of-interest questions.

Latin America's *colégio* laws have become a hot political issue in the Americas, and even the halls of the United Nations. Most U.S. news organizations view *colégio* laws with disfavor. They frequently view them as government attempts to manipulate their brethren in Latin America. Many Latin American publishers view *colégio* laws as restraints on their hiring autonomy. *Colégio* laws are regularly condemned during Inter American Press Association (IAPA) meetings as a covert form of government licensing of journalists. The IAPA is the major media "watchdog" group in the Western hemisphere that adheres to a philosophy of an independent press free of government intervention. Dr. Julio Muñoz (personal interview, January 26, 1990), who heads the IAPA's Technical Institute, claimed that he is not against all aspects of *colégios,* and in fact finds many commendable. However, he and his organization strongly oppose "compulsory" *colégio* laws. UNESCO supports *colégio* laws, as does the International Organization of Journalists (IOJ), based in Prague, Czechoslovakia, and aligned with the Soviet bloc.

The various groups from the political right and left that have gotten involved in the debate about *colégio* laws have framed the issue, not surprisingly, in political terms, dealing with such heady matters as national and cultural sovereignty, the free flow of information, and journalistic autonomy. Latin American journalists, however, have traditionally viewed the matter of *colégios* largely in economic terms as a form of job protection. *Colégio* laws, if enforced, would effectively limit the market for journalists and raise their salaries (Knudson, 1979; Pierce, 1979). Temple University Professor Jerry Knudson (1979) studied the development of Bolivia's *colégio* during the 1970s and reported that it contributed to improved economic conditions and tended to reduce a number of unethical practices.

Today, numerous Latin American nations have laws requiring journalists' membership in *colégios.* As of 1987, 11 Latin American nations had *colégio* laws (Cifrino, 1989):

Bolivia	Brazil
Costa Rica	the Dominican Republic
Guatemala	Ecuador
Honduras	Haiti
Peru	Panama
Venezuela	

The laws are unevenly enforced and have different provisions. In Venezuela, there is no effective way to deal with infringements against the *colégio* law (Knudson, 1989). In Peru, by contrast, journalists accused of violating the code of ethics of the *Colégio de Periodistas del Peru,* established in 1980, stand before a tribunal of professional journalists that can mete out punishment ranging from a simple warning to expulsion from the *colégio.* The code includes provisions against publishing obscenities and revealing the privacy of sources. Interestingly, the code also includes a provision against working for wages below the established minimum (Rodriguez, 1989). In recent years, Costa Rica has strictly enforced its *colégio* law and has prosecuted violators.

Critics of *colégio* laws, such as Prof. Gardner of Michigan State University, a long-time observer of the Latin American press, have observed that authoritarian governments on both the political left and right have enforced *colégio* laws to silence the press. But not only have authoritarian governments enforced *colégio* laws. Costa Rica, "the Switzerland of Central America," regarded as one of the most democratic nations in the region, has the region's most famous—or infamous—*colégio* law. Costa Rica's *colégio* law was the center of a major press controversy in 1983 as a result of a failed legal challenge brought against the law by an American journalist practicing in Costa Rica.

THE STEPHEN SCHMIDT CASE

Costa Rica's *Colégio de Periodistas* (Association of Journalists) was established in 1969. Members of the *colégio* must graduate from the University of Costa Rica's (UCR) journalism school, or possess a degree from a university recognized by the UCR (Fonseca, 1977). Anyone else who practices journalism faces a prison sentence for "the illegal practice of journalism" (Youm, 1989).

The publicity surrounding Costa Rica's *colégio* law stems from a lengthy legal battle brought by American reporter Stephen Schmidt. In 1983, Schmidt was convicted by the Costa Rican Supreme Court for the "illegal practice of the profession." The officers of the University of Costa Rica urged the Costa Rican government to prosecute Schmidt. Schmidt had been working as a reporter for the *Tico Times,* an English-language weekly with a circulation of about 7,500, since 1975, without membership in the *colégio.* He held an undergraduate degree in physics and mathematics and a master's degree in journalism. His master's degree was obtained at the Autonomous University of Central America. Schmidt might not have been prosecuted had he not openly dared the *colégio* to prosecute him for practicing journalism in Costa Rica without membership in the *colégio.* At the annual meeting of the IAPA in San Jose in 1980, Schmidt declared: "I'm covering this meeting illegally. Let me work or sue me" (Ostroff, 1986, p. 59).

Schmidt won his case in a lower court. However, he lost on appeal brought by the *colégio* before the Costa Rican Supreme Court. The Supreme Court sentenced Schmidt to a 3-month jail sentence, which it immediately suspended. Schmidt, with the assistance of the Inter American Press Association (IAPA), then appealed to the Inter-American Commission on Human Rights (IACHR) for a nonbinding advisory opinion. Costa Rica was a member of the IACHR, which heard human rights disputes in the hemisphere. The IACHR ruled that the licensing of journalists was incompatible with Article 13 of the American Convention on Human Rights. The article guarantees the right to freedom of expression. The court asserted: "(A) law licensing journalists, which does not allow those who are not members of the '*colégio*' to practice journalism and limits access to the '*colégio*' to university graduates who have specialized in certain fields, is not compatible with the Convention" (Youm, 1989, p. 5).

The implications of the IACHR decision were not immediately clear. Because the IACHR's decision was nonbinding, the Costa Rican Supreme Court's decision stood. Although critics of *colégio* laws hailed the decision and claimed that as a result Costa Rica and other Latin American nations with *colégio* laws would be reluctant to enforce *colégio* laws in the future, Costa Rican representatives claimed that they would enforce the law. Bill Williamson, executive director of the IAPA, compared the IACHR decision to the landmark journalism case of John Peter Zenger in the United States, in which the New York editor who had been charged with seditious libel in 1735 had been acquitted because truth was a recognized defense. However, Costa Rica's minister of information and communication, Armando Vargas, described the IACHR decision as "just a document of scientific and academic value" (Ostroff, 1986, p. 59).

It would be incorrect to view the Schmidt decision solely as a freedom-of-the-press incident. The University of Costa Rica and many of the nation's journalists support the *colégio*. They have obvious financial motives for supporting the *colégio*. Richard Dyer (1988, 1989b, 1989c), publisher of the *Tico Times,* naturally sided with Schmidt. Dyer claimed that the law restricted Costa Rican publishers' freedom to hire employees. Dyer also said that he asked the *colégio* to provide him with reporters with a command of English, but the *colégio* ignored his requests (Maeckle, 1983).

It should be obvious, however, that Costa Rican publishers had more to gain from a Schmidt victory than just asserting their hiring autonomy. If they did not have to hire members of the *colégio,* the labor market for journalists would be larger and journalists could be paid lower salaries. Nevertheless, Dyer was correct in asserting that the existence of *colégio* laws did not guarantee high professional standards. As an example, Dyer (1988) cited a banner headline in the February 1988 edition of *Primera Plana* that read: "THE NORTH AMERICAN PRESS (is) IN THE HANDS OF JEWS" (Salwen et al., 1991, p. 309).

For its part, the president of Costa Rica's *colégio* asserts that the *colégio*'s critics, and the Inter American Press Association (IAPA) in particular, are launching a propaganda campaign to portray the *colégio* as an obstacle to press freedom. The *colégio,* he maintained, does not restrict freedom of expression "because the law allows people to write opinion and commentary" (Maeckle, 1983). The *colégio,* he further asserted, performs a "social function" by disciplining unethical journalists and working for the betterment of the profession and the economic security of its members. "It is simply a case of regulation concerning university degrees in the case of Costa Rica and of watching over professional practice, a guarantee of better protection of human rights" (Valverde, 1989, p. 8).

Since the Schmidt case, Costa Rica has become one of the most active nations in the region to enforce its *colégio* laws. The active participation of the *colégio* in enforcing the law accounts for the number of convictions in Costa Rica. In September 1989, with the 7-month sentence of popular radio-TV commentator Flavio Vargas Castaing by the First Criminal Court of San Jose, Costa Rican courts had convicted four people for "the illegal practice of journalism." The conviction was met by a chorus of cheers by members of the *colégio* who packed the court (Dyer, 1989a).

While Costa Rica, through the efforts of the *colégio,* was working to put some teeth into its *colégio* law, the Supreme Court of the Dominican Republic declared mandatory membership in the *colégio* unconstitutional in 1989. Six daily newspapers, all members of the Dominican Daily Newspaper Association, brought a joint complaint against the section of the *colégio* law, Law 142, that they said constitutes the licensing journalists (Anon., September 23, 1989).

The decision came 5 years after members of the Dominican Daily Newspaper Society agreed to ignore the law. The Dominican *colégio* required media organizations to employ a set number of people in their news departments with degrees, or in lieu of degrees journalists with a minimum of 5 years of experience. The Dominican *colégio* law also mandated a 1.25% tax on advertising revenues that went to the nation's *colégio*. The Court ruled the tax was unconstitutional because it violated constitutional provisions that tax levies should not be directed against specific groups or used to benefit specific groups. The decision did not totally end the dispute. The *colégio* claimed it would challenge the Court's decision in the IACHR.

THREATS AND VIOLENCE

With the rise of democratically elected governments in many regions of Latin America during the 1980s, journalists generally have had legal recourse when they felt wronged by the government and could freely appeal to public opinion during times of government pressure. But threats to journalists come not only from governments, but from private terrorist groups, drug lords, and quasi-governmental hit squads as well. Numerous news organizations have been ransacked, bombed, and destroyed by nongovernmental opponents. Dozens of Latin American journalists have been murdered for their beliefs and for writing articles that contain those beliefs.

Joel Solomon (personal communication, May 14, 1990), an associate specializing in Latin America for the New York-based Committee to Protect Journalists, has observed the following:

> While the nature of many governments in Latin America has changed in recent years,
> it is impossible to draw general press-related conclusions from that fact. It is interesting

to note that more journalists were killed in Latin America last year than in all other regions of the world combined, and most of the deaths occurred in countries generally considered democracies.

Colombia is widely regarded as among the most dangerous nations in the world to practice journalism. Table 3.1 displays the extent of violent acts that *murdered* journalists in Colombia and other Latin American countries in 1988–1989. Press self-censorship exists in Colombia, imposed by terrorists. "Within the vast problem of drug trafficking and drug use, there is an aspect that directly affects the press," *El Espectador* publisher and editor-in-chief Luís Gabriel Cano said in 1989. It is "the new, macabre method of press censorship by the drug mafia and its criminal organizations" (Cano, 1989, p. 18). Cano has direct experience with this form of nongovernmental censorship. His brother, Guillermo, the former publisher, was shot to death by a drug lord hitman outside of *El Espectador*'s office in 1986. His newspaper's building and equipment were destroyed by a truck bomb in 1989 that also killed one person.

Peru, along with Colombia, is one of the most dangerous places in Latin America to practice journalism. The nation's most notorious terrorism group, the *Sendero Luminoso* (Shining Path), associated with the teachings of Mao Tse-tung, is responsible for many of the threats to journalists. In late 1989, American journalist Todd Smith of *The Tampa Tribune,* who was on assignment in Peru, was killed by Shining Path guerrillas. Smith intended to write a story while on vacation about drug trafficking and terrorism (Harrison, 1989).

The mysterious leader of the Shining Path, Abimael Guzmán, known as "Chairman Gonzalo" and "Presidente Gonzalo," has received some celebrity status in the nation's media. He has not been seen in public since 1981, and there are those who doubt that he is still alive. Every once in a while a newspaper claims to report an interview with him. The authenticity of these reports are questionable (Shakespeare, 1988).

According to the right-wing newspapers, Guzmán is reported to have taught his initiates to kill their victims, usually wealthy landowners, and then to drink their blood. Left-wing newspapers dub him with Robin Hood status, a defender of the poor against the exploitative wealthy classes. All newspapers, no matter what their political tendencies, exploit Guzmán's reputation with sensational coverage to improve their circulations. According to the newspapers, Guzmán had been spotted in Brazil, Bolivia, or New York. One Lima newspaper carried a headline, "ABIMAEL VISITS HARRODS" (Shakespeare, 1988).

The spread of terrorism in Peru and elsewhere has led to responses by Latin American governments that some fear could lead to restraints against press freedom. In Peru, the democratic government has imposed measures to silence news media sympathetic with the Shining Path guerrillas. In December 1988, Luís Arce Borja, a former editor of the leftist newspaper *El Diario,* was arrested and charged with "apologia of terrorism," a criminal offense, for publishing an anti-government

TABLE 3.1
Violent Deaths of Journalists in Latin America, 1988–1989

The Committee to Protect Journalists (CPJ) is a New York-based organization that studies conditions under which journalists worldwide must function. Violent acts against journalists are a major concern. In its "Reports of Journalists Killed and Disappeared in Latin America During 1989 and Counts for 1988," the most severe recent cases of violence against journalists in Latin America are documented.

This report was compiled by Joel Solomon, Latin America specialist for Committee to Protect Journalists (personal communication, May 14, 1990).

BRAZIL (2)

• Luiz Alberto Montenegro: Reporter and national editor at Baudru-based daily journal *Jornal da Cidade,* in Sao Paulo state, shot and killed on January 8. Motive unclear.

• Maria Nilce Magalhaes: Columnist with the daily *Jornal da Cidade,* based in Vitoria, Espirito Santo state, shot to death on July 5. It appears she was killed for reasons related to work.

The Committee to Protect Journalists (CPJ) reports two other deaths in 1988.

COLOMBIA (10)

• Luis Daniel Vera Lopez: Radio journalist with the Bucaramanga-based Radio Metropolitana de Bucaramanga, shot in a drugstore on April 22.

• Hector Giraldo: A lawyer and journalist with the Bogotá daily *El Espectador,* shot on March 29 while at a stoplight in Bogotá. Colleagues believe that his death may be related to his legal work in the murder case of the newspaper's late editor, Guillermo Cano.

• Carlos Enrique Morales Hernandez: Reporter with the biweekly *Radar Colombiano,* found strangled to death on May 21 after being kidnapped from his home by armed men. Motive unclear.

• Adolfo Perez Arosemena: A journalist working in the press department of the Red Cross in Cali. He also contributed to various media. Found strangled and shot on May 21 after being kidnapped by armed men. Motive unclear.

• Juan Caro Montova: A journalist who contributed articles to the Medellín daily *El Mundo.* Shot to death in Medellín on August 15. Motive unclear.

• Guillermo Gomez Murillo: Reporter with *El Espectador* in Buenaventura, shot to death on September 16, apparently because of his investigations on local corruption.

• William Bendeck Olivella: Radio journalist with La Voz de Montería and La Voz del Sino, shot to death on October 13. Motive unclear.

• Roberto Sarasty: Radio journalist who also wrote and published *El Cronista Demócrata,* a Medellín magazine that appeared on an irregular basis. Shot and killed on October 10 as he was leaving the Caracol radio station.

• Diego Vargas Escobar: Radio journalist with La Voz de las Americas, a Medellín station, shot to death on October 17. Frequently criticized organized crime and other local problems.

• Jose William Espejo (also reported as José Wencesalo Espejo): Editor of the newspaper *El Tabloide* of Tulua, southwest of Bogotá, shot to death on December 10.

CPJ reports four other deaths in 1988.

ECUADOR (1)

• Francisco Jaime Arellano: Print journalist who went by the name of Pancho Jaime and published a satirical weekly criticizing politicians and others. Shot to death in Guayaquíl on September 6.

CPJ reports no deaths or disappearances in 1988.

(Continued)

TABLE 3.1
(*Continued*)

EL SALVADOR (13)

- Roberto Navas: Photographer for Reuters, shot and killed on March 18, after passing an air force checkpoint outside the Ilopango Air Base on the outskirts of San Salvador.
- Mauricio Pineda: Soundman with local Channel 12 television, shot and killed on March 19 when a soldier opened fire on a clearly marked press van. A soldier has been arrested in the case.
- Cornel Lagrouw: Cameraman with Dutch Interchurch Broadcasting (IKON), wounded in crossfire between government forces and guerrillas on March 19. Colleagues attempted to take him to a hospital in a clearly marked press car, but military aircraft repeatedly strafed the vehicle, forcing its occupants to halt and take cover. Lagrouw died before receiving medical treatment.
- Ignacio Ellacuria, Ignacio Martin-Baro, Segundo Montes: Jesuit priests and editorial board members of the monthly *Estudios Centroamericanos,* killed along with three other priests, their cook, and her daughter on November 16 by men believed to be members of the military. Ellacuria was also editor-in-chief of the monthly and a contributor to the weekly *Proceso.*
- David Blundy: British journalist with the *Sunday Correspondent,* shot and killed by an unknown sniper on November 17 in the San Salvador neighborhood of Mejicanos. It is unclear whether Blundy was targeted.
- Jose Caballos, Anibal Dubon, Oscar Herrera, Alfredo Melgar, Elibardo Quijada: Journalists with the government's Centro de Información Nacional, organized to disseminate information during the FMLN guerrilla offensive, disappeared on November 29. Last seen in a building under assault by guerrillas.
- Eloy Guevara: Salvadoran Agence France-Presse photographer, shot and killed December 1 after entering Soyapango with other journalists and the Red Cross. It is unclear whether Guevara was targeted.

CPJ reports no deaths or disappearances in 1988.

GUATEMALA (1)

- Danilo Barillas: Shot and killed on a Guatemala City street on August 19 shortly after becoming a major stockholder of *Por Que,* for which he also wrote.

CPJ reports no deaths or disappearances in 1988.

HONDURAS (0)

CPJ reports no deaths or disappearances in 1989. It reports one death in 1988.

MEXICO (0)

CPJ reports no deaths or disappearances in 1989. It reports four deaths in 1988.

PANAMA (1)

- Juan Antonio Rodriguez: Photographer for Madrid-based *El País,* shot and killed on December 21 during crossfire by U.S. troops during U.S. invasion of the country.

CPJ reports no deaths or disappearances in 1988.

PERU (5)

- Juvenal Farfán: Part-time radio and print journalist in Ayachucho in the southern part of the country. Gunmen broke into his home on January 30, killing him, his wife, and two children. Motive unknown.

(*Continued*)

TABLE 3.1
(*Continued*)

- Luís Piccone: Radio journalist in Ica, about 170 miles south of Lima, killed by a lone gunman on January 26. Press reports blamed the attack on Shining Path guerrillas, whereas a witness blamed a government-linked assassin.
- Barbara d'Achille: Journalist specializing in ecology issues for the Lima-based *El Comercio,* beaten to death on May 31, presumably by members of the Shining Path guerrillas. Was investigating a development project outside Huancavelica.
- Guillermo Lopez Salazar: Worked for Radio Tingo Maria until shortly before he was murdered on April 19. He had also contributed to other media and acted as a guide for journalists in the region. Motive unknown, but colleagues suggest that he may have been killed for his journalistic activities.
- Todd Smith: Reporter for Florida's *Tampa Tribune,* found strangled to death in Uchiza on November 21. Reports point to Shining Path guerrillas and drug traffickers as the murderers. He had been captured 4 days earlier, apparently by Shining Path guerrillas.

CPJ reports one other death in 1988.

pamphlet. The anti-terrorism law went into effect just a few days before Arce's arrest. Arce was arrested 4 months earlier for publishing an interview with Abimael Guzmán (Collett, 1988; Smith, 1988). In June 1989, *El Diario*'s interim director, Janet Talavera, was temporarily detained by police on the apologia-for-terrorism statute.

El Diario has been described as a mouthpiece for the Shining Path. The paper claims that although it is sympathetic with the guerrillas, it is not a mouthpiece. *El Diario* began as a news magazine for leftist intellectuals in 1975. It began presenting the viewpoints of the Shining Path in 1986. It eventually published documents of the Shining Path's first party congress in 1988 and carried ads for the guerrilla organization (Smith, 1988).

When the anti-terrorism law was directed only at left-wing media, such as *El Diario,* there were few complaints from the nation's establishment news media. But when a local lawyer attempted, without success, to invoke the law against the editor of the prominent magazine *Si,* many Peruvian journalists spoke out against the statute (Anon., February 1990).

Even Colombia, regarded as one of the continent's most stable democracies, has been so wracked by drug violence and terrorism in recent years that it passed an Anti-Terrorist Statute in January 1988. One of its articles that may affect the press sets penalties against those who have contacts with armed groups and refuse to reveal their whereabouts. The Colombian government maintains a degree of control over broadcast coverage of terrorism, imposing restrictions on identifications of witnesses to terrorist acts and the reporting of on-going terrorist activities (Anon., February 1990).

The growth of Mexico as a drug transportation center into the United States during the 1980s accounted for much of the violence against Mexican journalists. What is more, the Mexican government's willingness to solve the murders has been questioned. It has even been suggested that there is governmental complicity in the murders. In May 1988, the Human Rights Committee of the United

Nations questioned the Mexican government's willingness to investigate the murder of journalists who wrote about taboo subjects. Mexico's UN ambassador responded that only one of the 31 Mexican journalists killed between 1981 and 1988 had been murdered for political reasons—a charge rejected by the Human Rights Committee (Jackson, 1989a, 1989b).

The most notable case of a murder of a Mexican journalist was that of Manuel Buendía, an independent muckraking journalist whose column "Private Network" appeared in over 200 newspapers. Buendía, the victim of an assassin's bullet in 1984, wrote about illegal drug activities in high public places, arms dealers, Central Intelligence Agency involvement in Mexican politics, paramilitary organizations run by police and top government officials, corruption in the state oil industry, and so forth.

After his murder, many journalists maintained that he was killed by government officials. Many doubted that the Mexican government would seriously investigate Buendía's murder. For 5 years after Buendía's death no one was charged. Journalists claimed that the government was intentionally lax in its investigation. Not until the fifth anniversary of Buendía's murder did President Carlos Salinas de Gortari concede possible governmental complicity in Buendía's death and promise to thoroughly investigate the killing. Four days after Salinas' promise, an arrest warrant was issued against Jose Antonio Zorrilla, the former head of the now-defunct federal secret police (Mexico's FBI) who was captured after a shoot-out (Jackson, 1989a; Rohter, 1989a). In April 1990, President Salinas presented Buendía's widow 250 million pesos (about $90,000 U.S.) and announced the establishment of a scholarship fund in Buendía's name.

In Guatemala, reform-minded President Vinicio Cerezo has been working to expand press freedom since he was elected in 1985. After his election the violence committed by death squads, reactionary members of the military, almost disappeared. However, by 1989, human rights groups reported the reappearance of death squads. Many of these squads' activities were aimed against the press. Cerezo apparently could not control the death squads. The authoritarian structures created by 32 years of military rule before Cerezo's election was difficult to overcome. In June 1988, *La Epoca* was the victim of a bomb attack and entry of its office by 10 armed men. Right-wing forces bombed the offices of the Soviet news agency Tass and the correspondent of Cuba's Prensa Latina was threatened (Buckman, 1990a).

*   *   *

SPOTLIGHT

Colombian Journalists: Their "War" With the Cartel

As the decade of the 1990s was ushered in, Colombia found itself in a declared "state of war" with the nation's drug cartel in which journalists were among prime assassination targets. During most of the 1980s, members of Colombia's drug cartel lived openly and enjoyed ostentatious lifestyles. Many were even pillars of their communities who made generous donations to charitable causes. They were able to successfully sway judges and even Supreme Court members to keep them from being prosecuted by means of bribes, intimidation, and assassination threats. One former attorney general described the drug lords as having created a "superstate."

But even by Colombian standards, the cartel violated the unwritten rules for acceptable violence when it assassinated leading presidential candidate Luis Carlos Galan in August 1989. Galan ran on a campaign in which he promised to crack down on the cartel. President Virgilio Barco rounded up 11,000 suspects within a week and confiscated mansions, airplanes, and limousines of the drug lords. Before the month was over, the government had confiscated enough limousines, mansions, livestock, helicopters, airplanes, firearms and other booty to pay off the nation's $16 billion national debt.

More importantly, Barco issued an emergency decree that in effect took extradition power away from the Supreme Court and gave it to the executive branch. An extradition treaty between Colombia and the United States was suspended by the Colombian Supreme Court in 1987 under heavy pressure from the cartel, which assassinated dozens of judges, a Supreme Court justice, and a justice minister. The killing of Galan, meant to intimidate the nation, actually galvanized support to rid the nation of the cartel, at least for the short term. Many newspapers, which had gingerly handled stories about the cartel, took strong stands against the cartel. Leaders from 30 media organizations signed declarations of support for Barco's "confiscate-and-extradite" campaign.

The evening Galan was assassinated, the nation's news media had to make some difficult decisions. The editors of Bogota's *El Tiempo* met to determine how to cover the story. The most important question concerned whether they dared to report what everyone already knew—that Galan was assassinated by the cartel. They agreed to accuse the cartel with the murder. As one *El Tiempo* editor said, "The death of Galan has changed a lot of attitudes. We've never gone that far before" (Marquis, 1989a, p. 16a). Other Bogotá newspapers that formerly played down cartel violence were also inspired by Galan's assassination to speak out against cartel violence.

On August 24, 1989, the cartel issued a typewritten statement over letterhead identifying themselves as "The Extraditables." In the letter, "The Extraditables" threatened to wreak havoc on the nation if cartel members were extradited to the United States:

> We declare an all-out and absolute war on the government, the industrial and political oligarchy, journalists who have attacked and insulted us, judges who support extradition, union leaders and all those who have persecuted and attacked us. . . . We will not respect the families of those who have not respected our families. (Marquis, 1989a, p. 16a)

After the declaration of war, journalists joined politicians and judges in seeking increased security. Some journalists understandably avoided confrontational reporting that might upset the cartel. This was especially the case in violence-wracked Medellín, a major drug center where the daily *El Colombiano* had been intimidated into silence. Medellín's newspapers took a more prudent stand in reporting the "war" than Bogotá's newspapers. Rather than directly attacking the cartel, they reported straightforward accounts about attacks and often did not assign blame. What views were expressed frequently reflected the views of Medellín's mayor that some sort of dialogue with the cartel was needed to resolve the problem.

This view was typical of many mayors and police chiefs in rural cities who felt they might become victims of violence if they defied the cartel. Some rural mayors and police chiefs were sympathetic with the cartel, whose leaders purchased large tracts of rural land over the years and became prominent "narco-ranchers," creating jobs and pumping money into local economies. By contrast, Bogotá's newspapers seemed to grow more defiant in the weeks after Galan's assassination. They supported President Barco's crusade against the cartel and portrayed Medellín's politicians and newspapers as cowards. Those in Medellín felt the Bogotá newspapers were taking a moral view the Medellín press could not afford to take.

Bogotá's *El Tiempo,* although not running a banner headline, did report the cartel's declaration of war in the last three paragraphs of a page-3 story headlined "NARCO TERRORIST WAVE IN MEDELLÍN." *La Prensa,* a small Bogotá daily, published the entire text of the war declaration. "It's true, we've all got ulcers," *La Prensa* editor Gonzalo Guillen said. "But we have to get out of bed every morning and do our jobs" (Marquis, 1989a, p. 16a). *El Espectador,* a leading proponent of the extradition of cartel members, published a number of investigative reports about the cartel. *El Espectador* came under criticism from its competitors for its "preaching" to avenge the assassination of its former editor, Guillermo Cano, at the hands of the cartel (Marquis, 1989a, 1989b, 1989c).

If ever there was any doubt that journalists were major targets in the war, that doubt was dispelled when *El Espectador*'s offices were bombed in 1988. The car bomb injured almost 100 people, left one dead, and caused $2.5 million damage.

In a show of unity, the Inter American Press Association contacted newspapers, news agencies, press organizations, and private individuals from around the world and urged them to purchase advertising space in *El Espectador* expressing their solidarity with *El Espectador.* With the help of other newspapers, makeshift operations were created and *El Espectador* was ready to resume publishing within hours after the bombing. The next day the newspaper put out a 16-page edition that sold 500,000 copies, more than twice the usual daily circulation. Luís Gabriel Cano, the newspaper's editor-in-chief and publisher, made a trip through the United States and Canada after the bombing, seeking financial assistance from news organizations to keep his newspaper publishing. After the bombing, *El Espectador* had to publish its newspapers under the protection of government troops stationed inside and outside the newspaper building. The cartel not only threatened *El Espectador,* but the paper's advertisers as well. According to Luís Gabriel Cano (personal interview, January 25, 1990), *El Espectador*'s representative in the United States, department stores that advertised in *El Espectador* saw their businesses bombed.

During April 1990, newspapers and journalists continued to be targets of assassinations. *El Espectador* was feeling pressure by the violence. On April 3, the newspaper announced on its front page that it was temporarily suspending publication of all editorials as a result of threats against the newspaper and its employees until President Barco returned from a United Nations conference on the drug problem in Europe (Anon., June 1990a). In mid-October, another newspaper, the daily *Vanguardia Liberal* in Bucaramanga, about 175 miles north of Bogotá, was bombed. Four newspaper employees died and most of the building was destroyed. The explosion caused $1.5 million damage. The bombing of *Vanguardia Liberal* brought the number of journalists murdered to eight in less than a week.

In June 1991, the government reached an arrangement with the cartel. The law permitting extradition of cartel members was declared unconstitutional. In response, leading cartel members, including the notorious Pablo Escobar, turned themselves in to the government.

New World Information
and Communication Order

Many of the United Nations Educational, Scientific, and Cultural Organization's (UNESCO) first efforts to implement a New World Information and Communication Order (NWICO) were aimed at Latin America. To critics of the NWICO, the very term *information order* conjures up Orwellian images of self-serving media manipulation by governments. To supporters, the NWICO promises developing nations the opportunity to develop their own mass media systems and to become self-reliant. Much of the rhetoric about the NWICO debate comes from Latin American scholars who, during the 1960s, asserted that Latin America is a victim of "media imperialism" because it is dependent on foreign mass media for its information and culture. Latin American media are developing a few cultural centers such as Mexico and Brazil to supply the region with news and entertainment from within the region. In recent years, much of the debate centering around the NWICO has subsided.

Former proposals for what would come to be known as a New World Information and Communication Order (NWICO) started being discussed in the United Nations Educational, Scientific, and Cultural Organization (UNESCO) during the 1970s. UNESCO regarded improvement and equality in world communication issues as one of its major responsibilities since its establishment in the late 1940s. Since the mid-1970s, however, the worldwide debate over communication issues in UNESCO became political and frequently contentious. Representatives from Western news organizations feared that discussions about a NWICO would be used as a rationale by governments to justify government intervention in news media (Muñoz, 1983).

The NWICO lacks a clear definition and does not represent any single idea. The concept encompasses an amalgam of ideas outlined through numerous UNESCO declarations and resolutions over the years aimed at correcting the uneven flow of communication between and within nations. The UNESCO resolutions and declarations that involve the NWICO have to satisfy a number of constituencies that comprise, quite literally, the entire world. As a result, many UNESCO documents are so ambiguous that they mean different things to different people. For instance, depending on how different parties in the NWICO debate view the issue of *colégios* (discussed in the previous chapter), they may be described as "licensing" or "protection" of journalists (Youm, in press-b). As one observer wrote of the NWICO:

> The New World Information and Communication Order means sharply different things to different people. . . . It seems clear that the term NWICO has become a symbol around which or against the varying sides to the controversy have rallied. As a symbol, the NWICO is now associated with a movement or cause, rather than a specific entity. (Shea, 1984, p. 4)

Beyond the perfunctory rhetoric of calling for a more equitable international news flow, the calls for a NWICO have also embraced solutions for correcting news flow problems. These include the creation of national and regional news agencies and the establishment of journalism training and education programs in developing countries. These proposed solutions have usually been accepted by all parties as reasonable. Many Western news organizations, ordinarily critics of the NWICO, have not only endorsed but embraced the concept of journalism training programs for Third World journalists. In addition, Western news agencies have provided financial and technical assistance for the establishment of news agencies in developing nations, including those in Latin America and the Caribbean.

The "debate," however, has centered on questions dealing with to what extent, if at all, national governments should take active roles in correcting news flow problems. Some supporters of the NWICO claim that governments must be actively involved in correcting news flow problems, whereas Western press theory takes a dim view of any role for governments in media policies. Although Western news agencies and news media organizations may support the establishment of national and regional news agencies in developing nations, they stress that these agencies must be independent of governments.

Although much of the debate over the NWICO has quelled in recent years, the topic is far from dead. Despite the ambiguity concerning the NWICO, it has proven to be a valuable concept for analyzing mass media in developing nations. The NWICO has also contributed a decidedly and much needed Third World point of view to international communication issues.

Partly as a result of what Western nations regard as UNESCO's dangerous solutions for correcting world communication problems, the United States and Great Britain withdrew from the organization in 1984 (followed later by Singapore). William Harley (1984), a media consultant to the U.S. National Commission for UNESCO in the Department of State, claimed the United States withdrew from UNESCO because its continued participation in the organization might be viewed as

> a kind of Good Housekeeping seal of approval to anti-free press behavior. . . . Though it is true that any number of resolutions may be passed by UNESCO, no nation can be forced to comply with them. However, sanction by UNESCO of the kind of restrictions on the media which are constantly being proposed in that forum could lend respectability to actions by authoritarian regimes. (p. 20)

THE ROOTS OF THE NWICO

Calls from developing nations for a NWICO stem from Western researchers' failed attempts to facilitate modernization in developing nations through mass media during the 1950s and 1960s. These Western researchers, with Daniel Lerner, Wilbur Schramm, Lucian Pye, and Everette Rogers the most prominent among them, believed mass media played a significant role in promoting national development. The most important role that these researchers saw for the mass media in national development was that of creating positive dispositions toward development and modernization among peoples in developing nations. It was also believed that if economic development could be achieved, social and political development (i.e., democracy) would soon follow (Fair, 1989; Stevenson, 1988). Latin America was viewed as a testing ground for Western theories dealing with the role of mass media in modernization (McNelly, 1966).

By 1963, Lerner conceded weaknesses with the theory. He argued that the press in developing nations may have stifled national development by fostering unrealistic goals about economic development, and thereby raising expectations. Other U.S. researchers stressed the importance of an independent press in national development (Gardner, 1963; Nixon, 1960).

By the late 1970s, Everette Rogers (1976), a leading American scholar long concerned about the role of media in promoting development in developing societies, claimed a "new paradigm of development" was approaching. The problem with the old or "dominant paradigm" of economic development, he argued, was that it viewed indicators of development such as per capita income as measures of "quality of life."

The dominant paradigm, Rogers asserted, overlooked such important matters as the equitable distribution of wealth and maintaining traditional cultures. The rapid rush for national development in developing nations, spurred by promises from Western scholars and local politicians, followed a "growth-first-and-let-equality-come-later mentality" (Rogers, 1976, 1980). Rogers claimed that the new paradigm would involve popular participation from all sectors of society, equitable distribution of wealth, self-designed development strategies, and compatibility between modern technologies and traditional values.

Scholars from the political left, many from Latin America, were among the first to outline the form they believed this "new paradigm" would take (Atwood, 1986; Mattelart, 1976; Reyes Matta, 1981). In addition to outlining a new paradigm, they spent much of their time castigating the old one. Atwood (1986) charged that the early Western development researchers' paradigm supported "ethnocentric rigidity, mercantile or imperialistic motives, and methodological inadequacy" (p. 13).

As these aspersions suggest, much that has come from the NWICO has involved a good deal of rhetoric. Bolivian communication scholar Luis Ramiro Beltrán (1978), ordinarily a supporter of the NWICO, agrees that too often the supporters of the NWICO engage in "catchy slogans" that are "meant to elicit prompt and uniform—and almost instinctive—reactions of a given nature . . . (which) function as agents of emotion and dogmatic preconception, banning sensible dialogue in favor of aggressive monologues" (p. 183).

LATIN AMERICA AND THE NWICO

Latin American scholars during the 1950s and 1960s put forward the notion of "*dependency theory.*" The theory grew from their frustrations with Latin American nations' seeming inability to achieve self-sufficiency despite considerable economic advancement. According to dependency theory, nations in the political *Core* (e.g., the United States and other Western European nations) kept nations in the political *Periphery* (e.g., Latin American nations) perpetually dependent on the Core nations (Cordoso & Falleto, 1979). This political and economic theory serves as the theoretical framework for *media imperialism* and *cultural imperialism,* central terms in NWICO debates. According to these two forms of imperialism, mass media exported from the Core to the Periphery support modern-day imperialism through propaganda rather than military force and occupation (Beltrán, 1978). Supporters of the NWICO further assert that as a consequence of media imperialism and cultural imperialism, communication messages primarily flow one way from developed nations to developing nations.

Although even some of the more conservative media scholars in the United States agree that there exists a primarily "one-way" flow of information from the developed nations to Latin America, they do not concede the immediate dangers of this imbalance. Further, they see nothing nefarious in the uneven flow (McGregor, 1984; Merrill, 1981). Most Western scholars and practitioners maintain that the uneven flow is the result of the natural economies of scale enjoyed by the industrialized nations (Hoskins, Mirus, & Rozeboom, 1989). For instance, Prof. John C. Merrill (1981), a frequent critic of the NWICO, asserted that "unevenness of flow is a basic characteristic of news—and not only of news flow, but of water flow, oil flow, money flow, population flow, and food flow" (p. 156).

Some dependency scholars from the political left, however, assert that the uneven news and information flow has nothing to do with economies of scale. Instead, they argue, the uneven flow is the result of a "conspiracy" to keep developing nations forever dependent on the industrialized nations. Bolivian scholar Luis Ramiro Beltrán (1978) summarized this conspiracy view when he asserted that "cultural imperialism through communication is not an occasional and fortuitous event . . . (I)t is a vital process for 'imperial' countries to secure and maintain economic domination and political hegemony over others" (p. 185).

Many of these scholars from the political left in Latin America and elsewhere have advocated varying degrees of government involvement in national communication policies as a means of correcting the uneven flow. According to these scholars, the government is frequently seen as a benevolent force concerned with people's needs. In addition, the government can also serve as a counterveiling power to dangers posed by wealthy private media owners, both indigenous and foreign. In fact, these scholars criticize what they view as the *laissez-faire* policies of Latin American governments as failures of the governments to work for the best interests of their citizens. As one Latin American supporter of this view wrote: "The existence of the state presupposes the existence of (state) policies. The absence of explicit policies merely indicates that policy-making has been moved from government agencies to the boardrooms of corporations" (Roncagliolo, 1986, p. 169).

Representatives from developed nations and their respective media organizations view government involvement in "national communication policies" as the worst imaginable solution for addressing national communication problems. They assert that such solutions are merely rationales for governments to control their news media to maintain favorable coverage of government achievements and silence critics.

Although many Latin American governments and scholars looked favorably on the NWICO, many of the large Latin American media organizations reacted coolly, if not hostilely. There are some distinct differences between Latin America and other developing regions that account for this hostility. Unlike most developing nations in Africa and Asia, many of which were European colonies up to the end of World War II, most Latin American nations have long histories of political independence dating to the early 19th century. In addition, the concept of privately owned mass media, including broadcast media, is well established in Latin America, and the region has a relatively large number of well-developed, privately operated media outlets. For what are generally thought of as developing nations, levels of media penetration are high in most Latin American nations, as shown in Table 4.1. Finally, unlike other developing regions, Latin America has a number of wealthy families and entrepreneurs with the economic resources to maintain independent media organizations. Not surprisingly, Latin American media entrepreneurs take a dim view of the role of governments in national media policies.

TABLE 4.1
Media Penetration in Latin America and the Caribbean

Country	Daily Newspaper Readers Per 1,000	Radio Receivers Per 1,000	TV Sets Per 1,000
Anguilla	22*	—	—
Antigua	80*	247	234
Argentina	115	727	202
Bahamas	154	514	156
Barbados	145	706	201
Belize	41*	450	—
Bolivia	46	571	59
Brazil	44*	355	122
Cayman Islands	35*	944	167
Chile	87*	300	113
Colombia	39	122	89
Costa Rica	77	84	86
Cuba	118	317	164
Dominican Republic	42	44	78
Ecuador	64	319	61
El Salvador	54	336	64
French Guyana	23*	781	172
Grenada	28**	327	—
Guadaloupe	98	115	112
Guatemala	24	43	26
Guyana	85	352	—
Haiti	4	21	4
Honduras	61	48	13
Jamaica	46	386	84
Martinique	99	163	127
Mexico	140	292	111
Montserrat	—	483	—
Netherland Antilles	208	674	169
Nicaragua	50	274	67
Peru	77	161	50
Puerto Rico	139	582	238
Saint Kitts-Nevis	22*	309	66
Saint Lucia	33	746	16
Suriname	84*	582	103
Trinidad & Tobago	140	291	250
Turks and Caicos	—	667	—
Uruguay	188	577	126
Venezuela	176*	408	126
Virgin Islands (Br.)	—	850	200
Virgin Islands (USA)	145	776	466

*1979.

**1970.

All others 1982.

Source: Anon. (1986).

Note: For comparison, with newspapers, Japan is 562, The Soviet Union is 422; United Kingdom is 411, West Germany is 348, the United States is 267, and Canada is 220. With radio, the United States is 2,030, United Kingdom is 993, Canada is 821, Japan is 710, the Soviet Union is 516; and West Germany is 401. With television, the United States is 785, Japan is 562, Canada is 479, West Germany is 360; United Kingdom is 328, and Soviet Union is 310.

GOVERNMENT-CONTROLLED
COMMUNICATION POLICIES

Latin America was one of the first regions where UNESCO's "experts" sought to first implement the NWICO (Fox, 1988a). UNESCO sponsored the First Intergovernmental Conference on National Communication Policies in San José, Costa Rica, in 1976. The purpose was to make recommendations for national media policies in Latin America. The conference, attended by 20 Latin American nations, endorsed the establishment of government-controlled communication policies. One of the few recommendations that was eventually implemented was the establishment of an intergovernment information service, the Association of National Government Information Systems (ASIN), in 1979, and a regional Latin American feature news service, the Latin American Feature News Service (ALASEI), in 1983.

The San José conference's recommendations were vigorously condemned by many Western and Latin American publishers and broadcasters. They maintained that UNESCO solutions were guided by "statist" policies, which were thinly disguised rationalizations for governments to regulate the press (O'Brien, 1980). In a UNESCO meeting in Bogotá 2 years after the San José conference, members restated their distaste with private media and their hope that national governments could correct the excesses associated with private media:

> The formation and execution of national communications policy should be the exclusive concern of the State: commercially owned media, by providing the people "with amusement and means of escaping from reality which tend to deaden their critical faculties and stultify their potential for action to bring about social change" fail to promote development. (O'Brien, 1980, p. 7)

Although U.S. media organizations were concerned about UNESCO declarations, the U.S. government was not upset. During the Bogotá meeting, the Inter American Press Association (IAPA) expressed "deep concern and dismay" at the absence of a U.S. government observer at the meeting. A low-level State Department official told IAPA that UNESCO declarations were not very important:

> We think the conference has very limited significance. . . . The recommendations have no force beyond what the nomenclature signifies. . . . Recommendations of regional conferences are not binding upon member states even when they are adopted by the General Assembly. (Gonzalez, 1978, p. 82)

A U.S. newspaper trade publication, *Editor & Publisher,* charged that the State Department had taken a naive view toward UNESCO press policies. The publication asserted that many governments take UNESCO declarations seriously, adding that governments frequently rely upon these resolutions to legitimize government control of the press. The chair of the World Press Freedom Committee, who attended the Bogotá meeting, agreed with *Editor & Publisher*'s assessment:

> Some fifteen non-regional nations had registered with their ambassadors and they were seated at long tables with signs indicating each country. I was distressed to find the U.S. unrepresented. I inquired of the Embassy and was told that they had received no instructions from Washington to attend. And in fact, they didn't know of the meeting until they read it in the Bogotá press, they said. (Gonzalez, 1978, p. 82)

Several years later, however, as UNESCO took a more active role in devising communication policies, the United States government no longer viewed UNES-CO declarations as irrelevant. The United States withdrew from UNESCO for a host of reasons, including allegations of inept financing. But communication issues were among the factors for the withdrawal.

Supporters of the NWICO order in Latin America frequently single out Western media organizations, particularly the "Big Four" international news agencies (Associated Press, United Press International, Reuters, and Agence France Presse), for Latin America's continual—and they would say perpetual—"dependency" upon Western news media. The Associated Press, because of its worldwide dominance, probably takes the brunt of these criticisms. However, in Latin America, where United Press International is the predominant international news agency, UPI takes its share of criticism.

Bolivian communication scholar Luis Ramiro Beltrán (1978), among others, asserted that Latin Americans are being overwhelmed with information from an "alien culture," and as a result are losing their cultural heritages. Beltrán also decried developing nations' inabilities to influence news disseminated about them in the world press. Some leaders in the region see more immediate dangers from their countries' dependency upon foreign news than long-term cultural loss (Hosein, 1976; Johnson-Hill, 1976). Former Jamaican Prime Minister Edward Seaga appeared before the Inter American Press Association and accused the North American news media of exaggerating the extent of upheaval in Jamaica during January 1984. Seaga asserted that there were no "riots," only "demonstrations." He also claimed that Jamaica suffered $30 million in lost tourism revenue within five months after the upheaval (Anon., June 1985, p. 41; Cuthbert & Sparkes, 1978).

Since the United States' withdrawal from UNESCO, much of the rhetoric has mellowed. Even some former critics of UNESCO, such as Leonard Sussman (1990), the executive director of the World Press Freedom Committee, had argued that UNESCO had abandoned many of its anti-press NWICO policies and returned to the "free flow of information" ideology. As the 1990s began, the United States' perceptions toward UNESCO shifted. United States participation in the organization was now under discussion.

IMPACT OF THE NORTH AMERICAN PRESS MODEL

In addition to the influence of Western news media in Latin America, local Latin American news media have been viewed as having been influenced by Western news values. During the height of the "yellow press" in the United States during the late 19th and early 20th centuries, leading Latin American editors and publishers journeyed to the United States to study under the likes of William Randolph Hearst, Joseph Pulitzer, and others. Agustín Edwards Ross, who purchased the prestigious *El Mercúrio* of Santiago, Chile, studied the practices of James Gordon Bennett, Jr. in the United States (Knudson, 1987a). Caribbean press scholar John A. Lent (1987) dated U.S. media influence in the region to U.S. colonial times. He noted that Benjamin Franklin helped establish Antigua's first newspaper, *The Antigua Gazette*. Lent described Franklin's press arrangement in the Caribbean as "the first international media combine" and one of the first instances of "media imperialism" (p. 245).

A number of researchers have sought to empirically demonstrate or refute Latin America's state of dependency and victimization of cultural imperialism. These studies suffer because the concept of "cultural dependency," unlike its counterpart "economic dependency," cannot be easily quantified. Measurable "indicators," such as Latin American news media reliance on foreign news agency reports for international news (Reyes Matta, 1977) or "capitalist themes" in Donald Duck comic books (Dorfman & Mattelart, 1971), are sometimes used to quantify cultural dependency. Just because the concept of cultural dependency cannot be easily quantified does not mean such studies should not be done, only that the findings from these studies must be interpreted with caution. Typical among such studies that examined the "quantity" of the flow, Mexican communication scholar Fernando Reyes Matta (1978) analyzed 16 daily newspapers in 14 Latin American countries. He reported that more than 80% of the foreign news originated from the "Big Four" international news agencies. This is a straightforward finding that illustrates an easily measurable indicator of the "imbalanced" flow. But it does not shed light on the "quality" of the flow.

In another study that examined the "quality" of the flow, Reyes Matta (1977, 1979a) analyzed South American newspaper coverage dealing with Suriname's independence on November 26, 1975. He examined 16 leading South and Central American newspapers from November 24–27. Although the birth of a new independent nation on the continent was a major regional story, not one of the newspapers sent a correspondent to Suriname to cover the story, nor did one of the newspapers give the story front-page coverage. What news coverage Suriname's independence received in the Latin American press originated from news agency reports, mostly United Press International (UPI). The UPI report, Reyes Matta observed, was written for the North American reading public. The report stressed Suriname's central importance as a supplier of bauxite to the United States.

During the period of Suriname independence, most of the major newspapers in South America reported the major international news stories in Europe and the Middle East, the same stories important to the United States and European readers. Reyes Matta argued that this lack of news coverage about Latin America and failure to provide Latin American "angles" to news stories was the result of the continent's dependency on the international news agencies for world news. Because the international news agencies did not treat Suriname independence as an important story, Reyes Matta reasoned, neither did the Latin American newspapers. In other words, the international news agencies set the news agenda for what would be regarded as newsworthy in Latin America, and this held true even for stories about Latin America.

Reyes Matta reported that during the week of Suriname's independence, 60% of the 1,308 international stories that he coded in the 16 newspapers originated from UPI (39%) and AP (21%) combined. Reyes Matta added, however, that this was considerable improvement from 80% dependence on UPI and AP since the 1960s. But Reyes Matta's (1979a) study hardly yielded overwhelming support for Latin American dependency on the foreign news agencies in determining news values. Reyes Matta himself presented data on the world's cities most widely reported in the newspapers. Madrid and Lisbon led the list, respectively. Although Reyes Matta argued that the coronation of Juan Carlos may have contributed to Madrid's importance that week, the event was of no greater importance than the many other occurrences in the news during a given week.

The fact that a Spanish-speaking European nation received the most coverage in a continent where Spanish is the dominant language and mother culture, and a Portuguese-speaking European nation received second most coverage where Portuguese-speaking Brazil is a dominant regional power, tended to refute Reyes Matta's own assertions. These findings suggest that Latin American gatekeepers may have been selecting stories about cities from the news agencies' files that reflected local cultures and interests. In addition, Reyes Matta himself reported that some Latin American cities such as Buenos Aires and Santiago received considerable coverage.

Reyes Matta claimed his findings supported dependency theory (in what he referred to as "information inertia"). He argued that economic difficulties among Latin America's news media alone could not account for his finding of Latin American media dependency on Western news agencies because, unlike other developing regions, Latin American news media organizations in some large nations such as Argentina, Mexico, and Brazil have the economic wherewithal to gather and distribute their own news in Latin America. Reyes Matta concluded that Latin American dependence on the Western news agencies accounted for the state of Latin American journalism.

Another study, a comparative content analysis of prestigious North American and South American newspaper coverage of El Salvador's civil war, provides evidence for the contention that Latin America's newspapers reflect the conservative views of their owners. Canadian researchers Sodurlund and Schmitt (1986) analyzed the coverage of Argentina's *La Nación* and *La Prensa* and Chile's *El Mercúrio* and *La Tercera* during a sample period in 1981. The results were compared to the coverage of *The New York Times* and *The Washington Post* in the United States and the Toronto *Globe and Mail* and Ottawa *Citizen* in Canada.

The South American newspapers in Sodurlund and Schmitt's study portrayed El Salvador's military-led junta, accused of numerous human rights abuses, in mixed or neutral terms, whereas the North American newspapers reported the junta in decidedly negative terms. The South American newspapers even portrayed U.S. involvement in El Salvador's civil war in far more positive terms than the U.S. newspapers. A caveat is needed that the study was conducted at a time when brutal military dictatorships existed in both South American nations. As a result, it is possible that the conservative coverage in the South American newspapers may have been a function of overt or subtle pressure from their military governments.

Another empirical study by Buckman (1990b) examined Latin American newspaper and magazine coverage of cultural issues (e.g., cinema, art, theater, television, history, and so forth). Buckman examined about 6,400 stories reported in a sample of 14 "elite" Latin American newspapers during 1949 and 15 during 1982. The dates were chosen to reflect a sample year before the introduction of the cultural medium of television into the region and another sample year that was the most recent year available to the author. To the extent possible, Buckman examined the same newspapers during both sample years, but was unable to exactly duplicate the samples because of newspaper closings and unavailability of newspapers to the author. Buckman also examined about 1,225 stories and 1,725 short "vignettes" (capsulated items) in 11 Latin American magazines during 1983. Each story and vignette was coded as either "domestic," "U.S.," "European," "other Latin American," "other region," or "mixed."

Buckman found no support for both his hypotheses that (a) "measurable U.S. cultural coverage in the sample newspapers and magazines is significantly greater than the coverage of domestic culture" and (b) "measurable U.S. coverage is significantly greater than measurable European cultural coverage" (pp. 136–137). He found that for both sample years examined in the newspapers, most of the newspapers reported more domestic cultural coverage than U.S. coverage. If there was any cultural dependency, Buckman cautiously suggested that during 1949 the newspapers displayed some dependency on European culture. In the 1982 newspaper sample and the 1983 magazine sample, Buckman reported that all the newspapers and magazines he examined reported more domestic cultural reports than U.S. or European reports.

DEVELOPMENTAL JOURNALISM

The concept of developmental journalism is closely associated with the NWICO. The concept, however, is as vague and ambiguous as the NWICO. Developmental journalism is closely associated with "nation-building." It is unclear, however, whether developmental journalism calls on news media to report only "good news" or whether it also includes critical news (Ogan, Fair, & Shah, 1984; Salwen & Garrison, 1989). One writer has described developmental journalism as "an amorphous and curious mixture of ideas, rhetoric, influences, and grievances." In some instances, it represents "aspects straight out of Lenin and the Communist concept of the press" (Hachten, 1981, p. 81).

Perhaps journalists and Western media scholars can be accused of making too much fuss about press freedom, in the form of an independent, unencumbered press. Other freedoms are important too. Supporters of "developmental journalism," who focus on the active role of the press in addressing long-standing social and economic problems, claim that too often the banner of press freedom is waved by wealthy media owners who simply want to be left alone by their governments to rake in profits. This has particularly been true in Latin America, where many media owners have sided with conservative, and even reactionary, elements who foot the media's advertising bills. Beltrán (1988) summed up this view:

> The state is not the only enemy of democratic freedom in modern Latin America. Conservative and exploitative interests, native and from outside the region, have built a private and commercial mass communication system that, on several counts, falls short of being democratic. (p. 1)

If supporters of a free and unencumbered press put too much faith in private ownership of the press, some supporters of "benign" government intervention in the news media tend to overlook the possibility that governments, if given the opportunity, may attempt to extend and abuse their powers to control the press. A freedom-of-the-press analysis rests on the assumption that in an unfettered media marketplace, where anyone may publish or broadcast whatever he or she pleases, a number of different views about all issues will be publicly aired and considered. For instance, Marvin Alisky, in his 1981 book *Latin American Media: Guidance and Censorship,* observed that freedom of the press in Latin America is important because it precedes other freedoms: "Press freedom in Latin America does not guarantee that problems will be solved, but the converse holds that when press freedom is lacking both leaders and citizens do not face problems openly or solve them in ways that are equitable for all citizens" (p. 4).

LITERATURE, POLITICS, AND DEVELOPMENTAL JOURNALISM

Although the concept of developmental journalism is relatively new, many of its supporters claim that its Latin American roots are old. Because Latin American journalism has a history of advocacy for social causes and is closely intertwined with literature and politics, a number of observers have argued that Latin American journalists have practiced variations of developmental journalism long before developmental journalism was popular.

One scholar has argued that Cuban poet, writer, and journalist Nicolás Guillen displayed aspects of developmental journalism in his writings (Irish, 1976). During the 1930s, and through the 1940s and 1950s, Guillen wrote about a number of social problems in the Americas. As a Cuban of African extraction, in a nation where people of African heritage were long victims of discrimination, he wrote about prejudice against Blacks and mulattos in Cuba, Haiti, South America, and the United States. In 1949, he wrote a stinging satire against Cuban dictator Fulgencio Batista in the Communist *Noticias de Hoy,* which he edited, that resulted in the closure of the paper (Irish, 1976).

In Cuba, since the days of the wars of independence against the Spanish in the late 19th century to Fidel Castro's revolution, journalism has played an important role in the island's revolutions and social causes (Jensen, 1988). The Cuban statesman and martyr Jose Martí founded *Pátria* while in exile in 1892 to lead the clarion call against Spanish occupation of the island. After Marti died in 1895, the newspaper's operations was taken over by the well-known journalist Enrique Jose Varona (Hedman Marreo, 1969). Under the leadership of Castro's confidante Ernesto "Che" Guevara, the newspaper *El Cubano Libre* was founded in 1957 while the rebels were in the Sierra Maestra mountains. Guevara published in the newspaper under the pseudonym Franco Tirador. In 1958, the clandestine radio station *Radio Rebelde* was founded by Guevara to broadcast rebel versions of the news to the Cuban people (Szulc, 1986).

A number of Latin American literary figures, associated with political positions, began their careers in journalism. These included Jorge Amado, Carlos Fuentes, and others. To this day, Latin American newspapers occasionally carry serialized novels, short stories, poetry, and cultural criticism, a practice that disappeared long ago from North American newspapers (Bogart, 1990). No Latin American literary figure's name is invoked more often by the region's journalists than the Colombian Nobel prize-winning author Gabriel García Marquez, author of *One Hundred Years of Solitude* (1982) and *Love in the Times of Cholera* (1987), among other works. García Marquez has been described as a Latin American journalist in the developmental journalism tradition (Pierce, 1988). As a former journalist on some of Colombia's largest daily newspapers, García Marquez wrote about the lives and customs of the people in Colombia's remote areas.

García Marquez began his journalism career in 1948 at age 20 writing for newspapers in the resort town of Cartagena. By 1954, he joined the staff of the prestigious *El Espectador* in Bogotá. According to Luís Alberto Cano (personal interview, January 25, 1990), the U.S representative of *El Espectador,* many Colombian journalists at *El Espectador* and elsewhere in Colombia still view García Marquez as an inspiration for what journalists can accomplish in Latin American societies. According to Cano, García Marquez also illustrates the romanticism attached to Colombian journalism. Many young journalists starting at *El Espectador* aspire to become leading national journalists or literary figures, and a newspaper career is seen as a route to accomplishing that goal.

García Marquez's major journalistic coup came when he detailed the account of a Colombian sailor washed overboard during a storm on a Colombian freighter and presumed dead. The sailor survived for 10 days on a raft without food or supplies. When he was found alive, he was received as a hero by the Colombian people and government for his courage. García Marquez held 20 separate in-depth interviews with the sailor. García Marquez's revelation that the sailor was washed overboard not by the storm alone but by sliding boxes of contraband (luxury items such as refrigerators and washing machines) resulted in a national scandal, exposing a major flaw in the political and economic system.

Colombian dictator Gustavo Rojas Pinilla, however, did not see García Marquez's journalism as valuable for pointing out a national problem with contraband goods. Rojas Pinilla was so upset by the series of stories that resulted from García Marquez's interviews that pressure was put on the newspaper to reassign García Marquez in another nation. He was made a foreign correspondent and sent to Europe. García Marquez published the sailor's account in a *Chronicle of a Death Foretold* (Pierce, 1988).

Another living South American writer, Mario Vargas Llosa, also mixes literature with politics. In April 1990, he was the Democratic Front's candidate for president of Peru. He garnered the plurality of the votes in the April election but lost in a run-off election 3 months later. Vargas Llosa's lack of political experience was considered a plus in Peru, where politicians were vilified. The nation's economy was near collapse, as inflation ran in the thousands of percent and many Peruvians maintained extra-legal employment to avoid paying taxes. Meanwhile, the Shining Path guerillas terrorized the countryside. Vargas Llosa's Democratic Front exploited Peruvians' disgust with traditional politicians by running a series of controversial television commercials showing how politicians were destroying Peru. One commercial depicted a "bureaucratic" monkey defecating on a desk (Marquis, 1990a).

An admirer of British Prime Minister Margaret Thatcher, Vargas Llosa ran on a platform of encouraging free-market capitalism, eliminating state subsidies, and reducing the national bureaucracy. In Latin America, the political opinions of intellectuals such as Vargas Llosa and García Marquez carry enormous weight. Support for Cuba's Fidel Castro has often been viewed a prime indicator of a person's politics. Vargas Llosa once shared García Marquez's leftist politics, until the late 1960s and early 1970s when Castro cracked down on leading Cuban literary figures. This crackdown culminated with the arrest of poet Herberto Padilla in March 1971. Although Padilla was released a month later after protests from leading literary figures, including García Marquez, Padilla's obviously forced recantation of his "anti-revolutionary" ways angered many writers.

The rift between Vargas Llosa and García Marquez came to physical blows when, in 1976, Vargas Llosa broke García Marquez's jaw in a Mexico City movie theater. Although the dispute may have been over a woman, it also highlighted the political differences between the two men. When Vargas Llosa turned to the political right, he became something of a pariah in Latin American literary circles. But since then, there has been a waning of support for Castro among intellectual circles, especially after Eastern European nations started separating from the Soviet Union during the late 1980s. As a result, García Marquez found himself as one of the few major Latin American writers to remain uncritical of Castro. In a rare interview with a *Miami Herald* reporter during 1990, García Marquez shifted from his previous unwavering support for Castro. He called on Castro to implement "profound reforms" (Oppenheimer, 1990b).

THE NWICO IN PRACTICE

Despite all the discussion about the role of the press and journalists in NWICO debates, few examples exist that clearly illustrate NWICO policies in practice in Latin America. All one can do is point to examples that illustrate various aspects of what might represent NWICO policies in practice. To some extent, media policies under Argentine dictator Juan Domingo Peron could be viewed as illustrating NWICO policies.

On June 4, 1943, a military junta seized power in Argentina. Although Gen. Pedro P. Ramirez was president (June 7, 1943 to March 9, 1944), it was clear that Gen. Peron, the vice president, was the real power. In 1946, the charismatic Peron was elected president until he was ousted by a military coup in 1955. Peron returned from exile to take power again in a 1973 election, in which his third wife, Isabelita, became vice president.

The Peron dictatorship, unlike many others in the region, was marked by active government involvement in media affairs rather than simply cracking down on critical media. Peron sought to actively use the media to promote his ideas of national development. In 1973, just a few months before Peron's death, a presidential decree ordered newspapers to devote 50% of their news space to news about Argentina and 30% to news elsewhere in Latin America. The decree was never enforced because of the impracticability of allocating news content by regions (Alisky, 1981).

Did Peron's press policies represent developmental journalism? It certainly contained some aspects of what some supporters of developmental journalism contend developmental journalism is about. The government took an active role in media policymaking, and, it claimed, promoted educational and cultural development. Other supporters of developmental journalism, however, would argue that developmental journalism involves media exposure of social problems, in the form of Western-style investigative journalism (Aggarwala, 1978, 1979).

The military dictatorship in power in Brazil from 1964 to 1985 also illustrates aspects of developmental journalism. The Brazilian dictatorship actively sought to use the media to stimulate the economic growth of the nation. The dictatorship achieved rapid economic development, the so-called "economic miracle." However, this economic development was achieved at a heavy cost to Brazilian society, and the economic advancements were far from equitable (Mattos, 1982). The media were among the industries that witnessed rapid growth during the period of the dictatorship, particularly in the broadcast media, in the form of the Globo television network.

A reform-minded Peruvian military that came to power during a 1968 coup also illustrated aspects of developmental journalism. From July 1974 to March 1976, the leading daily newspaper *El Comercio* of Lima, which belonged to the powerful Miro Quesada family, as well as other newspapers, were nationalized and handed over to peasant organizations. The move was part of a mass media policy promulgated by Peruvian leader Gen. Juan Velasco Alvarado (1968–1975). Critics charged the takeover represented an egregious violation of freedom of the press; but more sympathetic views maintained that there was never freedom of the press in Peru, which was run by a small clique of wealthy families (Gilbert, 1979). The Velasco government undertook plans for nationalizing Peru's news media. According to Chapter 24 of the revolutionary government's plan, the government had the right to nationalize the media in order to promote "freedom of the press."

Unlike nationalization of the news media elsewhere, where governments took over and operated media, the Peruvian government hoped to turn the news media over to the people through "organized sectors of society" such as farming organizations and worker communes. The first major attempt to nationalize a leading newspaper took place in 1970, when the Ministry of the Interior announced plans to expropriate two Lima dailies, *Expreso* and *Extra*. The newspapers were turned over to boards representing the journalists and printers. Later that year, the government expropriated *La Crónica* and its radio station, *Radio Crónica*. But the government waited several years before expropriating the nation's two most prestigious dailies, *La Prensa* and *El Comercio* (Alisky, 1976).

The government ordered *La Prensa* publisher Pedro Beltrán to sell his stock to his employees on a legal technicality after he had violated a section of the 1970 Press Statute. The statute prohibited a publisher from leaving the nation for more than 6 months during a 1-year period. The newspaper became an organ for industrial workers. In 1974, *El Comercio* was expropriated and became an organ of peasant organizations.

Under peasant leadership, *El Comercio* made special efforts to carry the views of local artists and writers and present a variety of views. In the area of news, efforts were made to provide in-depth news about the region instead of relying exclusively or primarily on the foreign news agencies. Newspaper employees were guaranteed space to vent their criticisms against their employers in the newspaper that could not be edited by management (Cardenas, 1980).

In 1975, Gen. Francisco Morales Bermudez ousted Velasco in a coup and was soon afterwards named president. Morales (1975–1980) allowed closed publications to re-open and exiled journalists to return. He promised to ease government control over the news media but vowed that reform would continue. By 1980, Fernando Belaunde Terry (1980–1985) won the presidency (he also served from 1963–1968) and started phasing out government control over the nation's news media and reverting ownership back to the original owners.

The "Chilean Experiment" during the rule of elected Marxist President Salvador Allende, like the other examples mentioned so far, also failed to take the extreme step of Cuba and nationalize all media (Schiller & Smythe, 1972). As a result, the private media that were permitted to operate with various degrees of government control were often among the most vitriolic critics of the Allende government (Fagen, 1974).

A similar situation appeared to be taking place in Nicaragua before the defeat of the Sandinista government during a 1990 presidential election. Although the Sandinistas insisted that their revolution involved "socialist ideals," they did not impose all-encompassing, centralized state control over the economy. Their media policies attested to that. The Sandinistas maintained a government-owned media with the stated goals of promoting social justice while permitting opposition media to co-exist as a check on government power. But the leading opposition newspaper, *La Prensa,* apparently took its opposition role too seriously for the Sandinista government. The government frequently used heavy-handed measures to silence it, including violence, censorship, and prior restraint.

The "Cuban experiment" deserves attention, if only for its longevity. During the 1960s and 1970s, Fidel Castro's Cuba was lauded as an alternative model for how a small nation could assert its independence and achieve progress and social justice. In line with Communist governments elsewhere, the Cuban government expropriated privately owned mass media to use the media to promote national goals. Cuba's revolutionary rhetoric has lost much of its appeal in Latin America and the rest of the world during the 1980s. Although Cuba appears to have lost its central position in the communist world, Cuba's political policies had changed very little during the 1980s from previous years. Part of Cuba's problem during the 1980s stemmed from greater attention to Cuba's human rights abuses, exposed exaggerations of its economic successes, its military and economic dependency on the Soviet Union, and its military adventures abroad. But Castro's main public problem was public relations oriented. He was unable to change with the times as Communist nations throughout Europe liberalized their governments.

This defect in the Cuban model was especially apparent in comparison with Soviet leader Mikhail Gorbachev's attempts to show "the human side of Socialism" through *glasnost* (openness). Gorbachev's *glasnost* policies created a rift between Cuba and the Soviets (Bryan, 1989). Castro remains firmly committed to central planning and strengthening the authority of the Communist Party. In a number of speeches and interviews, Castro described his commitment to Marxist policies as "a sacred international mission," and viewed himself as a defender of Communism "when it is having international difficulties" (Treaster, 1989, p. 4).

The rift between Havana and Moscow became apparent when, for the first time since Castro came to power, Cuba banned two leading Soviet magazines. In 1989, the Communist Party newspaper *Granma* announced that the weekly *Moscow News* and the monthly *Sputnik* would no longer be available in Cuba. In unusually harsh terms, the party organ accused the Soviet magazines of "justifying bourgeois democracy as the highest form of popular participation" (Anon., August 9, 1989, p. 5).

The Communist Party's ban of the Soviet publications did not mean that Cubans were not receiving news about reforms in other communist nations. Rather, the Cuban government did not want the positive coverage of reforms portrayed in the Soviet publications. It was impossible to totally silence news about reforms. In fact, Cuban newspapers, television, and radio reported about the reforms, albeit with a negative angle. The Cuban media stories often included Castro's attacks on the reforms. Much of the news about the reforms were also apparently meant to warn the Cuban people of difficult economic times ahead with the Soviets withdrawing economic aid and Eastern European nations demanding fair market prices for their consumer goods exported to Cuba (Whitefield, 1989).

Soviet media criticisms of Cuba became increasingly bold by early 1990. Some openly criticized the country's lack of human rights and mismanaged economic system. A particularly harsh attack by the *Moscow News,* by now banned in Cuba, questioned the value of continued Soviet aid to Cuba. This led a spokesperson at the Cuban Interests Section in Washington, DC, to compare attacks from the Soviet media with that of the harsh criticisms of Cuba from anti-Castro publications by Cuban exiles in Miami (Whitefield, 1990b).

* * *

SPOTLIGHT

Guyana's New Information Order Experiment

The nation of Guyana is an example of the NWICO in action in the region, not because Guyana fits the model any better than other cases, but because the government explicitly claims to implement a local version of the NWICO (Sidel, 1984).

Guyana, about the size of the state of Idaho, has a population of 800,000. It is the only English-speaking nation on the South American continent and is an unfamiliar place to most North Americans. East Indians are the dominant group (about 51%), but Afro-Guyanese (43%) hold most of the political power. The rest of the population is comprised of Chinese, Europeans, and Amerindians. The small nation's claim to fame among the American public came in 1978 when a U.S. congressman from California was murdered in the nation's interior by followers of the cult leader Rev. Jim Jones, leading to the suicide of 910 of Jones' followers.

Since its independence from Britain in 1966, Guyana's leaders have advocated policies that presaged UNESCO's New World Information and Communication Order debate. Even before Guyana gained its independence from Great Britain, former Prime Minister Dr. Cheddie Jagan and his American-born wife planned a Marxist–Leninist government. Jagan so frightened President John F. Kennedy with his rhetoric during a White House visit in 1961 that Kennedy asked Great Britain to do something about Jagan. The British reacted by revamping Guyana's electoral system to provide proportional representation. Jagan's party, however, received a plurality 46.5% of the vote during the 1964 election (Steif, 1988).

After independence, most of Guyana's industries, including the mass media, were nationalized. The government started to purchase a number of newspapers and radio stations during the early 1970s (Hosein, 1975). The government had acquired the nation's two radio stations and only daily newspaper. To justify the government's monopoly of the media, the government recalled how the British colonialists controlled the radio airwaves and catered to the wealthy European sugar producers (Thomas, 1987). Now, Guyana's leaders proclaimed, the mass media would cater to the Guyanese people by promoting "national development." In 1974, Kit Nascimento, the Minister of State, said, "As much as we might like, we cannot simply import the libertarian ideas of and concepts of press freedom first voiced by men like Descartes, Locke and Milton, into countries such as ours without examination. . . ." (Anon., December, 1974, p. 14).

The nation became committed to a policy of Development Support Communication (DSC), which mirrored many of the goals expressed by UNESCO's New World Information and Communication Order declarations. To ensure that Guyanese journalists were trained to communicate news about DSC, they received intensive ideological training through a government-subsidized, 2-year public communication program at the University of Guyana.

During 1974, Guyana was the site of a UNESCO conference on development communication. At the conference, Prime Minister Linden Forbes Burnham (later president) insisted that Guyana's media policies did not constitute simple authoritarian control of the press, but instead reflected the spirit of the NWICO. He noted that Guyana's policy was not to tell the nation's mass media what *not to print or broadcast,* but instead to specifically direct the media as to what to print and broadcast. As Burnham told the conference members, the government . . .

. . . has a right to own sections of the media and the government has a right, as a final arbiter of things national, to formulate a policy for the media so that the media can play a much more important part than it has played in the past in mobilizing the people of the country for the development of the country. (cited in Lent, 1979, p. 4)

Under Burnham, the media were not only used to promote "national development" within Guyana, but Burnham's personal ambitions. His ambitions extended well beyond Guyana's borders. Burnham sought to transform Guyana into the "undisputed leader" of the Caribbean region. As one observer noted, "It was common knowledge that, from childhood on, Forbes Burnham had nurtured a dream of becoming the first Caribbean prime minister" (Brotherson, 1989, p. 19).

Ten years after the election that brought Jagan to power, Jagan found himself as the leader of the opposition. In this position, Jagan questioned Burnham's sincerity in purchasing the nation's daily newspapers and radio stations to promote "development communication."

The government's primary tools in implementing development policies through the mass media are the Guyanese (radio) Broadcasting Corp., the Guyana News Agency (GNA), and the government's daily newspaper, the *Chronicle.* The GNA was created in 1981 and charged with implementing "Development Support Communication" policies (also called the "New Local Information order") by increasing the news flow in the nation's rural regions and distributing daily bulletins for foreign correspondents.

The *Chronicle,* an eight-page tabloid with an estimated circulation of about 40,000, is the government's principal development vehicle. News about political matters in the *Chronicle* rarely veer from the party line, although there have been occasions when the newspaper has carried a multiplicity of views and has stimulated debate (Brown, 1976). Important milestones in the lives of Marx and Lenin receive wide attention in the *Chronicle* and the newspaper regularly praises the policies of North Korean leader Kim Il Sung (Sidel, 1984).

In addition to purchasing media, the government also imposed a number of harsh controls on opposition media, especially the opposition-owned weekly *Mirror.* The former daily was reduced to occasional publications in 1985. It eventually became a Sunday newspaper. The government restricted the availability of imported newsprint and technical equipment to the *Mirror* and resorted to searches and prior restraint orders.

The *Catholic Standard,* a weekly Jesuit publication with a circulation of about 10,000, was not nationalized. During a July 10, 1978, political referendum that would aggregate the president's powers, the *Standard* called for a boycott of the referendum. The referendum was eventually approved in an election plagued by widespread vote rigging. The *Standard,* however, may have contributed to the worldwide interpretation of the election as a defeat for President Burnham because only 15% of the eligible voters turned out (Chandisingh, 1983). As a result of government pressure to silence the *Standard,* the newspaper was unable to obtain newsprint, and it was printed on bond paper instead. During July 1979, when Father Andrew Morrison, the editor, was in Barbados, government thugs physically attacked the acting editor and another Jesuit, who died of a bayonet wound.

Guyana was one of the last nations in Latin America to officially adopt television in 1988. Before the official adoption of television, Guyanese could sometimes receive television broadcasts from neighboring Suriname. There was, and still is, a large market for VCR tapes brought back by returning Guyanese from New York City, Toronto, and Miami. Limited-access subscription-type television was instituted in the capital in 1983.

Government approval of the two television stations stipulated that the stations would not broadcast news programs. The stations are also required to broadcast 15-minute government news summaries each day that are produced in government studios and praise government policies (Obermayer, 1989b).

Guyana's late adoption of television resulted from the government's stated interest to keep out foreign culture that might hinder national development. Ironically, the television stations are legally permitted to pirate American programming, in violation of international copyright laws, to which Guyana is a signatory. President Hugh Desmond Hoyte, who succeeded Burnham upon his death in 1985, justified this policy by saying that "America should be paying the Guyanese to distribute its world events perspective" (Obermayer, 1989b, p. 44). According to a recent study of television programs in Guyana during 1988, the program fare contains heavy doses of U.S. programming, including "Dallas," "The Newlywed Game," "The Flintstones," "CNN News," and "The Jeffersons" (Sidel, 1988).

Since the death of President Burnham in 1985, a less hostile press–government relationship has emerged. Several opposition newspapers exist. In 1986, the bi-weekly *Stabroek News,* with a circulation of 15,000–18,000, began publication with the promise of no government interference. On several occasions, however, the newspaper claimed it was restricted from obtaining information from the public sector (Sidel, 1989). The *Catholic Standard,* edited by Morrison, remains the government's strongest media critic. It is financially supported by overseas religious groups.

Still, the press can hardly be described as free and vibrant. Frank Pilgrim, who became editor-in-chief of *The Chronicle* in July 1987, believed that as a result of the relatively more open atmosphere created by President Hoyte, Guyana was ready for a government publication that would offer "constructive criticism" of government policies. On the nation's celebration of Republic Day, February 23, 1988, the newspaper featured an exchange of opinions about Mass Games celebration, in which thousands of school children displayed their gymnastic prowess. The celebration was modeled on games in North Korea.

A commentator in the *Chronicle* charged that the games strained the nation's economy, overworked the children, and interrupted their school studies just at a time when area-wide exams were scheduled. The organ of the People's National Congress (PNC) called the criticisms in the *Chronicle* "brass-faced quaking" and "blind class prejudice" (Anon., January 1989). The controversy subsided after the author of the article, still refusing to recant, welcomed the "constructive suggestions."

Controversy stirred again in December that cost Pilgrim his job. The *Chronicle* called on the government to permit greater freedom of expression. The newspaper singled out problems with public access to public information and particularly access to information about police brutality. President Hoyte was so enraged by the allegations that he publicly called the allegations "faceless and gutless" (Anon., January 1989).

Even in 1990, the government sought to implement a local version of the NWICO and exert pressure on the press that challenged government policies. In March, the government inaugurated the Guyana Public Communications Agency (GPCA) for the stated purpose of organizing "the government's information services in a manner which will permit public access to vital information about development priorities, plans and performance" (Sidel, 1990, p. 6). In April, the editor-in-chief of the critical *Catholic Standard* was pressured by the government into taking an early retirement because of his "error of judgment" for refusing to publish a government press release four months earlier (Anon., April 8, 1990).

Overall, Guyana's attempts to implement a new information order have been a failure. An excellent and sympathetic summary of Guyana's policies by then University of Florida Prof. M. Kent Sidel (1984) argued that Guyana's attempt to free itself from its colonialist past trapped the nation's leaders in a "downward spiral" that led to economic stagnation and reduced media credibility. Another sympathetic treatment by Prof. Erwin Thomas (1982) claims that Guyana has never developed clear communication policies. For instance, Thomas noted that government journalists have been so obsequious and favorable in their reporting that the news media enjoy little credibility. As a result, the Ministry of Information has had to advise journalists to also report some negative stories about the government.

A less sympathetic analysis of Guyana's experiment comes from Ken Gordon, managing director of the *Trinidad Express* and chair of the Caribbean News Agency (CANA), a Third World agency developed with UNESCO support. In a 1983 interview with the magazine *Caribbean and West Indies Chronicle,* Gordon described Guyana's experiment with a new information order as a failure that other Caribbean nations should avoid: "If you look at Guyana today you find a country that is spiritually and financially bankrupt" (Anon., October–November 1983, p. 6).

As the 1980s drew to a close, Guyana's per capita income was declining, power shortages occurred daily, street crime was rampant, basic social services went unprovided, and the nation's best and brightest were leaving for jobs in the Caribbean and the United States. Ironically, it has been suggested that Guyana's economic woes may have actually contributed to greater freedom of expression. Since 1985–1987 there has been a clear loosening on government restrictions over the press (Cambridge & Hazzard, 1988; Sidel, 1988). Observers noticed increasingly more criticism of the government in the press. The Guyana Press Association was reactivated in 1988. And some regional and international periodicals carrying critical news about Guyana became regularly available.

William Steif (1988), a columnist for the *Virgin Islands Daily News,* wrote that as a result of the nation's $1.7 billion foreign debt, of which not a penny has been paid on the principal since 1981, the human rights situation has improved in Guyana. Steif claimed that President Hoyte cannot afford to offend his creditors with human rights violations and is "down on his knees, begging the United States, Britain, Japan and multinational agencies for funds to bail out his nearly bankrupt nation" (p. 24).

News Agencies

A small handful of news agencies in the industrialized nations dominate the "news flow" in Latin America. A similar situation exists in most developing regions. Latin America probably has a greater diversity of news agencies than most regions of the world. As a result of the assistance of UNESCO and western media organizations, a number of regional news agencies of varying quality have been established in Latin America in recent years. Some news agencies have reported news with definite political slants; others have attempted to provide impartial news reports. The Caribbean News Agency (CANA) has been singled out as a "Third World model." In addition to the western and regional agencies, a number of "second-tier" agencies from Spain, West Germany, and Italy supplement the region's news needs.

The news services provide the news media with news and information about national and international affairs. Numerous studies repeatedly report that the "Big Four" news agencies (The Associated Press and United Press International of the United States; Reuters of Great Britain; and Agence France Presse of France) dominate international news coverage in Latin America, as they do in much of the world. As a result, the large Western news agencies have been singled out by some supporters of the New World Information and Communication Order (NWICO) as among the primary culprits for Latin America's dependency on the Western news media.

In addition to the news agencies, large Western television news agencies are immensely powerful and influential. Visnews (Vision News, created in 1957 by the British Broadcasting Corporation, BBC) is by far the world's largest supplier of international news video (King, 1981). Its closest competitor is WTN (World Television News), headquartered in London.

DEVELOPMENT OF WIRE SERVICES

The Big Four agencies, and later television news services, derive their economic strength and influence from a long history of international news reporting that dates back to the 19th century. The concept of the news agency is frequently attributed to Charles Havas of France, the founder of the Havas agency. Havas employed correspondents throughout Europe to collect news primarily for businessmen and diplomats. By using carrier pigeons, Havas was able to provide important news to his clients more quickly than the mail. He was able to get same-day information from England and Belgium for his French clients. Years later, several newspapers recognized the value of Havas' service and became clients. By 1870, Havas made use of Samuel Morse's electromagnetic telegraph and hot air balloons to report the Franco–Prussian War.

The Associated Press (AP) of the United States claims to be oldest news agency. Although the European agencies pre-date the AP, the AP claims to be the oldest agency established *specifically* to gather news for public consumption, not private business interests (Read, 1976).

Former Havas employees established agencies elsewhere in Europe—Bernard Wolff in Germany and Paul Julius Reuter in Great Britain. The opening of a cable between France and England in 1851, followed by the Atlantic cable in 1866, made rapid communications possible (Cuthbert, 1980; Hachten, 1981).

With the high cost of collecting information from all over the world, it did not take long for the three dominant European agencies—Havas, Reuters and Wolff—to see the economic benefits in avoiding cutthroat competition. By 1859, the three agencies formed a cartel agreement (Agency Alliance Treaty). According to the terms of the agreement, the three agencies divided the world into territories for exclusive distribution of cartel news. Although this arrangement permitted the agencies to work more profitably, it meant that newspapers and news consumers in various regions were usually limited in their access to international news to the news and views of a single European news agency (Altschull, 1984).

Meanwhile, in the United States, the rapidly expanding AP was asserting its power and influence. The AP joined the cartel as a junior member in the late 19th century. Under the original terms of the arrangement, the AP was only permitted to distribute cartel news in the United States. Like the other members of the cartel, the AP had to share whatever news it gathered with the other cartel members. In return, the other cartel members agreed not to compete against the AP in the United States.

Under the cartel's arrangement with the AP, the AP was the primary source of foreign news in the United States. Needless to say, most U.S. newspapers wanted to become members of the AP cooperative. Within the next two decades, the AP's economic power would grow, and it would demand and receive from the other cartel members the right to expand its influence in the hemisphere to Canada,

Mexico, Central America, and the West Indies. If the cartel members would not cede to the AP's demands, the AP threatened to bolt from the cartel, tearing asunder the cozy economic arrangement (Cuthbert, 1980).

The AP's monopoly on international news in the United States caused resentment among some U.S. newspaper groups whose newspapers could not join the AP cooperative because of the AP's bylaws. Two powerful U.S. media barons— Edward W. Scripps and William Randolph Hearst—decided to do something about the AP's *de facto* monopoly on international news. In 1907, Scripps formed the United Press (UP) association to service his chain of newspapers and whoever else was willing to purchase UP news. Two years after the creation of UP, Hearst formed the International News Service (INS). In 1958, the UP and INS merged and became United Press International (UPI).

Scripps and Hearst were particularly angered by the AP's "exclusivity arrangements" within the United States. These arrangements kept many Scripps and Hearst newspapers from receiving the AP's news. The AP was, and still is, a "cooperative" comprised of its members. According to the AP's bylaws at that time, if any member of the cooperative objected to a new member, a vote could be demanded. For the new member to join, at least 80% of the members had to approve the new applicant. It was this exclusivity clause that effectively kept many Scripps and Hearst papers from having access to the AP wire (Cuthbert, 1980).

The AP's reputation and worldwide influence expanded during World War I. The United States was officially neutral during the early years of the war. As a result, some newspapers in neutral Latin American nations believed the AP provided more balanced reports about the European war than the European agencies. The U.S. State Department recognized the value of the AP as a propaganda tool for the United States. It assisted the AP in establishing bureaus abroad. The State Department was particularly interested in having the AP establish bureaus in Latin America, where State Department officials feared German propaganda influence (Renaud, 1985).

The cartel divided up territories of the world in such a way that the French agency Havas had the cartel's exclusive news distribution rights in all of South America. Publishers from two of Argentina's most prestigious daily newspapers, *La Nación* and later *La Prensa,* still in existence today and managed by later generations of the same families, sought to obtain international news from the AP.

In 1914, Jorge Mitre, the director of *La Nación* of Buenos Aires, sought to persuade the German agency Wolff to provide it with news. Mitre correctly believed that the French agency was reporting a pro-French view about the European war and sought to balance this biased view with a German view. Havas, which was under French government censorship, refused to distribute German war communiques through its wire. Wolff refused *La Nación*'s request to supply it with news. It did not want to endanger its valuable position in the cartel. *La Nación* made a similar unsuccessful plea for news to the AP.

La Nación then turned to the UP. At this time, UP was a relatively small but aggressive American agency not bound by the cartel agreement. UP jumped at the opportunity to provide news in Latin America. Argentina was among the world's wealthiest nations with a relatively sophisticated, independent media system. UP hoped that this connection with *La Nación* would lead to other opportunities in the region. By 1916, UP and *La Nación* arranged a successful joint service to supply news to other Latin American newspapers (Morris, 1957).

By 1918, Mitre had broken his contract with the UP and attempted to service clients in Latin America by himself. The move caused bitterness between *La Nación* and UP. Meanwhile, the AP realized that it had to expand into Latin America. The AP had reached an arrangement with the war-weakened European members of the cartel to expand into South America without losing its connection with the cartel. In effect, the AP agreed to reimburse Havas for any loss of clients in the region as a result of the AP's entry into Latin America. By the end of 1918, as the War was drawing to a close, the AP established 25 clients in Latin America, including the prestigious *La Nación* and *La Prensa* of Buenos Aires (Morris, 1957).

The UP was almost destroyed in Latin America as a result of the combination of *La Nación*'s breach of contract and AP's entry into the region. Undaunted, the UP kept pressing *La Prensa* to subscribe to UP, pointing out that UP could provide *La Prensa* with distinctly different international news than AP was providing to its competitor, *La Nación*. Finally, during June 1919, *La Prensa* agreed to use UP's special news service on an experimental basis. During this time, in which *La Prensa* was "testing" the UP, the UP excelled to provide *La Prensa* with more complete and timely news than the AP. UP's big break came when it scooped the AP in reporting the signing of the Versailles treaty, in which Germany surrendered to the allies. *La Prensa* signed a contract with the UP. The contract virtually saved UP from becoming relegated to a negligible force in the region. As a result of the *La Prensa* deal, UP (now UPI) has become the major news agency in Latin America (Read, 1976).

La Prensa paid UP over $500,000 a year to receive comprehensive world reports on a daily basis. *La Prensa* was particularly interested in receiving news about post-War Spain and Italy because Argentina was receiving many immigrants from these countries. UP was then free to sell these reports to other clients in other nations. The injection of revenue from *La Prensa* allowed UP to increase its news staff in Europe and expand its client list in Latin America. Because of its large clientele in Latin America, UP attempted to provide more Latin American angles to European news than the other international agencies.

Meanwhile, the AP's worldwide reputation and international influence continued to grow. With this growth, the AP continued to demand from cartel members the right to distribute its news in more territories. The European members of the cartel reluctantly ceded to the AP's demands rather than chance the dissolution of the cartel. In 1934, the AP withdrew from the cartel. The AP's withdrawal marked the effective break up of the cartel (Boyd-Barrett, 1980; Cuthbert, 1980; Smith, 1980). Although the AP has become the United States' largest news agency, its relatively late entry into South America allowed the UP to gain a foothold in the region that has made it (in the form of the UPI) the pre-eminent international news service in Latin America today.

INFLUENCE OF THE BIG FOUR TODAY

The international news cartel no longer formally exists. Nevertheless, a large proportion of the international news disseminated in Latin America today still originates from today's "Big Four" agencies. Because of this seeming dependence on the Big Four agencies for international news, a number of critics who claim that Latin America is still a victim of "media imperialism" have called for the establishment of national and regional news agencies.

UNESCO lent its support to the creation of a number of regional news agencies in Latin America during the 1970s. To date, these regional agencies have had only modest impact on the region's news flow, although their supporters emphasize that they were never conceived as competition for the international news agencies (Smith, 1980).

There have been some allegations that the international news agencies' reliance on native "stringers" (locals within various nations hired on a part-time basis) results in biased news reports. It has been charged that these local stringers have been "compromised" by Latin American governments, a charge the agencies vigorously deny (Stein, 1988). In nations such as Mexico and Panama, there have been some fears that native agency correspondents are on government payrolls. The charge gained some attention during the 1988 annual Inter American Press Association convention in Salt Lake City, Utah, when Roberto Eisenmann, the then-exiled Panamanian publisher of the opposition newspaper *La Prensa,* claimed that native stringers for the agencies were compromised. According to Eisenmann: "When press agencies hire domestic stringers it is normal for them to be compromised by payoffs, scare tactics, or threats" (Stein, 1988, p. 28).

DEVELOPMENT OF REGIONAL NEWS AGENCIES

Many news media organizations in Latin America support the development of nongovernmental regional agencies. The media organization's owners do not subscribe to the rhetoric of leftist-oriented dependency theory and media imperialism, and they generally see little value for government news agencies (Diaz-Rangel, 1967). Latin American newspaper publishers, who are relatively well off by the standards of most developing nations, generally subscribe to the notion of an independent "watchdog" press. As Jonathan Fenby (1986) wrote in his book about the international news agencies: "Calls for the establishment of an alternate news agency regional service reflected the Latin Americans' desire to cover the continent for themselves, rather than political discontent with North American agencies by media owners'' (p. 207).

According to University of North Carolina Prof. Robert L. Stevenson (1984), when the 1980s began, the notion of national and regional news agencies in the developing world was so popular that national and regional agencies ''were to the 1980s what television was to the 1970s and radio to the 1960s—a priority for communication planners and politicians, a magic machine to overcome the still growing information gap between the North and the Third World'' (p. 77). Stevenson (1988), however, had little that was positive to say about most national and regional news agencies. He viewed most of them as dull government organs. But in Latin America, which has a long tradition of private ownership of the media, Stevenson conceded that at least some of the national and regional agencies met high professional standards, served their readers well, and were not afraid to criticize their governments.

The need for a regional news agency became apparent to many Latin Americans after the so-called 1969 ''soccer war'' between El Salvador and Honduras. The war ostensibly started over a disputed call in a soccer match between the two nations. What was portrayed to the world as a seemingly humorous rationale for a war, reinforced stereotypes of Central America's ''banana republics.'' In fact, the news reports overlooked long-standing border disputes between the two nations. Further, it seemed to government leaders in Latin America that even the peoples of El Salvador and Honduras lacked an understanding of the events behind the war because of the incomplete news reports coming from the international news agencies (Fernandez, 1978).

Agencia Latinoamericana

In 1976, representatives from nine Latin American and Caribbean nations met in Mexico City and approved the formation of the Agencia Latinoamericana de Servicios Especiales de Informacion (ALASEI)—Bolivia, Cuba, the Dominican Republic, Ecuador, Haiti, Mexico, Nicaragua, Panama, and Venezuela (Salinas Bascar, 1986; Underwood, 1987). ALASEI was finally established on October 19, 1983. ALASEI circulated feature-oriented development news stories to the major newspapers through the various official national news agencies (Reyes Matta, 1986).

Technically, ALASEI is a ''mixed agency'' that permits participation from governments and private media, as well as from educators and researchers (Salinas Bascar, 1986). Headquartered in Mexico City, ALASEI's reputation suffers from the perception that various governments influence its content. However, ALASEI stresses that there is no government censorship and it acts to supplement the information of existing agencies in the region, not replace them (Underwood, 1987).

In 1984, the IAPA rejected an offer to serve on ALASEI's board of directors, asserting that "news agencies in whose management governments or international entities such as UNESCO intervene directly or indirectly (are) dangerous to the free flow of information" (Gardner, 1985, p. 91).

National Information Systems Network

Another early attempt to establish a regional agency was the formation of the National Information Systems Network, known by its Spanish acronym of ASIN (Accion de Sistemas Informativos Nacionales). It was initiated in 1979 by 10 national governments under the leadership of Venezuela. ASIN is a network of Latin American and Caribbean national agencies that served primarily as an exchange pool of information for Latin American governments. The news is heavily laden with "official" information from presidential information offices. ASIN President Luis Javier Solana, speaking before UNESCO's General Conference in 1980, spoke in favor of "the right of governments to inform and be informed directly, and to be more deeply integrated through information. . . . The so called 'mass communication' has been nothing more than a one-way street" (cited in Fenby, 1986, p. 226).

LATIN and ACAN

Two other regional agencies that, like ALASEI, have had only a modest impact on the news flow in the region are Agencia Latinoamericana de Informacion (LATIN) and Agencia Centroamericana de Noticias (ACAN). These agencies were established with the help of major international news agencies. LATIN received assistance from Reuters and ACAN from the Spanish agency EFE.

LATIN was established as a cooperative agency, privately owned by 13 newspapers from seven nations in the region during 1970 and went into operation in July 1971 (Anon., May 1990). LATIN was established with UNESCO support and assistance from Reuters. Reuters provided LATIN with assistance in the hiring and training of journalists. Under a contract with Reuters, LATIN was given an exclusive right to distribute Reuters' world news reports in Latin America. An analysis of LATIN's content by Latin American media scholar John S. Nichols (1975) revealed that LATIN may have been offering news content similar to the international agencies as a means to compete against the international agencies.

Although there was great hope for LATIN's success as a Third World alternative to the international agencies, it experienced financial difficulties since its establishment. By 1978 LATIN was nearly bankrupt. As a result, LATIN and Reuters integrated their operations, although they remained legally separate, and LATIN became a fading regional source of news and eventually disappeared

(Cuthbert, 1979). According to a history of Reuters in Latin America written internally by the Reuters organization, LATIN became dormant in 1981 (Anon., May 1990).

ACAN was established during the early 1970s to serve Central American news media. The organization, however, could not be described as a truly indigenous Central American agency because the Spanish news agency EFE owned one third of its stock and appointed the general manager (Fernandez, 1978). EFE, although not as wealthy and powerful as the Big Four international agencies, claims a special obligation to Spanish-speaking nations. It has committed substantial resources to covering Latin America, particularly the Central American republics (Graff, 1983).

EFE representatives assert that ACAN is an independent agency serving Central America's news needs. EFE representatives, however, concede that ACAN was established to provide Central Americans with a better understanding of events in Spain (Graff, 1983). The agency is comprised of newspapers and TV stations in five Central American republics, with Panama as an associate member. By the mid-1980s, ACAN was producing 70 to 80 correspondences a day (Kim, 1989).

Inter Press Service

Inter Press Service (IPS) and the Caribbean News Agency (CANA) are regarded as two of the more successful attempts to establish regional agencies. Although IPS originally started as a news service for Latin America, it has expanded to serve other regions and has lost much of its Latin American roots. Both IPS and CANA have managed to avoid being labeled as public relations agencies for governments. Further, both report in news styles other than what has been derogatorily described as "protocol news," a stilted, self-serving style that resembles that of official government documents (Stevenson, 1988).

Although IPS claims to be independent from the influence of governments, it has not escaped political controversy. IPS has experienced numerous complaints for its alleged anti-Western bias. The U.S. State Department once chastized IPS for its "anti-imperialist line" (Hall, 1983, p. 53). IPS reports, however, are not written by government employees and its reporters do not perceive themselves as public relations representatives for governments. However, IPS reporters apparently do not subscribe to the western model of objective journalism, and they frequently take strong political stands.

IPS management concedes that many of its reporters express leftist political views in their reports, a problem that management claims it tries to deal with during the editing process (Harris, 1981). IPS management expresses sympathy with developing nations and their struggles. It explicitly states that its editorial policies "are in line with the ideals of 'decolonization of information' " (Anderson, 1981, p. 340).

Giffard (1985), in his analysis of IPS content, concluded there was no evidence of an anti-Western bias:

> There is little to support allegations that the service is biased against the West; far more of its news reports are critical of the Third World. Although the proportion of national agency material carried on the networks is not high, it is substantial, and is in accord with the IPS philosophy of encouraging a pluralism of voices in international news exchange. (p. 44)

Both IPS and CANA fit Stevenson's (1988) description of a new breed of regional news agencies that successfully responded to the competitive challenges from the international news agencies:

> Those who ran the new services were beginning to recognize the reality that the Western agencies had learned years earlier; the news business was competitive— and becoming more so—and the product had to be acceptable to potential customers. If it wasn't, plenty of other services were prepared to produce one that was. (p. 149)

IPS has its headquarters in Rome. It was founded in 1964 by Latin American and European journalists as a means of creating an "information bridge" between Latin America and Europe (Giffard, 1984). The service was enormously successful and, by the late 1970s, it expanded from its Latin American base to other regions, but it is still strongest in its coverage of Latin America. By the mid-1980s IPS had bureaus and correspondents in 63 nations, including 40 in developing nations, 24 of which were in Latin America and the Caribbean (Giffard, 1984, 1985). IPS is linked with agencies in 55 nations, including 24 in Latin America and the Caribbean (Anon., 1989a).

According to its founder, Dr. Roberto Savio, IPS provides news stories about developing nations that are overlooked by the large international news agencies. It also explains how international events affect people in developing nations. As a result, IPS correspondents may interview villagers and village leaders instead of high government sources. According to Savio, the problem with the NWICO is that its proponents have put too much stress on information flow, which has resulted in attempts to obtain quantitatively more news, but not necessarily better news (Ogan & Rush, 1985).

Although many news agencies in developing nations rewrite reports from international and national news agencies, IPS prides itself on the fact that 70% of its news originates from its own correspondents (Giffard, 1985). In an analysis of IPS content, Giffard (1985) reported that 72% of the English-language copy during October 1982 was written by IPS correspondents. However, IPS's Spanish-language content was apparently not up to par with the English-language version. Only 57% of the Spanish-language copy originated from IPS correspondents. About 25% of the Spanish copy came from Latin American agencies, most of which represented government views.

Another systematic study of IPS news content reported less than flattering results about IPS' stated commitment to developmental news. Ogan and Rush (1985) analyzed a 2-week sample of IPS copy in 1984. They reported that slightly less than half the copy dealt with developmental news. According to the researchers, for an agency that claims to provide "alternative news," this was a disappointingly low percentage of developmental news.

Despite IPS's expansion outside of Latin America, IPS still has a strong Latin American focus. The Ogan and Rush (1985) study reported that 59% of the stories dealt with Latin America. No other region received more than 15% of the coverage. An earlier study by Giffard (1984) also reported that 59% of IPS copy dealt with Latin America.

By early 1983, it was estimated that IPS had grown to the world's sixth largest news agency in total communication links, behind the Big Four agencies and the Soviet Union's Tass (Hall, 1983). It grew so large that it played a role in the establishment of other news agencies, such as ASIN, a regional news pool comprised of national news agencies in Latin America and the Caribbean (Hall, 1983).

Caribbean News Agency

The Caribbean News Agency (CANA) has met with both financial success and, unlike IPS, relatively little political controversy. Headquartered in Bridgetown, Barbados, CANA is cooperatively owned by private and government media. It has frequently been praised as a "Third World model" news agency (Cuthbert, 1981a, 1981b).

Prior to the establishment of CANA, the major Caribbean print and broadcast media had a block arrangement to subscribe to Reuters World Service. In 1971, Reuters announced that it would increase the cost of its services by 63% over 3 years. The *Daily Gleaner* in Kingston, Jamaica, the largest daily newspaper in the Caribbean region and the newspaper that paid the largest single portion to the Reuters arrangement, balked at paying the price increase. The *Gleaner* announced its intentions to withdraw from the arrangement, believing it could obtain regional news from its own stringers and international news from the AP (Cuthbert, 1981b). The *Gleaner*'s threat to withdraw from Reuters meant the other members would have to pay even more to subscribe to Reuters.

The *Gleaner*'s decision to drop Reuters created a chain of events that led to the establishment of CANA. Reuters assisted in the creation of CANA. From the outset, it was decided that to maintain CANA's credibility, CANA must not develop into a propaganda tool for any government or governments. The agency was established by public and private shareholders, all media organizations in the region, from Barbados, Guyana, Jamaica, Trinidad and Tobago, and Montserrat. In addition, CANA had five media organizations from the region as subscribers.

CANA began as a joint venture between the Caribbean Publishers and Broadcasters Association (CPBA) and Reuters Caribbean Service in 1974, at a time when the English-speaking Caribbean islands considered confederating. In January 1976, CANA took over the Reuters' operation and became an independent agency (Cuthbert, 1976; Dunn, 1988).

CANA maintains its links with Reuters and distributes the Reuters international file to CANA subscribers. Meanwhile, Reuters purchases CANA's regional services and distributes it through its World Service. By the late 1980s, CANA had succeeded in quadrupling the volume of news exchange among the English-language media in the Caribbean (Dunn, 1988).

CANA quickly gained a reputation for quality and credibility unusual among Third World news agencies. Unlike most Third World news agencies, which frequently rewrite existing news accounts, CANA uses the reports of stringers and staffers to gather regional news. Since its creation, CANA had a staff of journalists trained under Reuters (Cuthbert, 1981b). CANA's reports are free from the self-serving, pro-government styles so common in "protocol news" (Stevenson, 1988).

In 1984, CANA introduced CANARADIO to provide a variety of radio reports of news, arts, and sports in the region. In 1989, the agency began publication of CANABUSINESS, a financial and business newsletter about the region aimed at business executives in the Caribbean, North America and Europe.

"SECOND-TIER" NEWS AGENCIES

In addition to the international news agencies serving Latin American media and Latin America's regional and national news agencies, there are the "second-tier" news agencies from Western European nations. Among the leading second-tier agencies are Deutsche Presse-Agentur (DPA) of West Germany, Agenzia Nazionale Associata (ANSA) of Italy, and EFE of Spain.

The second-tier agencies do not have the worldwide prestige or influence of the Big Four agencies. However, they do have considerable economic resources, and are experienced in news gathering and dissemination. EFE deserves to be singled out among the second-tier agencies because of its commitment to providing Spanish news, sometimes with Latin American angles, to Latin American nations. As of 1989, EFE had 500 subscribers in the western hemisphere. The service is widely used in many Latin American nations.

According to a study of leading newspapers in Brazil, Argentina, and Mexico, EFE is major source of international news in Mexico and Argentina. Mexico City's prestigious *El Universal* and *Excelsior* used EFE almost as often as UPI, AP, and AFP. In Argentina, *La Crónica* used more EFE reports than any other foreign news service. In Portuguese-speaking Brazil, EFE reports were rarely used (Link, 1984).

EFE was established in 1939 during the waning days of the Spanish Civil War by pro-fascist partisan "Nationalists" who sought to counter what they viewed as the negative image of Spain in the international press. Until the death of Gen. Francisco Franco in 1975, EFE was rightly perceived by international journalism scholars and the world media as a mouthpiece for the neo-fascist views of the Franco government. After Franco's death and the democratization of Spain, however, EFE made a rapid transition to a respectable second-tier news agency (Kim, 1989).

In January 1971, EFE laid the groundwork for the creation of ACAN by establishing a bureau in Panama City and correspondent offices in the capital cities of five Central American republics. The agency's relationship with ACAN provided EFE with extensive news about Central America. EFE's relationship with ACAN allowed EFE to compete with the international and second-tier agencies in supplying news about Central America (Kim, 1989).

EFE improved its standing among its Latin American clients in 1982 during the Falklands/Malvinas War. Although most Latin American nations disapproved of Argentina's brutal military dictatorship, they still sympathized with Argentina's territorial claim to the islands. Most Latin American nations also perceived a pro-British tilt in the coverage of the international news agencies. EFE offered its Latin American clients what it claimed was more "balanced" coverage than the pro-Anglo-Saxon coverage of the international news agencies (Kim, 1989).

NATIONAL NEWS AGENCIES

According to one comprehensive study of international news agencies, the competition of international, second-tier, and regional news agencies in Latin America "gave the continent the widest choice of news services of any area outside Western Europe" (Fenby, 1986, p. 206). In addition, a number of Latin American nations have established national or government news agencies. Some of the large Latin American nations have several national agencies. For instance, Argentina has three national agencies: Telam (official news agency), Diarios y Noticias and Noticias Argentinas (Banks, 1988). During the early 1980s, the government agency Telam expanded its services to bureaus and correspondents in the United States, Western Europe, and several other Latin American nations, including Bolivia, Brazil, Paraguay, Peru, and Uruguay (Anon., n.d.b). Telam maintains reciprocal agreements with a number of agencies, including EFE, ANSA, LATIN-Reuter, the China News Agency (Taiwan), Associated Press (Morocco), and Tanjug (Yugoslavia).

Many of the national agencies in Latin America are government operated and, not surprisingly, pro-government in their coverage. For this reason, many observers would not view these organizations as "news agencies" in the true sense, but instead as government agencies because of their close connections with their governments (Stevenson, 1988). By no means, however, are all national agencies government mouthpieces. Argentina's Noticias Argentinas was established in Argentina by independent newspapers in 1972 to compete against the government agency Telam, established as a mouthpiece for President Juan Domingo Peron's policies (Kraiselburd, 1978).

The Venezuelan government-operated agency Venpres is up front about its goals to promote a good image of the nation. The agency is operated by the Office of Central Information and is headquartered in the Ministry of Information and Tourism. Venpres disseminates government advertising and promotional material about government agencies (Ortega & Pierce, 1984). Brazil, as the hemisphere's only Portuguese-speaking nation, has developed a number of news agencies. Brazil has two major national news agencies, Agencia Nacional in Brasilia and Agencia Noticosa in Rio de Janeiro. Two large newspapers, *O Estado* and *Jornal do Brasil,* function as national agencies by selling their news to client newspapers.

The Cuban news agency Prensa Latina (PL), established in 1959, is the official voice of the Communist Party. It is the principal source of international news for Cuba's 16 daily newspapers, 60 magazines, 2 TV stations, 3 national radio stations, and 29 local radio stations. PL also rewrites and distributes news from foreign agencies within Cuba to conform with Cuban government political views (Carty, 1976, 1981). Although PL is a national government agency, it also serves as a regional agency supplying news to newspapers and other news media in Latin America and the Caribbean. It maintains bureaus in several countries, although it keeps small staffs and relies heavily on stringers in its foreign bureaus (Nichols, 1982).

In many Latin American nations, national agencies have few correspondents. The national agencies frequently act as "exchange services," exchanging national news with other national, regional, and international agencies. The national agencies sometimes receive, edit, and distribute news from international or regional agencies to local media and government agencies.

The trend toward privatization of national industries may affect government-owned Latin American national news agencies. During mid-1990, the Venezuelan government announced that 50% of its shares in Venpres would be offered for sale to the private sector in order to raise revenues to purchase new equipment and streamline operations (Anon., June 1990b).

JAMPRESS, Jamaica's official government news agency, established in 1984 to collect and disseminate news about the government's programs and policies, is typical of government agencies in the region. It claims to provide news about "national development" in Jamaica. Prior to 1984, official governmental news distribution was handled by the Jamaica Information Service (JIS), which also performed many other non-news functions. With the creation of JAMPRESS, the government gave special importance to relations specifically with the news media.

The agency is well aware of the dangers and criticisms leveled against official news agencies. In its own government literature, JAMPRESS asserts that "it is not some sort of make-the-government-look-good agency'' (Robinson, 1989, p. 3). JAMPRESS, which has a staff of a dozen reporters and editors and claims to distribute its correspondences with 150 clients within and outside Jamaica, asserts that it provides professional news about government activities:

> The final decision on any JAMPRESS release is not determined by any Minister of the Government or party official, but lies solely with the Agency's editorial staff. . . . JAMPRESS' purpose and objectives therefore is to ''operate as a news service'' engaged in the collection and distribution of such material locally and internationally. The fact that its principal news source is government does not mean compromising professional news values. . . . (Robinson, 1989, p. 3)

Oliver Clarke (personal interview, January 13, 1990), chairman of the board of the dominant *Daily Gleaner* in Jamaica is like most journalists from privately owned news media in the Caribbean and is skeptical of government news agencies. But Clarke gives JAMPRESS high marks. While he sees JAMPRESS as a government agency with a vested interest in the news, he stated that ''as these things go, Jamaica has a pretty good public information service. From time to time it is accused of being partisan, but it's not unduly so. We attempt to rewrite their stories or add other opinions to them, but we certainly use them. By and large, we find them very good.''

The problem with the national government agencies is not so much that they are false or misleading. Western and Latin American journalists, who rely on them for information, expect them to be false or misleading. Rather, the problem is that they frequently omit sensitive stories altogether. Mort Rosenblum (1978), the former AP bureau chief in Paris, recounted that during the early 1970s, when a group of Argentina's generals launched a military coup, the government agency Telam reported about sports news in the southern region of the nation instead of the coup.

Rosenblum was not bothered by Western journalists' reliance on national agencies as news sources so as long as the journalists' sources were clearly identified in the news stories. He also believed that Western journalists who develop close personal contacts with employees in national agencies may receive not-for-attribution advance warnings about political events that might be too sensitive to include in agency reports.

ASSOCIATED PRESS IN THE REGION

AP maintains 17 bureaus in Latin America today, as shown in Table 5.1. Most bureaus are small, but some cities such as Mexico City and Buenos Aires include large numbers of full-time staff. These figures do not include the bureau in Miami, which shares responsibility in covering the Caribbean region with the San Juan, Puerto Rico, bureau. AP's Miami bureau has 15 staff members

TABLE 5.1
Associated Press in Latin America

Country	Location	Staff Size†
	Caribbean Division	
Puerto Rico	San Juan	22
United States	Miami	20
	Central America Division	
El Salvador	San Salvador	5
Mexico	Mexico City	23
	Monterrey	1
Nicaragua	Managua	5
	South America Division	
Argentina	Buenos Aires	16
Bolivia	La Paz	2
Brazil	Brasilia	2
	Rio de Janeiro	10
	Sao Paulo	1
Chile	Santiago	12
Colombia	Bogotá	5
Ecuador	Quitó	1
Paraguay	Asunción	1
Peru	Lima	7
Uruguay	Montevideo	3
Venezuela	Caracas	8

†In some locations, figures include stringers.
Source: Susan Clark, Associated Press, New York (personal communication, January 23, 1990).

four photographers, and a bureau chief (Susan Clark, personal communication, January 23, 1990).

Although UPI is the leading news agency in Latin America, the AP has sought to extend deeper into Latin America. La Prensa Asociada (PA), AP's Spanish-language news service, serves 500 clients, including 50 Spanish-language broadcast stations and newspapers in the United States (Abreu, 1986). Like UPI, PA claims that its news for Latin America is not simple translations but largely original news for its Spanish-language clients.

An article written by PA's editor of Latin American service that appeared in the AP's house publication Associated Press *World* claims that PA's editors in New York, almost all from Latin American nations, select stories already in Spanish from AP's Latin American bureaus (Abreu, 1986). In addition, the PA editors sift through the English-language stories from the AP wire, looking for stories that may be of interest to Latin American clients. PA editors may follow up on these English-language stories of possible interest to Latin Americans with phone calls to get a unique Latin American perspective. PA also claims to provide news of special interest to individual Latin American nations, each with their unique cultures and idioms (Abreu, 1986).

* * *

SPOTLIGHT

UPI: "General Motors of News Services"

Latin America has been one of United Press International's (UPI) most successful and lucrative markets for many years. Regardless of the financial troubles that the news agency experienced in the last decade, UPI clients have remained fiercely loyal—partly because of service and partly because of long-time close relationships between UPI and Latin American publishers and editors (Garneau, 1988a, 1988b).

The most important recent development in press agencies in Latin America was the purchase of the deficit-ridden UPI, the world's second largest news agency, by Mexican media magnate Mario Vazquez-Rana for $41 million in 1986. Although Vazquez-Rana eventually sold control of the financially strapped news company in spring 1988, the significance of Vazquez-Rana's brief (1986–1988) ownership was not lost. Many Latin Americans took offense at what they perceived as the fear and even racism in much of the U.S. news industry over the suggestion that a journalist from Latin America was somehow unqualified or incapable of being in charge of a leading international news agency.

Only after Vazquez-Rana relinquished control of UPI did UPI management decide to move its Latin American desk (LATAM) in Washington to Latin America. UPI's LATAM has been the pre-eminent international news service in South and Central America for much of this century. Although UPI plays a secondary role to the AP in the United States (UPI served 300 newspapers and 2,300 radio and television stations in the U.S. when Vazquez-Rana took over), UPI thinks of itself as "the General Motors of Latin American news services" (Massing, 1979, p. 45). UPI differs from the other leading U.S. agency, the AP, in that it is a profit-making organization. AP, on the other hand, is a media-based news service. Its members share operation costs and news. UPI has extensive coverage in Latin America through a system of bureaus and correspondents. Table 5.2 shows the number of UPI bureaus in Latin America and number of news staff in each bureau.

The sale of the financially troubled UPI to Vazquez-Rana, Mexico's largest newspaper publisher, came under close scrutiny from U.S. journalists because of Vazquez-Rana's close ties with the Mexican government. Shortly after Vazquez-Rana purchased UPI, the Scripps League newspaper group, discontinued the ser-

TABLE 5.2
United Press International in Latin America

Country	Location	Staff Size†
	Caribbean Division	
Puerto Rico	San Juan	6
Dominican Republic	Santo Domingo	3
Guyana	Georgetown	1
Haiti	Port-au-Prince	1
Jamaica	Kingston	1
	Central America Division	
El Salvador	San Salvador	1
Costa Rica	San Jose	1
Guatemala	Guatemala City	2
Honduras	Tegucigalpa	1
Mexico	Mexico City	4
Nicaragua	Managua	2
Panama	Panama City	2
	South America Division	
Argentina	Buenos Aires	3*
Bolivia	La Paz	1
Brazil	Brasilia	1*
	Rio de Janeiro	1
	Sao Paulo	0**
Chile	Santiago	3
Colombia	Bogotá	2
Ecuador	Quitó	1
Paraguay	Asunción	1
Peru	Lima	2
Uruguay	Montevideo	1
Venezuela	Caracas	4

†In some locations, figures include stringers.
*Management total only.
**No correspondent, technical and administrative staff only.
Source: Pieter Van Bennekom, United Press International, Washington (personal communication, January 31, 1990).

vice. Gene Roberts, executive editor of the *The Philadelphia Inquirer,* also expressed fears about Vazquez-Rana, but added that many of the criticisms "strike me as an anti-Mexican, anti-foreign bias" (Beale, 1986a, p. 11).

Vazquez-Rana purchased the bankrupt *El Sol* newspaper group from the Mexican government in 1976 for $12.8 million. Over the next 10 years he doubled the size of the group from 34 to 62 newspapers with a daily combined circulation of 2.1 million. Vazquez-Rana's newspapers use one quarter of all newsprint used by Mexican newspapers and magazines. But Vazquez-Rana never was able to disassociate himself from allegations that he purchased the group at an unreasonably low price because of his friendship with then Mexican President Luis Echeverria Alvarez (1970–1976) (Oppenheimer, 1986).

Latin Americans, and Mexicans in particular, had mixed feelings about the scrutiny the Vazquez-Rana deal had received in the United States. Many Latin Americans believed the scrutiny suggested that Latin Americans could not be trusted to report news about themselves, not to mention international news, and must rely on foreigners. But even many Latin American media people conceded that Vazquez-Rana's past close ties with the Mexican government might cause ethical problems. One leading Bogotá daily, *El Tiempo,* initially terminated its service with UPI after Vazquez-Rana took over, but resumed the service later.

UPI started the 1990s controlled by Chairman Earl Brian and Vice-Chairman Joseph Taussig. Pieter Van Bennekom (personal communication, January 31, 1990), UPI's senior vice president of international operations, with more than 20 years of experience in Latin America, is acutely aware of the charges of "cultural imperialism" aimed against the international news agencies. He is particularly aware that at least in Latin America, UPI is often accused of cultural imperialism. He strongly disagrees with these charges. Harking back to the days of the international news cartel, of which UPI (then UP) was not a member, Van Bennekom (personal communication, January 31, 1990) noted that UP was the stimulus that led to the eventual break-up of the cartel, adding: "UPI has always stood for the free flow of information around the world and especially in the Western Hemisphere and has earned widespread loyalty, respect, and credibility."

Van Bennekom claimed that the majority of UPI stories disseminated in Latin America each day originate from Latin America. In addition, stories that originate from outside of Latin America and are disseminated to the region are often re-written to reflect Latin American angles and perspectives. Concerning the charges of cultural imperialism against the international news agencies, Van Bennekom stated:

> UPI's Spanish-language news service for Latin America is not some kind of sub-product of a news product for the American market but an authentic stand-alone product tailored to the information needs of the Latin American market. As such, we certainly plead "not guilty" to the charge, sometimes leveled in this context, that we practice any kind of cultural imperialism. We are a multinational company in the best sense of the word, in that we have a staff for the Latin American operation composed of nationals of all the countries in the Western Hemisphere.

Newspapers

Latin America has a number of regionally and internationally prestigious newspapers of diverse political leanings. Traditionally, many large Latin American newspapers are associated with leading families with conservative political views. However, a trend toward less political newspapers not identified with families is becoming increasingly popular. Latin American newspapers were slow to shed their partisanship, and many still remain strongly partisan to this day. Many newspapers go beyond simply being associated with one political orientation or another and are partisan organs, funded by political parties or individuals with strong political orientations who see newspapers as a means to influence public opinion. Many daily newspapers in Latin American metropolitan centers have adopted sophisticated production technologies. New computer-based systems produce full-color printing capabilities, high-speed news processing, and data storage.

The best Latin American newspapers tend to be located in the largest nations, but there are exceptions. Highly regarded newspapers are produced in Brazil, Mexico, Colombia, and Chile, but also in smaller nations such as Costa Rica and Uruguay. Many of these quality newspapers have reputations for defiantly challenging autocratic governments. Up-to-date figures on newspapers are difficult to obtain. Brazil may have as many as 600 newspapers (Muñoz, personal interview, January 26, 1990). In 1982, Mexico was reported to have had the most daily newspapers in the region, with well over 300. Others with large numbers of daily newspapers included Brazil, Argentina, Peru, Chile, Colombia, Uruguay, Ecuador, and Cuba (Wilkie & Ochoa, 1989).

LATIN AMERICA'S LEADING NEWSPAPERS

In each Latin American country, a handful of newspapers has emerged to form the "prestige" or "elite" press. These newspapers have varying political orientations and are at times in and out of favor with their governments. Louisiana State University Prof. John C. Merrill (1968) said elite newspapers "represent the serious, informed, and influential journalism of their respective nations" (p. xiii).

Merrill added that an elite international press should also be complete in foreign coverage, concerned with interpretation, graphically dignified, serious and lack sensationalism, impartial, and imaginative among other criteria. Although attempts to classify newspapers by their prestige often seems arbitrary, the fact that there is considerable agreement among the experts suggests that there is some validity and reliability to these ratings (Garrison & Muñoz, 1986).

Table 6.1 lists what we believe are the major newspapers in the Latin American and Caribbean region today. Table 6.2 lists the number of newspapers by country in the region from 1965 to 1984. The following sections give brief descriptions of the region's leaders.

Argentina

In democratic Argentina, inflation has been the press' worst enemy. Economic troubles at the beginning of the 1990s have seriously hampered the progress of Argentine newspapers. Only the strongest have been able to survive the national economic crisis. With most existing dailies in serious financial trouble at the beginning of this decade, some new publications failed. In 1989, for example, *El Heraldo* in Buenos Aires was killed by inflation that has affected the costs of supplies such as newsprint, ink, photographic paper, and film.

Argentina's *La Prensa*, *La Nación*, and *Clarín* are widely rated as among the best in the region. The three are part of nearly 200 daily newspapers published in Argentina (Boyle, 1988). *La Prensa* was founded in 1869 by José Carlos Paz as an independent family-owned newspaper that carries the motto: "Truth, honor, freedom, progress, civilization." The newspaper has been described as resembling the *Times of London* in its appearance and *The New York Times* in its prestige and influence (Bailey & Nasatir, 1968). During the rule of the dictator Juan Domingo Peron, *La Prensa*'s fight with the dictatorship captured world headlines, but it was eventually taken over by the government.

During the military dictatorship that ruled Argentina until 1983, *La Prensa* typified a classic case of the "lapdog" press, intimidated by the regime and unwilling to criticize the government. Perhaps it would have been expecting too much of *La Prensa* to criticize the brutal government that was known to murder its critics. After the democratically elected government of Raúl Alfonsín came to power in

TABLE 6.1
A Selected List of Latin America's Leading Newspapers

Newspaper Name	Location	Publication Cycle	1990 Daily Circulation
	Central America		
Costa Rica			
La Nación	San Jose	MS	135,000
El Salvador			
El Diario de Hoy	San Salvador	MS	88,000
La Prensa Gráfica	San Salvador	MS	106,000
Honduras			
El Tiempo	San Pedro Sula	M	35,000
La Prensa	San Pedro Sula	MS	50,000
Mexico			
Excelsior	Mexico City	MS	175,000
El Heraldo de Mexico	Mexico City	MS	300,000
El Nacional	Mexico City	MS	120,000
Novedades	Mexico City	MS	190,000
Novedades de la Tarde	Mexico City	E	111,000
La Prensa	Mexico City	MS	300,000
El Sol de Mexico	Mexico City	M	120,000
Ultimas Noticias de Excelsior	Mexico City	M	108,000
El Universal	Mexico City	MS	185,000
Uno Mas Uno	Mexico City	M	70,000
El Norte	Monterrey	MS	100,000
Nicaragua			
La Prensa	Managua	D	74,000
Barricada	Managua	D	6,000
Panama			
La Prensa	Panama City	D	35,000
La Estrella de Panamá	Panama City	MS	40,000
Panama America	Panama City	D	—
	South America		
Argentina			
Clarín	Buenos Aires	MS	670,000
La Nacion	Buenos Aires	MS	285,000
La Prensa	Buenos Aires	MS	70,000
Ambito Financiero	Buenos Aires	M	67,000

(Continued)

TABLE 6.1
(Continued)

Newspaper Name	Location	Publication Cycle	1990 Daily Circulation
Brazil			
Jornal O Dia	Rio de Janeiro	MS	300,000
O Globo	Rio de Janeiro	MS	400,000
Jornal do Brasil	Rio de Janeiro	MS	176,000
Tribuna da Imprensa	Rio de Janeiro	E	1,970,000
O Estado de Sao Paulo	Sao Paulo	M	179,000
Chile			
El Mercurio	Santiago	MS	325,000
La Tercera	Santiago	MS	340,000
La Epoca	Santiago	M	—
Colombia			
El Espectador	Bogota	MS	227,000
El Tiempo	Bogota	MS	350,000
El Colombiano	Medellin	MS	89,000
Ecuador			
El Comercio	Quito	MS	140,000
Hoy	Quito	D	41,000
El Universo	Guayaquil	MS	190,000
Paraguay			
Diario ABC Color	Asunción	D	75,000
Peru			
El Comercio	Lima	MS	185,000
Expreso	Lima	MS	140,000
Uruguay			
El Día	Montevideo	MS	100,000
El Diario	Montevideo	E	170,000
Venezuela			
El Universal	Caracas	MS	150,000
El Nacional	Caracas	M	150,000
Diario de Caracas	Caracas	D	103,000
	Caribbean		
Cuba			
Granma	Havana	MS	675,000
Juventud Rebelde	Havana	E	250,000

(Continued)

TABLE 6.1
(Continued)

Newspaper Name	Location	Publication Cycle	1990 Daily Circulation
Jamaica			
Daily Gleaner	Kingston	MS	75,000
Puerto Rico			
El Nuevo Día	San Juan	MS	207,000

W = weekly; M = mornings (Mondays–Saturdays); E = evenings (Mondays–Saturdays); S = Sundays; D = daily.

Sources: Velez (1990) and Williamson (1989).

TABLE 6.2
Number of Daily Newspapers Published, 1965–1984*

	1965	1975	1978	1979	1982	1984
Argentina	171	164	141	133	191	188
Bolivia	9	14	14	14	12	13
Brazil	ND	299	328	328	ND	322
Chile	ND	47	37	37	37	ND
Colombia	39	40	39	38	28	31
Costa Rica	ND	6	4	4	4	5
Cuba	ND	15	9	9	17	18
Dominican Republic	7	10	7	7	9	7
Ecuador	23	29	37	38	18	16
El Salvador	ND	12	12	12	6	6
Guatemala	ND	10	9	9	9	5
Haiti	6	7	7	4	4	4
Honduras	ND	8	7	7	6	6
Mexico	220	256	ND	ND	374	312
Nicaragua	6	7	6	8	3	3
Panama	10	6	6	6	5	6
Paraguay	ND	8	5	5	5	5
Peru	69	49	57	59	68	60
Uruguay	ND	30	29	28	24	21
Venezuela	33	49	55	69	36	61
United States**	1751	1775	1774	1787	1710	1687

All data originally come from several UNESCO documents, summarized in Wilkie and Ochoa (1989, p. 72).

ND refers to no data.

*A daily is defined as publication at least four times a week.

**Figures from the United States included for comparison.

1983, *La Prensa* used the new freedom to harshly criticize the Alfonsín government in its editorials (Bradley, 1988). Although some authorities believe *La Prensa*'s hemispheric influence has waned, it remains influential with national and hemispheric political and economic decision makers. *La Prensa*'s circulation of 70,000 daily and 145,000 Sunday is relatively small compared with other leading Argentine newspapers (Banks, 1988).

El Clarín, founded in 1870 and also based in Buenos Aires, has become one of the two leading newspapers in Argentina in terms of importance and influence. *El Clarín*, with 670,000 copies sold daily and over 1 million on Sundays, is the largest newspaper in Buenos Aires. *La Nación*, also published in Buenos Aires, is also a leading newspaper. It has a circulation of about 285,000 copies daily and 350,000 on Sundays.

In the past, Argentine newspapers endured pressures from governments they opposed. There was little if any overt censorship during the government of President Alfonsín (1983–1989). However, even Alfonsín's democratic government attempted to coerce the press at times (Golden, 1989a). A 1984 law was passed at Alfonsín's urging that requires those who feel maligned by the press a right of reply in a newspaper (Boyle, 1988).

During 1985, Argentina was thought to have the highest newsprint tariff in the world, 38%. This discouraged the growth of the newspaper industry (Ruth, 1985). Although the high tariff was not used by the Alfonsín government to silence any particular publication, the potential existed. The tax policy on newsprint was meant to increase profits for Papél Prensa, Argentina's largest newsprint mill, in which the government is a 25% owner. Three other Argentine newspapers have a combined 65% interest in Papél Prensa, from which they purchase newsprint at reduced rates, resulting in what many see as an unfair advantage. The three newspapers purchased newsprint at $350 a ton while other newspapers typically paid $600 a ton.

Bolivia

In 1990, Bolivia had about 12 daily newspapers. The most important newspapers in Bolivia are *El Diário*, with a circulation of about 45,000; *Hoy*, with a circulation of 20,000; and *Ultima Hora*, with a circulation of 30,000 daily. They are located in La Paz.

Presencia, the Catholic Church newspaper founded in 1952, is growing in influence in Bolivia. It is a daily with 65,000 circulation and 92,000 on Sundays. It is published in La Paz.

Brazil

With the fifth largest land mass in the world and the largest population in Latin America, newspapers flourish in Brazil's urban areas. During 1990, Brazil had more than 325 daily newspapers.

In fact, *Tribuna da Imprensa*, an evening daily in Rio de Janeiro, reported a circulation of 1,970,000 copies. This makes *Tribuna da Imprensa* the largest newspaper in Latin America. *Tribuna da Imprensa* was founded in 1949.

However, *Jornal do Brasil, O Estado de São Paulo*, and *O Globo* are often rated as the three best newspapers in Brazil. *O Estado de São Paulo* is considered one of the region's most outstanding newspapers. *Jornal do Brasil* and *O Globo* are based in Rio de Janeiro, whereas *O Estado* is in São Paulo. *O Globo*, with a daily circulation of 400,000 and over 500,000 on Sundays, is part of the Globo media conglomerate that owns Radio Globo, with nearly 2,000 transmitters, and TV Globo, the fourth largest commercial television network in the world.

The Caribbean

There are six major newspapers serving the Caribbean at the beginning of the 1990s. The dominant privately owned newspaper in the region is *The Daily Gleaner* and its companion edition, *The Sunday Gleaner*, published in Kingston, Jamaica. A relatively new newspaper, *The Jamaica Record*, is also produced in Jamaica. There are about 10 different newspapers published in Jamaica (Anon., 1989b). Also serving the Caribbean islands are *The Nation* and *Advocate* in Barbados, and the *Guardian* and *Express* in Trinidad and Tobago.

The Daily Gleaner was founded in 1834. So influential is the *Gleaner* in Jamaica that Jamaicans use the word "gleaner" as synonymous with "newspaper" (Brown, 1976). The Gleaner Company Limited, its owner, also produces *The Star* and prints thousands of school textbooks each year. The morning *Gleaner* circulates 74,000 and 107,000 on Sundays. The afternoon *Star* circulates 55,000 evenings. The Gleaner Company actually produces 12 different newspapers—including foreign editions, weekly compendium editions, and London and Toronto editions. About 55% of the circulation of the Gleaner Company newspapers is in the Kingston area. The *Gleaner* and *Star* have about 100 newsroom employees and about 430 employees in the entire company (Clarke, personal interview, January 13, 1990). Jamaica also has a number of weekly and monthly newspapers as well as newspapers published by religious groups.

The Gleaner was frequently at odds with Jamaica's socialist leaders during the 1970s. When the People's National Party declared a policy of "democratic socialism," which included friendly relations with Cuba and support for the Marxist rebels in Angola, the *Gleaner* accused the government of subscribing to an "alien ideology" (Cuthbert, 1976). During 1980, the *Gleaner* and the government were at odds when the newspaper called for the expulsion of the Cuban ambassador. Prime Minister Michael Manley himself led a protest march against the *Gleaner* (Habermann, 1985).

El Nuevo Día and *El Vocero de Puerto Rico*, both located in San Juan, Puerto Rico, dominate daily circulation in this U.S. territory. *El Nuevo Dia* is the larger and regarded as the better of the two newspapers.

The Caribbean does not have a region-wide newspaper. In 1989, a group of Canadian and American investors announced plans to begin publication of a weekly full-color tabloid newspaper for the Caribbean region. Communications Inc. hoped to sell 60,000 copies of *Caribbean Week* each week and take in $1.5 million (U.S.) a year from advertising revenues alone. The paper would be printed and edited in the Barbados (Anon., October 9, 1989).

Chile

Former Chilean President Gen. Augusto Pinochet (1973–1990) loathed the press, regardless of whether it was Chilean or foreign. It was in this difficult environment that some 37 daily and 128 non-daily newspapers and periodicals operated. But, as the decade ended with Pinochet's resounding defeat in a December 1989 election, and the inauguration of a democratically elected president in 1990, more freedoms, including press freedom, have come to Chile. The new democratic Chile is expected to offer a less hostile atmosphere for the nation's press.

Santiago's *El Mercurio* was founded in Valparaiso in 1827. It is the oldest Spanish-language newspaper published in the world today. It was established in 1824 in Valparaiso by Pedro Félix Vicuña with the assistance of Thomas G. Wells. Wells was a student of Benjamin Franklin, a typesetter and owner of a small press, when he joined Vicuña in 1827 (Campbell, 1962).

The newspaper was acquired by Agustín Edwards in 1880, who built it into the nation's most prestigious daily. In 1900, Edwards launched a Santiago edition. The newspaper has had an unbroken record of continuous publication until the government of Salvador Allende (1970–1973) closed it for one day on June 16, 1973 (Knudson, 1981). It is published today by the third and fourth generations of Agustín Edwards, father Agustín E. Edwards and son Agustín J. Edwards.

El Mercurio Newspapers, now at least 14 newspapers including *El Mercurio de Valparaiso*, have a daily combined circulation of 520,000 and a Sunday combined circulation of 643,000. The conservative *El Mercurio* was once recognized as one of the best daily newspapers in the southern hemisphere. As far back as 1942, Euleau described the conservative stand of *El Mercurio*:

> In its attitude toward domestic political questions the paper stands on the right, is a defender of strong governmental authority and Catholicism. A large society section suggests that *El Mercurio* is read in leading society circles by the rich landowners and by the still strongly entrenched aristocracy. (p. 292)

Despite this portrayal of *El Mercurio* as a defender of the wealthy class, Euleau added that *El Mercurio* deserved credit for taking a strong stand against fascism during and before World War II, even though this ideology enjoyed a good deal of support in Chile and much of South America's southern cone.

El Mercurio's image has been severely tarnished over the years because of its close association with the Pinochet dictatorship and the disclosure that it took money from the U.S. Central Intelligence Agency to help in Allende's overthrow. In 1986, Agustín J. Edwards, assistant editor of *El Mercurio* and a director of the chain, criticized an IAPA report condemning Pinochet's press controls during the organization's convention in Vancouver, Canada (Stein, 1986a).

Colombia

By and large, Colombia's newspaper journalists have not distinguished themselves with aggressive, in-depth reporting of the nation's social and political problems, although the situation is improving. Today, for instance, Bogotá's *El Tiempo* is regarded as one of the best investigative reporting newspapers in the region. Given the intense violence in the nation, and the dangers that enterprising journalists face, it is difficult to fault them on this point. The political nature of the Colombian press also hampers the development of quality journalism. Many Colombian newspapers serve as organs of political factions. The directors of major dailies frequently serve blatantly political roles. They will arrange meetings among members of their own political parties or between political parties to resolve political crises (Hartlyn, 1988).

Drug wars have become a major concern of the press in Colombia. Narcoterrorists have made Colombia among the most dangerous nations in the world in which to practice journalism. Wealthy and dangerous drug lords often murder or injure journalists to express disagreement with stands taken on issues or displeasure with unwanted publicity. Colombian journalists' names often appear on hit lists circulated by right-wing death squads and drug cartels (Cano, personal interview, January 25, 1990).

El Espectador of Bogotá has distinguished itself because of its campaign against the Medellín drug cartel. *El Espectador*, with a morning daily circulation in excess of 227,000, is aligned with a Liberal group. The newspaper, founded in 1887, has been in the hands of the Cano family for over 100 years (Cano, personal interview, January 25, 1990).

In 1986, *El Espectador*'s editor Guillermo Cano was murdered while driving home from his office in Bogotá. At the time, police said they believed drug traffickers were responsible for the death of the editor of the second largest newspaper in the nation. Colombian President Virgilio Barco publicly accused drug trafficker Pablo Escobar for the murder. In 1989, *El Espectador*'s attorney and columnist, Hector Giraldo Galvez, who was involved in the investigation of the Cano murder, was also murdered. *El Espectador* vies with another morning paper in Bogotá, *El Tiempo*. *El Tiempo* is the largest circulation newspaper, however, with 350,000 daily and 425,000 Sundays.

As a result of these murders, many Colombian journalists have been intimidated into self-censorship. A leading Colombian human rights group, the Permanent Committee for the Defense of Human Rights in Colombia, polled 1,500 journalists and reported that 78% censor their own work. Many drop their bylines from stories. And editors regularly edit their own reporters' controversial articles and use similar stories from the foreign press when they are available. *El Espectador* and *El Tiempo* built international reputations in the 1980s for fighting corruption, especially against drug traffickers based in Colombia.

El Tiempo was founded by members of the Liberal Party in 1911. One-time publisher Eduardo Santos was also president of the country from 1938 to 1942.

El Colombiano, founded in 1912, is Medellín's largest newspaper, publishing about 89,000 copies mornings and 94,000 copies on Sundays. *El Colombiano* is situated in Colombia's narcotics trade center. It has understandably reported in a cautious fashion about the cartel's activities.

Costa Rica

Like much of the region, economic conditions have led to difficult times for the newspapers of Costa Rica. Even the nation's leading newspaper, *La Nación*, came close to declaring bankruptcy in 1982 when the country devalued its currency from 8.60 *colones* to the U.S. dollar to 50 *colones* to the dollar in just a few weeks. *La Nación* former publisher, the late Manuel Jimenez Borbon (personal communication, February 15, 1990) said the situation made journalism difficult at the time:

> *La Nación* had imported, and was in the process of paying for, a new $3 million printing press. Due to our financial arrangement with the Bank of America we had to pay the balance of $2 million. . . . It is almost impossible for newspapers to survive under such conditions.

Today, *La Nación* publishes 135,000 copies mornings and 150,000 copies on Sundays in a metropolitan area that has just 278,000 residents and a nation of just 2.8 million. *La Nación*, established in 1946, is not the nation's oldest publishing newspaper. That honor goes to *La Gaceta/Boletin Judicial*, which had been published since 1844. A legal newspaper, it circulates only about 5,300 copies on weekdays. Other major newspapers in Costa Rica include *La República*, a morning daily with 60,000 circulation, and *La Prensa Libre*, an evening daily with about 45,000 circulation.

One unique situation in Costa Rica is that newspapers in San Jose depend more on subscriptions than do newspapers in other Central American countries. *La Nación*, for instance, sells about 65% of its daily press run through subscriptions (Jimenez, personal communication, February 15, 1990).

Cuba

Cuba has no privately owned press; its official newspapers and magazines are owned and operated by the government, although a few crude clandestine newsletters and magazines are occasionally published.

Granma, named after the vessel that brought Fidel Castro and his 81 rebels from Mexico to Cuba in 1956 and launched the Revolution, was established in 1965 as a morning daily and Sunday newspaper in Havana with an estimated daily circulation of 675,000 in 1989. It is the official newspaper of the Communist Party. The newspaper is small (in terms of number of pages printed daily) compared to other Latin American and Caribbean newspapers, but this is in part due to newsprint shortages in Cuba. *Granma* publishes a two-color weekly review, an international edition, in four languages—English, French, Spanish, and Portuguese.

Cuba's largest afternoon newspaper is *Juventud Rebelde* (Rebellious Youth), which models itself after traditional Soviet youth publications to indoctrinate the young. It is published by the Union of Young Communists with content focusing on young people. Its circulation is around 250,000. Havana's third largest newspaper, *Las Trabajadores* (The Worker), circulates 120,000 daily. It is operated by the Cuban Federation of Labor.

In recent years, both newspapers have witnessed declines in readership, leading to the rare use of newspaper readership studies in Cuba to locate the newspapers' failings. A survey of 1,070 youth in some of the largest provinces, polled by the Research and Analysis Section of the Information Center of the Union of Young Communists, found that *Juventud Rebelde* was reaching primarily young professionals, not workers, and does not reflect the concerns of the nation's young people. In addition, like the situation elsewhere in the world, the research indicated that Cuban newspapers are having a difficult time competing against television (Carty, 1989b).

Ecuador

Ecuador had about 20 daily newspapers in 1990. *El Comercio*, of Quito, is the most highly regarded. With a circulation of 140,000 copies daily and 175,000 copies on Sundays, *El Comercio* is also Quito's largest newspaper. The largest circulation newspaper in all of Ecuador is Guayaquil's *El Universo*, with a circulation of 190,000 mornings and 210,000 on Sundays.

El Salvador

The nation's largest newspaper is the morning tabloid *La Prensa Gráfica* with 106,000 copies printed daily. It was established in 1903. *El Diario de Hoy* is published mornings and Sundays, and circulates about 88,000 copies daily and Sundays. Both newspapers are located in the capital of San Salvador.

Guatemala

With a population of 8 million, mostly rural and Indian, newspapers have a weak market compared to other Latin American countries (Skidmore & Smith, 1989). Literacy is still a problem in Guatemala, leaving newspapers read by the wealthy

·and well-educated citizens. For that reason, many newspapers in this nation of widespread poverty and illiteracy report gossip about the nation's most wealthy and famous citizens. In the capital, Guatemala City, the leading newspapers are *Prensa Libre* and *El Gráfico*.

Honduras

Honduras, with a population of just over 4 million, is also heavily rural. Like Guatemala, large portions of the population cannot read or write. Because of this, newspapers are read by government workers and an educated upper class. Two of the nation's major newspapers are centered in the capital city of Tegucigalpa. *La Tribuna* and *El Heraldo* dominate the city's modest newspaper sales. Two other newspapers in San Pedro Sula are also important at the national level. *La Prensa*, with 50,000 circulation, and *El Tiempo*, with daily circulation of 35,000 are highly regarded in Honduras.

Mexico

Depending on whose estimates are used, Mexico City is the largest or second largest city in the world. And, as Mexico's capital, it seems obvious that it would also be the newspaper publishing center for the country. Mexico has developed into a cultural and political center in Latin America, so, not surprisingly, a few of Mexico's 375 dailies in 1990 are among the best in the region. Of the dozens of newspapers published in Mexico City alone, only two are known for their nonpartisan orientations: *La Jornada* and *El Financiero* (Hossie, personal communication, February 15, 1990).

The quality of a few of Mexico's newspapers is surprising when one considers that the Mexican press has a reputation for avoiding criticism of public officials. Many newspapers are even viewed as publicity outlets for the ruling party (Hossie, personal communication, February 15, 1990).

Still, even in an environment where the government has developed a number of elaborate methods for gaining press acquiescence, several of Mexico's newspapers have established themselves as leading national publications. Since the 1950s, Mexico has seen the growth of respected newspapers in its provinces (Alisky, 1960). A few provincial newspapers, such as *El Norte* of Monterrey and *Zeta* of Tijuana, have attained considerable prestige for hard-biting journalism (Bailey, 1988).

Excelsior of Mexico City, with a daily circulation of about 175,000, is still regarded as an important newspaper, even though there are about a half dozen newspapers in Mexico City with larger circulations. *Excelsior* has sometimes been compared to *The New York Times* by some experts, primarily because of its role as the country's "newspaper of record" (Merrill, 1968).

Excelsior, which calls itself "el periodico de la vida nacional" (the newspaper of national life), was founded in 1917 as a conservative publication. Over the years it lost much of its conservative image. Moreso than most Mexican newspapers, *Excelsior* is associated with social causes and the problems of various social classes. Under the direction of Julio Garcia Scherer during 1968 to 1976, the paper was associated with leftist views and causes (Montgomery, 1985). *Excelsior* and two other Mexico City newspapers, *Novedades*, with a mornings circulation of about 190,000, and *Uno Mas Uno*, with a mornings circulation of about 70,000, are also rated among Mexico's best newspapers.

Monterrey's *El Norte* has established a reputation as a technological leader and it is fast becoming the nation's overall best newspaper. *El Norte* was founded in 1938 and circulates about 100,000 daily. *Novedades*, founded in 1934, is owned by Romulo O'Farrill, Jr. O'Farrill is president and publisher of Novedades Editores, S.A., in Mexico City, which publishes eight newspapers. However, he is also chairman of the board of Televisa, Mexico's major media conglomerate that owns 156 television stations throughout the country. O'Farrill also owns *Novedades de Baja California*, and other newspapers. *Novedades* is considered a mainstream or conservative newspaper associated with the nation's business interests (Montgomery, 1985).

Other important regional newspapers in Mexico today include *El Imparcial* in Hermosilla, *El Informador* in Guadalajara, and *Diario de Yucatan* in Merida (Muñoz, personal interview, January 26, 1990).

Uno Mas Uno was founded in 1976 by former *Excelsior* staff members. *Esto*, of Mexico City, is Mexico's largest newspaper, with circulation reported at 400,000 mornings and Sundays. The second largest newspapers in the nation are *El Heraldo de Mexico* and *La Prensa*, with circulations of about 300,000.

Another relatively new, but influential daily in Mexico City, *La Jornada*, is considered by some to be among Mexico's finest papers. It is read by such an elite few (circulation of about 25,000) that it has been referred to as "that letter among friends" (Bailey, 1988, p. 24). *La Jornada* fights the Mexico City press' tendency to publish government-written press releases as news stories. *La Jornada* published an English newspaper, *The Journal*, between 1987 and 1989 (Hossie, personal communication, February 15, 1990).

The Mexican government has expanded *El Nacional* into a national newspaper, its own version of *USA Today*. A daily, *El Nacional* represents "the official point of view of the Mexican government" (Montgomery, 1985, p. 765). The concept of this newspaper is similar to Gannett's *USA Today*, using printing plants in about 20 cities across the country linked by satellite. Although its news-editorial quality is sometimes uneven, the speed of satellite technology enables it to be available nationwide on the same day. Like *USA Today*, it features four-color process photos and graphics. The first three sections of each regional edition of the newspaper are prepared in Mexico City, while a fourth section is prepared locally (Anon., October 1986).

El Nacional, founded in 1929, has built a circulation of 120,000 mornings and Sundays. One advantage *El Nacional* holds over other privately held newspapers is newsprint supply. Because the Mexican government owns the only newsprint plant, *El Nacional* does not find newsprint availability a problem, as many other Mexican newspapers sometimes found before newsprint import restrictions were eased at the beginning of the 1990s.

Nicaragua

La Prensa, the largest newspaper with a current circulation of about 74,000, is published daily. Under the on-again, off-again censorship of the Sandinista government until 1990, when its publisher Violeta Chamorro was elected president of Nicaragua, government representatives stationed at the newspaper office frequently read the content of the newspaper before it could be printed. The newspaper was closed by the Sandinista government several times during the 1980s. The spotlight section in this chapter discusses *La Prensa* in more depth.

A new weekly newspaper in Managua has tried to bring the nation a new style of journalism. *La Crónica* (*The Chronicle*) began publication in November 1988 as an independent newspaper vowing to provide readers with an objective style of journalism not favoring either the left or right in Nicaragua. *La Cronica* debuted in competition with *La Prensa* (conservative daily of Violeta Chamorro), *La Barricada* (the official Sandinista daily under the previous Sandinista government), and *El Nuevo Diario* (the pro-Sandinista daily under the Sandinista government).

Panama

The newspaper industry in Panama was completely shaken when the United States sent its military forces into the country to bring down the government of Gen. Manuel Antonio Noriega. Until the democratically elected president, Guillermo Endara, was inaugurated during the last weeks of 1989, newspaper publishing in Panama was unsafe business. Publishers of opposition newspapers never knew when their publications would be closed, properties seized, or offices and facilities destroyed. With the new government in Panama, newspaper publishing flourished in 1990. Five newspapers, several of which were banned by Noriega, were published in just 6 weeks after the U.S. invasion on December 20, 1989 (Oppenheimer, 1990a).

Panama City's *La Prensa* is Panama's best-known newspaper. It is an independent daily with rapidly changing circulation—it was 90,000 on its first day of the post-Noriega era—in a city of about 800,000 residents. It was closed by the Noriega government for most of 1988 and 1989 (Oppenheimer, 1990a).

Because of the press' problems with Noriega, one of Central America's best-known editors lived much of those 2 years in the United States. I. Roberto Eisenmann, Jr., editor and president of *La Prensa*, resided in exile in Miami until Noriega was arrested and taken to Miami for trial on drug trafficking charges. Eisenmann returned to Panama to publish *La Prensa* when Noriega was flown out of Panama City by the Americans.

During February 1988, the Noriega government closed *La Prensa*. About 1,000 people lost their jobs when the government closed *La Prensa* and four other newspapers, three radio stations, and a television station. A year later, opposition to the action was marked by 150 demonstrators outside the closed newspaper. The event was the first opposition rally since May 1987, when protests were violently repressed by police. The exiled Eisenmann managed the newspaper when the Noriega government allowed it to publish by using his personal computer, a modem, a fax machine, and overseas telephone lines.

Panama America is also back in business after the 1989 departure of Noriega. Based in Panama City, this operation produces three daily newspapers including one in English. With a large English-speaking element in the Canal Zone area, the market for an English-language newspaper is significant.

La Estrella de Panamá, founded in 1853, is a morning and Sunday daily with daily circulation of about 40,000. It remains one of the leading newspapers in the country as well. *La Estrella de Panamá* supported Noriega, but offered support to Endara's new government. Nevertheless, as a result of its association with the past Noriega government, its circulation was falling in the first days of 1990 (Oppenheimer, 1990a).

Paraguay

Paraguay, with population of about 3.8 million, experienced much change at the end of the 1980s. The major newspaper, *Diario ABC Color*, resumed publication in 1989 after forced closure by former dictator Gen. Alfredo Stroessner (1954–1989) in 1984. Located in Asunción with a daily circulation of about 75,000, *ABC Color*'s battles with the government throughout the 1980s generated considerable international attention. Although the amount of newspaper reading among Paraguayans may increase now that Stroessner has been deposed, during the years of Stroessner's rule Paraguay had among the lowest newspaper readerships in the continent.

The 34-year rule of Stroessner came to a sudden end when he was replaced by Gen. Andrés Rodríguez during a military-led coup in early 1989. The provisional president promised to bring democracy, including freedom of expression, and vowed not to arrest journalists for carrying out their duties. One of his first actions was to permit *ABC Color* to reopen exactly five years to the day after it was shut down.

Peru

With a 15% literacy rate in a population of 20 million, Peru's 30 daily and 13 non-daily newspapers still find substantial markets for their varied content. There are 16 dailies in Lima alone, a city of 5 to 6 million people, that are kept alive by low production costs (Boyle 1988). Most of these Lima papers circulate widely throughout the nation.

There are several contenders for what is the oldest newspaper in Latin America. Peru may be the home of Latin America's first daily newspaper, the short-lived *El Diario de Lima* which was established in 1790 (Altschull, 1984). The oldest existing newspaper in Peru is *El Comercio*. It is a morning (185,000 copies circulation) and Sunday (225,000 copies) publication that celebrated its 150th birthday in 1989. *El Comercio*, which was once Peru's pre-eminent newspaper, now competes against a variety of popular newspapers (McClintock, 1988).

Most of Peru's newspapers reflect the conservative views of their owners, among the best known families in the nation. *El Comercio* is owned by the Miro Quesada family, a major force in Peruvian business and politics. During the 1930s, *El Comercio*'s editorials were so far to the political right that columnists were praising Hitler and European fascist movements (Pierce, 1979). *La Crónica/La Nueva Cronica*, owned by the Prado family, controls a large financial empire centered about the nation's second largest bank. The family contributed four national presidents to the country. The morning newspaper has a circulation of 208,000.

La Prensa was built into one of the nation's leading dailies during the 1920s and 1930s by Pedro Beltrán, a right-wing conquistador-descended aristocrat. During the 1930s, the newspaper represented the interests of large plantation owners along the nation's coast. Beltrán, an orthodox economist who dressed in flamboyant, colorful clothes in the style of Oscar Wilde and Benjamin Disraeli, was appointed premier during the late 1950s and saved the crumbling Peruvian economy by eliminating food subsidies, cutting imports, enforcing tax collection, and restricting credit. His achievement in stabilizing the economy may have helped the nation's wealthy, but it meant little to the poor, who had to sacrifice their already low standard of living for the economic good of the nation. Beltrán appeared to brag when he once said, ''I am the most hated man in Peru'' (Anon, 1960, p. 42).

An exception to the usually conservative Peruvian press is the leftist tabloid *El Diario*, which not only reports about, but eulogizes, the Shining Path guerrillas (Collett, 1988). As Altschull (1984) wrote of the traditionally conservative Peruvian newspapers:

> Thus, the newspaper industry that arose in Peru in the nineteenth century was a mirror of a larger feudal social order. . . . Each of these families was a powerful source in Peru; their newspapers all situated in Lima, were only divisions of their banking, commercial, and industrial empires. (p. 162)

Uruguay

In 1990, Uruguay had about 25 daily newspapers with a combined circulation of 750,000. Based in Montevideo, the conservative *El Diario* has a circulation of about 170,000 daily and is the largest newspaper in Uruguay. However, *El Día* associated with the Social Democratic party, is regarded as the best newspaper in the nation.

El Día was founded in 1886, at first representing the liberal view and more recently a conservative view. The newspaper helped lay the foundation for a number of social reforms that occurred in Uruguay during the first 20 years of this century. *El Dia* circulates 100,000 each morning.

A military regime established in 1973 forbade newspapers to report internal security matters. More than 30 newspapers were closed by the dictatorship, and those that remained open experienced numerous short-term closings. In November 1974, the dictatorship closed the last opposition publication, the weekly *Marcha*, read throughout the continent. Press freedom was not restored until 1985. Although many Latin American nations experienced military dictatorships during the 1970s, liberals throughout Latin America point to the Uruguayan experience to illustrate how a peaceful nation with a well-established democracy could subvert its freedom by allowing the military to wield wide power to fight terrorism and bring about social stability.

Venezuela

Since the fall of dictator Marcos Perez Jimenez in 1958, Venezuela has enjoyed considerable press freedom. Despite that, Venezuelan newspapers have been described as ''pallid and subservient'' to the government (Anon., December 1988, p. 32). Part of the reason may be the pressure on the press to stay close to the government line by practicing *autocensura* (self-censorship).

The divorce proceedings of president Jaime Lusinchi created Venezuela's worst period of *autocensura* in recent times. Lusinchi filed for divorce on December 18, 1986. The press in this Catholic nation, which looks askance on divorce, did not mention anything about it until September 10, 1987. In response, the government withdrew its advertising from the newspaper *La Región* of Cumaná, which broke the story. In January 1988, more than 2,500 journalists marched in protest against what they described as increasing government attempts to muzzle the press (Knudson, 1989).

El Universal, one of eight dailies published in Caracas, is one of the nation's major dailies. It was founded in 1909 and draws its reporting strength from stories on energy and iron ore. *El Universal* circulates about 150,000 copies mornings and over 195,000 copies on Sundays, but it is not the nation's largest newspaper. The largest is either *Meridiano* or the sensationalist tabloid *Ultimas Noticias*, both of Caracas, with reported circulations of about 300,000 each.

Venezuela boasts a strong provincial press. Unlike many Latin American nations, which have a few strong predominant dailies in the capital and perhaps one or two in other large cities, Venezuela has over 60 provincial dailies. Some of these fast-growing provincial dailies are attaining considerable national influence (Knudson, 1989).

NEWSPAPER PRODUCTION TECHNOLOGY

Some of the leading Latin American newspapers have traditionally sought to be in the forefront of publishing technology. These publications have the financial resources to invest and even experiment in new technology. Development of new computer-based technology at newspapers could be one of the most significant publishing developments in recent years, said the late Manuel Jimenez Borbon (personal communication, February 15,1990), publisher of Costa Rica's *La Nación*:

> The most exciting aspect of the technical development in Costa Rican newspapers, and I presume in the rest of Latin America, is the use of the computer in all facets [of production]. This results in a much improved product for the advertisers and public relations agencies, not to mention the improvement of interdepartmental communications of newspaper publishing companies.

Some companies, desiring to make technological progress as new equipment and production techniques are developed, simply have not had the financial resources to keep up with new publishing technologies. They have had to depend on second-hand equipment, some of it purchased from the United States. In some countries, governments have severely restricted availability, ownership, and use of new technologies such as satellite earth stations. The smaller regional newspapers use equipment obtained on the resale market from the United States and elsewhere in Latin America.

New publishing technology, as in other parts of the world, is a major concern of publishers in Latin America today. Publishers and production managers frequently travel to the annual American Newspaper Publishers Association summer meeting and exhibition devoted to technology. Some Latin American newspapers, like their North American counterparts, are installing satellite dishes and printing at multiple sites using satellite and laser technology.

In recent years, with the help of the Inter American Press Association Technical Center, private foundations, and other organizations, many Latin American publishers have held their own development seminars and exhibitions to focus on the latest publishing equipment and services provided by international publishing companies based primarily in North America and Europe.

The seminars, featuring experts from around the world, focus on offset printing, typography and design, personal computer-based graphics, color, press operation, satellite transmission and earth stations, electronic picture editing, database development, and electronic editing and reporting systems.

The adoption of new technologies to advance the newspaper industry is a high priority for leading Latin American newspapers. University of Miami Prof. Bruce Garrison (1984) studied adoption of new technologies at major Latin American daily newspapers and reported that two-thirds or more of the newspapers responding to his survey had adopted new technologies, including electronic editing and reporting systems, computerized phototypesetting, and platemaking equipment. Presses and mailroom (distribution) equipment was also high on the modernization list. Furthermore, from one quarter to one third of the newspapers were adding information-retrieval and storage capabilities, new darkrooms, and even first-generation pagination systems.

Modernization among Latin American newspapers occurs because editors and publishers are experiencing trouble managing the large amounts of information their newspapers process daily. Furthermore, publishers are interested in cost effectiveness and improving the quality of their newspapers. The impact of modernization occurs most frequently in the area of graphics. Newspapers either increased use of color or began using color for the first time in the 1980s. Today, many major Latin American newspapers are at the cutting edge of graphics and color printing. But new technology also enhances speed and efficiency in production of the newspapers (Garrison, 1984).

Most Latin American newspapers experience problems with technology, however. In most cases, problems relate to repair and maintenance of equipment once it is in use. The leading problem is obtaining replacement parts or late delivery of replacement parts which frequently come from companies in the United States, Canada, or Europe (Cano, personal interview, January 25, 1990; Garrison, 1984). Because of the difficulty in obtaining replacement parts, Bogotá's *El Espectador* maintains a Miami office that doubles as a magazine shop, headed by Luís Alberto Cano.

El Mercurio in Santiago, Chile, is typical of modern production plants in South America. Its spacious facilities at the edge of the city are the envy of visiting North American journalists. With state-of-the-art production equipment in a large, modern design building, the company produces its flagship newspaper and two other newspapers. Other newspapers owned by the company have their own plants.

Mexico's *El Norte*, based in Monterrey, is also a leader in technological innovation and is currently developing data bases and satellite technology. *El Norte* uses PCs, and in 1988 earned revenue by selling data and news stories originally published for the newspaper via PC link-ups to customers in the Monterrey vicinity (Anon., August 1988, p. 45).

Peru's *El Comercio*, founded in 1839 in Lima, has been one of the traditional technological leaders. *El Comercio* was the first newspaper in Peru to install a rotary press, use a Linotype, transmit by cable, and receive radiophotos (Anon., June 1989).

* * *

SPOTLIGHT

La Prensa: The Story of a Newspaper Family

The story of Central America's most famous newspaper, *El Diario La Prensa* in Nicaragua, is also the story of one of the most famous families in the civil war-torn country—the Chamorro family. The Chamorro family and the newspaper *La Prensa* have been linked since the 1920s.

The newspaper has long been known for leading the fight against government censorship of the press under both the Somoza government and the Sandinista government. The Chamorro family has also been known for its leadership, contributing five presidents to the nation, the most recent being Violeta Chamorro, wife of slain martyr Pedro Joaquín Chamorro and publisher of *La Prensa*. She was elected in February 1990. The demands of the presidency forced her to turn over control of the newspaper to her daughter, Cristiana, and the newspaper's board of directors.

The assassination of Pedro Joaquin Chamorro Cardenal, *La Prensa*'s publisher and a fierce opponent of Somoza, on January 10, 1978, turned every sector of the nation against Somoza, and the Sandinistas were able to assume power in the fray. Before the Somoza family came to power in 1936, four Chamorro family members had served as president of the nation. When the country was torn asunder by warlords jockeying for power after Nicaragua's independence from Spain more than 150 years ago, Fruto Chamorro Pérez forged a coalition as the first president (1853–1855).

In the early years of the Sandinista revolution, Violeta Chamorro supported the Sandinistas and gave the Sandinistas financial support. She even served in the ruling junta until she resigned in disgust in 1980 over what she regarded as the Sandinistas' autocratic rule and betrayal of the revolution (Christian, 1985; Moody, 1989). Part of her disgust with the Sandinistas stemmed from what she viewed as their disregard for press freedom.

Shortly after the revolution, in July 1979, all news media were taken over by the government, including *La Prensa*. Only one newspaper, the Sandinista organ *Barricada*, and a Sandinista radio station were permitted to operate. *La Prensa* and other newspapers were permitted to open again a month later, but with constant pressure and censorship from the government. By January 1980, *La Prensa* became the only opposition newspaper when the government shut down a Worker's Party newspaper, *El Pueblo* (Brownlee, 1984).

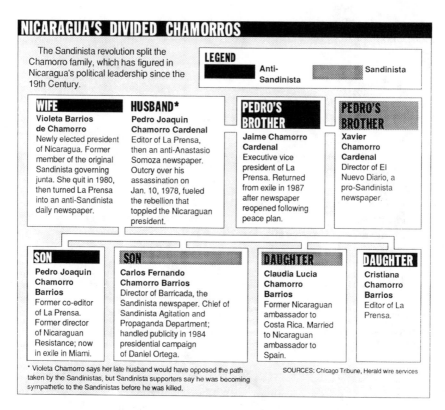

FIG. 6.1. Copyright © 1990 Knight-Ridder Tribune Graphics Network, Inc.

Just prior to Violeta Chamorro's 1990 inauguration, the Nicaraguan National Assembly voted to abolish the national news media law that gave the government a monopoly on television and the power to fine and close opposition newspapers. The law was often invoked by the Sandinista government to shut down *La Prensa* for its strong anti-government articles (Marquis, 1990a; Otis, 1990). Although the Sandinistas received praise for nullifying the law, cynics charged that the action was taken because the Sandinistas would soon become the opposition, and as the opposition they did not want to have to live with the repressive press law that they created.

During Sandinista rule, the Chamorro family was a politically divided clan. One of Violeta Chamorro's four children, Carlos Fernando, served as editor-in-chief of the Sandinistas' official organ, *Barricada*. During Daniel Ortega's presidency, *Barricada* regularly ran editorials referring to the former leader of the Contra rebels as a traitor. The man he called a traitor was his brother, Pedro Joaquin Jr., who edited a fiercely anti-Sandinista newspaper in Costa Rica called *Hoy*. One of their sisters, Cristiana, was the director (the frequently used Latin American term for editor-in-chief) of *La Prensa*, and the other, Claudia, once served as the Sandinista ambassador to Costa Rica. In 1980, Xavier Chamorro Cardenal, the brother of Pedro Joaquin, became editor of the state-subsidized but independent newspaper *El Nuevo Diario*. Despite their political differences during this period, the Chamorros still met for family gatherings and agreed not to discuss politics at the dinner table (see Fig. 6.1).

El Nuevo Diario has become one of the most virulent critics of President Chamorro. *El Nuevo Diario* regularly accuses President Chamorro of being a tool of the U.S. government (Tamayo, 1990). It also takes advantage of new-found press freedom by reporting tantalizing sex crime stories and occasional nude photographs. The Sandinista-owned *Barricada* has not been so bold as to openly accuse President Chamorro of being an agent of the United States. However, it clings to its anti-American view. It runs articles claiming that with improved U.S. relations, Nicaragua will become a port for U.S. sailors, bringing with them AIDS (Tamayo, 1990).

Magazines and Books

Magazines in Latin America cover a wide range of subjects and reach a diverse range of audiences. Production and distribution occurs at national and international levels. Because of political, cultural, economic, and social common ground, a large number of magazines serve audiences in numerous nations. Both translated and specifically edited editions of successful North American and European magazines are popular in Latin America. Nevertheless, most magazine publishers have retained European-style distribution systems dependent on street and store sales. Although democracies have become more widespread in the region, legal and political environments are still troublesome, creating editing and production problems for publishers whose publications occasionally challenge long-time values of conservative governments and social institutions. Magazines, like other news and entertainment media in the region, must battle editorial manipulation by advertisers as well. Rapidly changing and generally unpredictable economic conditions affect circulation and marketing strategies. Among the most popular types of magazines in the region are general news and political commentary magazines, national general interest magazines, women's magazines, *fotonovelas*, and comic books. The leading Latin American magazine publishing companies include Brazil's Editora Abril and Bloch Editores and Spain's Anaya-Editorial America. Sobering economic conditions loom large in the minds of publishers in a number of countries. Yet changing political environments offer opportunities to publish magazines without government intervention in most of the region's countries. Book publishing in Latin America is enhanced by a common cultural background for the region. The major publishing centers are also the region's population centers: Colombia, Mexico, Brazil, and Argentina. Brazil dominates publishing in the region and exports many of its titles to other Portuguese-speaking nations in the world. Spain is the leading nonregional book publisher, exporting many books each year to Latin America. Some companies in the region are reprinters rather than publishers, focusing on producing inexpensive licensed copies of titles such as textbooks from other countries. However, internal distribution problems, dwindling financial resources, piracy of titles published in other nations, and illiteracy cause on-going problems for book publishers.

In every major city in Latin America and the Caribbean, tiny kiosks dot the street corners. Hanging from the outside walls and inside shelves of these micro-businesses are dozens of Latin American and Caribbean magazines, newspapers, and books. This European-style sales system that is reminiscent of the news stalls of Paris or Madrid takes advantage of the fact that Latin American and Caribbean residents tend to go into the streets more often than do North Americans. In addition, much of the region's sometimes unreliable mail service and higher per copy mail/private delivery costs also account for the success of kiosk sales (Hinds, 1980). Although kiosks are the major sales points for Latin American and Caribbean magazines, readers also find their favorite magazines sold in large numbers in bookstores, card shops, drug stores, department stores, hotel lobby newsstands, and grocery store check-out counters.

Mail-delivered magazines and newspapers, as well as home-delivered newspapers, are the exception rather than the rule in most of Latin America. For instance, Editorial América, one of Latin America's major international magazine publishers, circulates its magazines only by newsstand sales in Latin America. The organization, which is headquartered in Miami, offers mail subscription service only in Puerto Rico and in the mainland United States. The $60-million-a-year company has a staff of over 4,000 employees worldwide, including 125 full-time editorial staff (Mariaurelia, 1988).

Delivery time and frequent labor strikes are the major problems for Latin American magazine distribution, said *Cosmopolitan en Espanol* magazine editor Sara Maria Castany (personal interview, March 21, 1990). Because magazine publishers cannot be certain when their latest issue will be delivered, subscriptions are not sold by many magazines. Castany (1990) explained:

> It can take three days or three weeks. We just don't know. For instance, we get mail [in Miami] postmarked from Mexico two or three weeks earlier than when we received it. That's just not reliable for magazines by mail. Even if our magazines are mailed from within the country [where they are delivered], we still have problems.

There are more than 5,000 periodicals in Latin America and the Caribbean today. As can be seen from Table 7.1, many periodicals are transnational or pan-American in nature. These publications are sold throughout the region. Table 7.2 shows the approximate numbers of periodicals in each nation. In the United States, there are about 9,000 magazines available to the public and as many as 22,000 total public and private (e.g., in-house) magazines, depending on how you count them (Garrison, 1989). Like magazine marketing in the United States, most Latin American magazines are highly specialized publications serving specific information needs and audiences. There are, of course, growing numbers of popu-

TABLE 7.1
A Selected List of Leading Pan American Magazines

Magazine Name	Content	Publication Frequency	1988 Circulation
Buenhogar	Women	Monthly	205,938
Business Week	Business	Biweekly	820,000
Coqueta	Teen girls	Monthly	297,000
Cosmopolitan en Español	Women	Monthly	300,000
Electronics	Electronics	Alt. wks.	95,277
Engineering News-Record	Engineering	—	102,000
Geomundo	Geography	Monthly	184,840
Harper's Bazaar en Español	Women	Monthly	101,652
Ideas para su hogar	Home	Monthly	250,000
Mecánica Popular	Men, science	Monthly	184,567
Playboy	Men	Monthly	283,700
Popular Photography	Photography	Monthly	675,000
Ring en Español	Boxing	Monthly	125,000
Rotarian	Rotary Club	Monthly	502,000
Scientific American International	Science	Monthly	112,780
Selecciones	Reader's Digest	Monthly	—
Time	News	Weekly	125,000
Time Euroexecutive	News	Biweekly	85,000
Tu	Young women	Monthly	325,000
TV y novelas	TV	Biweekly	1.1 million
Vanidades Continental	Women	Monthly	—

Sources: Anon. (1989c), "Hispanic magazines growing" (1988), Montalbano (1987), and Sara Maria Castany (personal interview, December 27, 1989).

lar mass circulation magazines that are originally written, edited, and published and distributed in urban centers. Among the top-selling magazines are:

- Buenos Aires' *Siete Dias* (110,000 circulation);
- Rio de Janeiro's *Manchete Esportiva* (210,000) and *Fatos* (115,000);
- São Paulo's *Veja* (793,000), *Veja em São Paulo* (210,000), and *Visao* (151,000);
- Mexico City's *Almas* (250,000), *Contenido* (163,000), *Tu* (150,000), *TV y Novelas* (610,000);
- Lima's *Revista Gente* (120,000); and
- Caracas' *Dominical* (331,000).

In addition to these locally produced, mass circulation magazines, some translated U.S. and European magazines also enjoy wide popularity. For example, *Selecciones* (*Reader's Digest*), *Vision*, *Buenhogar* (*Good Housekeeping*), *Cosmopolitan en Español* (*Cosmopolitan*), and *Mecanica Popular* (*Popular Mechanics*) are written, edit-

TABLE 7.2
Periodicals in Latin American–Caribbean Countries

Country	Number of periodicals
Antigua	3
Argentina	1,360
Bahamas	—
Barbados	130
Belize	5
Bolivia	18
Brazil	—
Chile	—
Colombia	300
Costa Rica	—
Cuba	100
Dominican Republic	17
Ecuador	284
El Salvador	—
Guatemala	—
Guyana	—
Haiti	—
Honduras	40
Jamaica	5
Mexico	1,964
Nicaragua	—
Panama	143
Paraguay	20
Peru	595
Puerto Rico	14
Trinidad and Tobago	24
Uruguay	335
Venezuela	147

Source: Kurian (1982).

ed, and printed in the United States, then shipped by air freight for distribution throughout Latin America. *Marie Claire*, a well-established French fashion magazine, is produced in Spanish in the U.S. by Editorial America and then distributed in South America (Castany, personal interview, March 21, 1990).

Although these popular publications reach a large, diverse audience, the trend in Latin America, as in the United States, is market "segmentation." Over 100 periodicals alone are devoted to the highly specialized area of the analysis and study of mass communication and culture in Latin America (Jones, 1989). A handful of literary magazines published over the past century in the Caribbean has told the world about the region's best authors and literature (Rodriguez, 1985). These small-circulation publications have also helped foster development of the arts in various nations and regions.

PRODUCTION AND DISTRIBUTION

Despite the shared language and culture among nations in the region, transnational magazine producers and distributors must be sensitive to sometimes subtle differences among various nations and cultures in the region. The main areas of concern for producers and distributors of Latin American and Caribbean magazines are the legal and political environments, language complexities, editorial manipulation by advertisers, and individual issue pricing.

Matters of Taste

Laws affecting news and advertising content may force publishers into elaborate production planning for transnational magazines. Some transnational magazines must prepare different versions of some articles and advertisements to get past government reviewers—sometimes called *censors*—who can prevent distribution of an issue if its content violates laws regarding acceptable taste.

If, for instance, an article in a women's magazine discusses sexual behavior too explicitly, that month's edition may not be permitted to enter some countries. These reviewers check magazines as they are shipped into the country. Because these guidelines vary greatly from nation to nation, it is legally and logistically complicated to publish magazines from outside a country and to import them weekly or monthly.

Some highly conservative governments will not permit certain articles and advertising dealing with sexual matters, forcing producers of international magazines to be sensitive to these potential problems. In 1989 alone, Castany (personal interview, December 27, 1989, personal interview, March 21, 1990) said, she had difficulty with subjects dealing with female sexuality. Articles that describe a sexual act or sexual organs in detail are often unacceptable and must be "softened" before publication. These national restrictions can be either legal or by custom. Brazil and Jamaica are generally more liberal than most other Latin American and Caribbean nations regarding sexual matters (Castany, personal interview, March 21, 1990).

Castany's predecessor, Cristina Saralegui, told a reporter from *South Florida* magazine that she encountered resistance from Latin American women in adopting *Cosmopolitan*'s sexually liberated, independent "Cosmo woman" to Latin America (Mariaurelia, 1988). Latin American women could not understand why they should have to go to work when their husbands could provide for them, and they were shocked by discussions of frank sex. Saralegui explained that Latin America's *Cosmopolitan* stressed women's independence without sex: "I always like to think that my women are liberated from the neck up, because I believe that a woman's most important organ is between her ears" (p. 39).

For the Mexican edition of *Cosmopolitan en Español*, for instance, Castany (personal interview, December 27, 1989) must send facsimile copies of some articles to her company's representative in Mexico City for company review prior to publication. The Editorial America representative in Mexico serves as an unofficial liaison and often helps Castany in advance to avoid costly judgment errors after the magazine is published.

Language Complexities

The cultural tie that binds much of the southern hemisphere is language. But even the shared language is no guarantee against linguistic difficulties. As Castany's predecessor Cristina Saralegui said:

> I hear people who do ads for the U.S.-Hispanic markets say "We have a Puerto Rican majority in the Northeast (Northeastern United States), Cubans in Miami, Mexicans on the West Coast, and how can we make one ad that will appeal to all the ethnic groups in Latin America?" I laugh. We've been doing it for twenty-three years. (Mariaurelia, 1988, p. 39)

Seemingly simple things, such as the names of foods, vary from country to country making food and dining feature articles difficult to select, write, edit, and produce. Articles of this type must be edited for the particular national edition of a given transnational magazine.

Editors of Latin American magazines directed toward several Latin American markets are often trained to find common language. Because there are some different Spanish phrases for subjects such as fashion or food that are unique to a specific country or region and others common to certain nations, editors must find the lowest common language denominator. For instance, the Cuban version of the Spanish word for "pig" is *puerco*, whereas Salvadorans and Nicaraguans call it *chancho* and the more general term for pork is *cerdo*. Editors would use *cerdo* because it is more commonly understood.

Editorial Manipulation by Advertisers

In addition to the need for different articles and versions of the same article to satisfy national laws and to appease government reviewers/censors, advertisers also have to be appeased. Certain advertisers do not want to be associated with controversial political content, suggestive sexual content, and other potentially offensive editorial and advertising material (Castany, personal interview, December 27, 1989). Two *Cosmopolitan en Español* advertisers from Mexico, one that sold bread and another that sold carpets, once pulled advertising because they were offended by a fashion photograph showing a popular Brazilian singer, Xuxa, in a skimpy bathing suit, cupping one of her bared breasts with her hand. Incidents such as this one do not happen often, Castany (personal interview, March 21,

1990) said, but do occur frequently enough to cause concern by editors and publishers.

As a result, advertisers make demands on publishers to edit or eliminate certain content planned for an issue. Editors and advertising managers, aware of these concerns through experience, become sensitive to potential lost revenue and at times will "negotiate" with a potentially troublesome advertiser before an article, photograph, or advertisement is published. With threats to withdraw their business, publishers, editors, and advertising managers are forced to listen.

Magazine Pricing

Often magazine prices are lower in Latin America than in North America. For instance, *Vanidades Continental*, the first international Spanish-language women's magazine, sold for $2.95 in the U.S. and Puerto Rico in 1989, but only for $1.50 in Mexico and $1.75 in Colombia (U.S.) during the same period. The magazine is published in Miami. Prices vary because publishers can only charge what the market will bear. Recent poor economic conditions in Latin America, made difficult by inflation, makes pricing almost an art form. Publishers must regularly review cover prices and decide what a reader will pay for a copy of the magazine.

As inflation takes more away from the consumer, and as the price of the magazine remains the same, fewer customers will be willing to purchase the magazine. Wise publishers will adjust their prices—even downward—when possible to keep circulation figures from declining. This boosts other revenue, in the form of advertising dollars because advertising rates are determined by circulation. Much of the cover price problem is related to readers' personal incomes. As spendable income improves, sales improve. As income is stung by inflation, sales suffer. If incomes were higher in Latin America, magazines could be priced higher (Castany, personal interview, December 21, 1989; Due, 1988).

Reliable circulation figures for magazines are quite difficult to obtain from Latin America because there is inadequate independent auditing conducted in the region. At present, there is no central auditing house in Latin America for magazines. Some publications, however, use the Audit Bureau of Circulation (ABC), a U.S.-based company.

NEWS MAGAZINES

The most successful news magazines and commentary magazines are national in scope and are supported by national political parties or national advertising bases as well as newsstand sales revenue. The focus is on national and local politics, foreign affairs, economic and finance news, business, industry, entertainment, and other regularly featured departments. Many news magazines imitate the successful formats of *Time* and *Newsweek* in the United States.

The two largest news magazines in Brazil are *Veja*, in Sâo Paulo, and *Manchete Esportiva*, in Rio de Janeiro. *Resúmen*, published each Monday in Caracas,

Venezuela, is also one of the leading news magazines in Latin America. Influential at all levels of the nation, *Resúmen* is widely read and quoted by politicians and journalists. One of the magazine's goals is to investigate government corruption. Founded in 1973, *Resúmen* publishes about 65,000 copies a week (Alisky, 1983; Gill & Smith, 1989).

Resúmen has been in fights with the government to defend its right to comment on public affairs. In a celebrated case in 1978–1979, *Resúmen* was partially confiscated after an issue reported charges of corruption in the government of the outgoing president. The issue was published prior to the election and a libel suit was filed by the president against the publisher and the magazine. The attorney general impounded about 6,000 copies before the election, but another 100,000 copies had reached subscribers. The publisher and the magazine were eventually cleared of the libel charges (Alisky, 1981).

During the height of the Brazilian military dictatorship of Gen. Joao Baptista Figueiredo (1979–1985), one political satire and humor magazine, *Pasquim*, developed an ingenious ploy for publishing criticisms of the military that got by the censors. Whenever the magazine meant to criticize the Brazilian dictatorship, it simply substituted the word ''Greek'' for ''Brazilian.'' At the time, Greece also had a military government. *Pasquim* published numerous articles of gross human rights abuses by the Greek military government. It took government authorities a year to figure out that the magazine was publishing criticism of the Brazilian government to a select segment of the audience that understood the ploy (Altschull, 1984).

Revista de Revistas is a Mexican weekly news magazine published by the prestigious Mexico City daily *Excelsior*. Its focus is pro-government with articles on government, public projects, business, and the urban lifestyle (Alisky, 1983). Another long-established general interest news magazine in Mexico is *Hoy*. A monthly, it was founded in 1937 in Mexico City (Gill & Smith, 1989).

Somos, founded in 1976 in Buenos Aires, is typical of many of the region's weekly news magazines today. Printed in Buenos Aires in full color by Editorial Atlantida, S.A., the magazine is sold in Argentina, Bolivia, Chile, Paraguay, and Peru. Its graphic design and organization are similar to *Newsweek*, with numerous major stories, regular departments each week, and a multitude of short items and boxed sidebar articles. Its contents regularly cover world and national politics, world and national leaders, national entertainment such as television and film, the arts, society and social issues, international and national sports, big business, banking and finance, and even the mass media.

POLITICAL COMMENTARY MAGAZINES

Like many of Latin America's major daily newspapers, politically oriented magazines often represent decidedly political views. Some publications are funded either in part or entirely by political parties. And like their U.S. counterparts—William

F. Buckley's conservative, pro-Republican *National Review*, for instance—these magazines depend on commentaries and criticism by seasoned journalists and political observers, interviews with prominent politicians and analysts, and discussions of the latest political news by the nation's intellectuals and philosophers. Most are supported by advertising. Although the theme is politics, the focus of these magazines can be either public or private sector activities involving the economy, finance, business, social problems, graft and corruption, and other current events affecting the course of the nation.

One popular commentary magazine in Mexico is the weekly *Proceso*. *Proceso* represents the leading voices of Mexico's political left (Bussey, 1989). The magazine was founded in 1977 by publisher Julio Scherer García, who was once publisher of the Mexico City newspaper *Excelsior*. *Proceso* follows the format of *Time* magazine, including some of its regular news departments. Its writers, including some who came with Scherer García from *Excelsior*, include recognized experts in a wide range of fields who produce regular analyses and interpretations of recent domestic and foreign events and policies (Alisky, 1981, 1983).

Siempre is another popular weekly commentary magazine in Mexico produced by the Popular Socialist Party. It has been known as a voice of the Marxist left and it is primarily read by Communist Party members (Alisky, 1983). Although *Proceso* and *Siempre* are associated with the political left, they have changed with the times as Communism and leftist politics changed throughout the world during the late 1980s and early 1990s. The magazines, once known for their lack of criticism and almost reverence toward Castro, have become more critical of Castro as world Communism undergoes significant changes.

Análisis-Confirmado is another Latin American magazine that follows the *Time* format. Published in Argentina, *Análisis-Confirmado* was created in 1961 (Alisky, 1983). *Gente y la Actualidad*, called *Gente*, is Argentina's leading news magazine with a circulation of about 250,000 copies (Windhausen, 1982). *Humor*, founded in 1978, focuses on political satire in its twice-a-month issues that are published in Buenos Aires. *Gente* and *Humor* are the best-selling political commentary magazines in Argentina.

Caretas, Opinion Libre, Marka, and *Oiga* are major publications in Peru. *Caretas*, a national weekly, was started in 1950 and concentrates its content on the economy, social problems, and crime. *Opinion Libre, Marka*, and *Oiga* are frequently filled with political criticism, but representing various points of view. *Opinion Libre* represents conservative thinking; *Marka* and *Oiga* represent more liberal views (Alisky, 1983; Gill & Smith, 1989). Peru's *Si*, founded in 1986, is published weekly in Lima, offering criticism and news about politics, the economy, and the national leadership of the country. *Si* even includes cartoon strips as part of its package of commentary and criticism.

Que Pasa, Revista Hoy, Analisis, and *Mensaje* in Chile served as "escape valves for political frustration" during the strict media control under Gen. Augusto Pinochet (1973–1990) (Alisky, 1983, p. 282). Published in Santiago, these magazines offer various perspectives on government policies, including those from foreign countries. Generally anti-government during the Pinochet years, these magazines provide political and economic news and social criticism. *Que Pasa* (founded in 1971) and *Revista Hoy* (1977) are weeklies and *Mensaje* (1951) is published 10 times a year by the Chilean Catholic church. All three publications average 50 to 60 pages per issue (Gill & Smith, 1989).

As the Chilean government relaxed its censorship of the news media during the late 1980s, some Chilean journalists, who for years lived in fear against retribution for what the government might regard as even mildly anti-government expressions, were unable to deal with the new openness. As Deputy Editor Fernando Paulsen, of the aggressive magazine *Análisis*, said of his staff

> Imagine reporters who for years lived in terror that (Attorney General) Ambrosio Rodriguez was going to have them jailed or beaten. Now we tell them "You have to go interview him to get his response." Many can't take it. They shout, "You want me to go to that son of a bitch? No way!" (Marash, 1989b, p. 27)

During this period of relaxation, the anti-Pinochet publications learned that simply being anti-Pinochet did not sell newspapers and magazines in the competitive marketplace. Paulsen said his magazine must also be well written, entertaining, and visually appealing: "We've streamlined our copy. Articles have been shortened. We now do far more sports, personality stories, features. And our reporting standards are now much higher" (Marash, 1989a).

In Cuba, political commentary magazines, like all mass media, are under the auspices of the Communist Party. Over 100 periodicals are published by various departments of the national and regional governments. Cuba offers citizens comment and humor through the weekly *Palante* (Forward!). This publication usually centers its satire, criticism, and attacks on political opponents of Cuba—such as the United States, Western Europe, and leading Cuban exiles in South Florida (Alisky, 1981).

Although Cuba's periodicals are each controlled by divisions of the national government, Prof. John S. Nichols (1982) said that different views may be expressed by the various divisions:

> The sponsoring group has sole responsibility for the organization, editorial policy and operation of its publication, although party ideological planners and central government officials have coordinating powers and considerable influence on matters of policy. (p. 261)

LEADING NATIONAL MAGAZINES

Mexico is the leading magazine publishing nation in Latin America. There are approximately 2,000 periodicals published in Mexico, the vast majority privately owned and distributed. *TV y novelas, Tú,* and *Almas* are among the largest magazines in Mexico. *TV y novelas* is a television listings book; *Tú* is a beauty and fashion magazine; and *Almas* is a Catholic Church publication covering church matters in Mexico and other countries of the region (Gill & Smith, 1989).

Panama and Honduras are also leading periodical publishing nations in Central America. Panama is home to about 140 periodicals. With the liberalization of publishing after the U.S. invasion and departure of Noriega in December 1989, the environment was good for additional growth. With the United States military and civilian presence after the invasion and occupation, and the on-going long-term involvement with the Canal Zone and large U.S. military bases, periodicals are commonly available in either Spanish or English. Panama's *Análisis*—different from the publication with the same name in Chile—is perhaps the best regarded political commentary magazine. Honduras produces about 40 periodicals. Perhaps the most influential is *Revista Militar*, a magazine published by the army. American news magazines and other general publications are widely available in major Honduran cities.

Chile's dominant magazine is *Hoy*. Some observers would argue that its national political influence rivals that of the prestigious conservative *El Mercurio*, the nation's leading daily newspaper. *Hoy* was founded in 1977 and has a circulation of about 32,000. In contrast to the conservative *El Mercurio, Hoy* was seen as an opposition publication during the rule of Gen. Augusto Pinochet (1973–1990).

In the Caribbean, magazines are regularly imported from North America, South America, and Europe. Local periodical publishing is centered in the urban areas of Barbados, Cuba, Trinidad and Tobago, the Dominican Republic, Puerto Rico, and Jamaica. A majority of Caribbean periodicals are special interest publications such as weekly television program guides or monthly tourism magazines distributed at airports, hotels, restaurants, attractions, and other high-traffic locations. Puerto Rico's largest magazine is *Vea TV Guide*, but *Bohemia* and *Avance* are also popular. Another large magazine in Puerto Rico is *Caribbean Business*, a regional published Wednesdays with circulation near 50,000 per issue. This publication highlights business news and features. Trinidad and Tobago publish about two dozen periodicals, with the leading publications weeklies such as *Sunday Punch* and *The Bomb*. These publications are really part newspaper and part magazine, focusing on exposés, gossip, and scandals.

The oldest national magazine in Cuba is the weekly *Revista Bohemia*, founded in 1908. It is also one of the largest circulation periodicals, with 311,000 copies printed per issue (Gill & Smith, 1989). Cuba's *Verde Olivo* is another national magazine, a weekly publication of the Revolutionary Armed Forces that has a circulation of about 100,000 (Lent, 1985).

Sports and sports magazines have always been popular in Cuba, even before the revolution. Cuba's major sports magazines not only report sports news, they also encourage Cubans to exercise for improved health. The major sports magazines are *Semanario Deportivo LPV* (Sport Weekly Listos Para Vencer) and *El Deporte - Derecho del Pueblo* (Sport—Right of the People) (Wagner, 1987).

BRAZIL'S EDITORA ABRIL AND BLOCH EDITORES

Brazil has the largest population and magazine readership in Latin America and the Caribbean. São Paulo's Editora Abril, S.A., and Rio de Janeiro's Bloch Editores, S.A., are the leading magazine publishers in Brazil and among the leaders in Latin America.

Editora Abril publishes about 100 technical and professional magazines. It also produces one of South America's largest news magazines, *Veja*. The company also publishes 19 other magazines including *Veja em Sao Paulo*, a localized edition of 209,000 circulation. Editora Abril publishes eight different categories of magazines, including

- *Placar*, a weekly sports magazine;
- *Exame*, a business magazine;
- the Portuguese edition of *Playboy*, the American men's magazine;
- *Nova*, the Portuguese edition of *Cosmopolitan*;
- *Elle*, the fashion magazine; and
- *O Pato Donald* and *Mickey*, both bi-monthly comic books.

Veja, which averages 132 pages an issue, is Editora Abril's flagship publication. It is the largest weekly in Brazil (circulation 793,000) and one of the most popular news magazines in Latin America. *Veja* publishes current events articles and criticism on politics, business and industry, and the arts (Alisky, 1983; Gill & Smith, 1989).

Veja was founded in 1968 by Mino Carta, an Italian immigrant who came to Brazil after World War II, one of Brazil's leading editors and publishers. Carta patterned *Veja* in the style of *Time* and *Newsweek*. The magazine gained popularity during the period of the military dictatorship that ran Brazil from 1964 to 1985 after it reported a number of exposes about government torture and corruption. After the Brazilian military decided to liberalize the dictatorship in 1977, another publication co-founded by Carta called *Isto E*, exposed stories about clandestine grave sites of Brazil's "disappeared" (Rocha, 1988).

Bloch Editores' best-known magazine is *Manchete Esportiva*, founded in 1952 as *Manchete*. It has a long-established reputation for its news content. Bloch Editores also publishes:

- *Fatos*, a general interest weekly magazine with circulation at 115,000 that was founded in 1961,
- *Desfile*, a monthly general interest magazine that originated in 1969, and
- *Amiga*, a weekly women's interest magazine started in 1970.

ANAYA AND EDITORIAL AMÉRICA

The leading publisher of transnational magazines in Latin America is the Spanish conglomerate, Anaya. Anaya, based in Madrid, Spain, is one of Spain's largest publishers. The corporation was founded in 1959 by Germán Sanchez-

Ruiperez, Anaya's president. In 1989, Anaya purchased Editorial América from the Venezuelan-based Bloque de Armas Publishing Group. As a result, Anaya now controls 40 different book and magazine publishing companies.

Anaya's subsidiary, Editorial América S.A., is headquartered in Miami and employs 1,900 persons—300 in Miami alone. Major distribution centers for its magazines are located in Guayaquil, Panamá City, Lima, Buenos Aires, Mexico City, Bogotá, and Santiago. The combined circulation of Editorial América's magazines is over 100 million copies each year. Editorial América also has offices in Chile, Colombia, Ecuador, Peru, Mexico, and Venezuela. Editorial América was founded in 1961 in New York by Cuban exiles (Hereter, 1989).

Miami is an ideal base for Editorial América. Geographically close to Latin America, Editorial América takes advantage of extensive international flight schedules for its South and Central American distribution. Furthermore, the wide influences of the Spanish culture on Miami make the area appealing for employees. Editorial América sales were about $67 million in 1988 (Hereter, 1989). Under its new ownership, Editorial América is also known as the América Publishing Group. Gustavo Gonzales-Lewis is president of America Publishing Group, following 25 years with *Selecciones del Reader's Digest*.

Editorial América publishes a group of seven women's magazines: *Vanidades Continental* (established in 1961), *Cosmopolitan en Español* (1973), *Buenhogar* (1967), *Tú* (1981), *Harper's Bazaar en Espanol* (1980), *Ideas para su hogar* (1978), and *TV y novelas* (1982). The firm's group of men's magazines includes *Hombre de Mundo* (1976), *Geomundo* (1977), and *Mecánica Popular* (1947).

The company also publishes *Coqueta* (for teens, 1978), *De todo un poco* (general-family, 1988), *Padres e Hijos* (general-family, 1980), *Muy Interesante* (science, 1984), *Ritmo* (music, 1982), *PC Magazine en Espanol* (computers), *PC Week en Español* (computers), and *Almanaque Mundial* (world almanac, 1955). In addition to these magazines and the almanac, Editorial América produces numerous special publications such as once-a-year editions, dictionaries, cookbooks, romance novels, and comic books.

Magazines are distributed throughout Spanish-speaking Latin America, but mainly in Mexico, Venezuela, Colombia, Peru, and Puerto Rico. Table 7.3 shows how the monthly *Cosmopolitan en Español* single copy and subscription sales are distributed throughout Latin America. Editorial América produces 40 magazines that are read in 23 countries. Its Spanish-language magazines reach all Latin American countries except Portuguese-speaking Brazil.

WOMEN'S MAGAZINES

One of the largest categories of Latin American magazine publishing is women's magazines. Sold at news stands and in groceries, these publications focus on family life, fashion, careers, consumer goods, entertainment and the arts, television soap operas (*telenovelas*), love and romance, food, and serialized fiction.

TABLE 7.3

Circulation and Distribution of *Cosmopolitan en Español*

Country of Distribution	Circulation on December 31, 1986
Bolivia	2,702
Colombia	32,616
Costa Rica	864
Dominican Republic	1,634
Ecuador	8,532
El Salvador	537
Guatemala	1,080
Honduras	922
Mexico	97,844
Panama	3,483
Peru	16,274
Puerto Rico	12,045
United States	31,595
Venezuela	31,709
Total	241,837

Source: Sara Maria Castany (personal interview, December 27, 1989).

Cosmopolitan en Español is one of the largest selling women's magazines in Latin America. Sold in a number of different countries and in two languages, the magazine follows the model of the English-language version published in New York. *Cosmopolitan en Español* circulated about 300,000 copies a month in 1990 throughout Latin America and the United States. *Nova, Cosmopolitan* in Portuguese, is published by Editora Abril in São Paulo, Brazil. It was founded in 1973.

Cosmopolitan en Español takes a slightly different philosophical approach than its New York relative. It attempts to be a "how-to" guidebook for women joining the work force instead of the sexual revolution leader that is edited by Helen Gurley Brown in the United States. The Spanish edition is edited, however, for young, modern, self-oriented women. Readers focus attention on relationships with men, fashion, travel, entertainment, and career advancement (Castany, personal interview, December 27, 1989; Due, 1988; Gill & Smith, 1989).

Amiga, a weekly, is one of Brazil's most popular women's magazines. *Vogue Brazil* is also widely read. *Perfil* is popular among women in Costa Rica. In Mexico and Venezuela, women frequently read *Kena* and *Tú*. *Páginas* is also popular in Venezuela. Cuba's major women's magazine is *Mujeres*, the monthly organ of the Cuban Women's Federation. Founded in Havana in 1961, it averages 66 pages per issue with a circulation of about 273,000. *Muchachas* is a Cuban magazine devoted to young women started in 1980 (Gill & Smith, 1989; Lent, 1985).

The women's magazines have been criticized by some scholars from Latin America's dependency school as well as feminists. Santa Cruz (1988) analyzed 27 popular "women's magazines" in five large Latin American nations (Mexi-

co, Brazil, Chile, Colombia, and Venezuela) and argued that the magazines promote a "transnational feminine model" of women and promote consumption of
consumer goods. She saw women's magazines as a means by which foreign cultures penetrate Latin American culture. Santa Cruz added that a particular danger
of cultural intrusion of the women's magazines was to be found in the advertising. The majority of advertisements originated from foreign advertisers. She
claimed that the advertising promoted foreign values and portrayed stereotyped
views of women.

Magazines as well as newspapers frequently "tie in" to the *telenovelas* by reporting about characters and events in *telenovelas* as if they were "news." If a major
character in a leading *telenovela* were to experience some tragedy, it would not
be unusual for the newspapers and magazines to report about such events as news.
Further hazing the distinction between fact and fiction, some observers have suggested that scandals in the news may be reported as if they were *novelas* (Katz,
1990). When Argentine president Carlos Menem was openly having marital
problems with his wife Zulema during 1990, all the details were covered in the
newspapers and magazines: He went to the World Cup soccer games in Italy
without her; she befriended his political enemies; he expelled her from the presidential compound. The media called the dispute the *dirty war*, a term used to describe
how the brutal dictatorship that ruled Argentina up to 1983 launched an internal
war against domestic enemies (Katz, 1990).

FOTONOVELAS AND COMIC BOOKS

Fotonovelas, live-action comic strip-type publications, are especially popular among
semi-literate, lower class women in Latin America. These publications are really
multimedia oriented, capitalizing on the success of *telenovelas*, Latin American-
style soap operas on television (Flora, 1980). *Fotonovelas* enjoy wide popularity,
and are not viewed as a children's medium. Many copies are exported from Colombia, a major center for the publication of *fotonovelas*, to Venezuela, Ecuador, Chile,
and Central America (Flora, 1980).

Fotonovelas have been analyzed by popular culture and feminism scholars (Bibliowiecz, 1980; Carty, 1989b; Flora, 1980; Volsky, 1989) because of the important gender, class, and sociopolitical roles they play in Latin America. One recent study concluded that the leading Mexican *fotonovela* industry is growing less
responsible to its readers' social and cultural needs as it expands into a multinational industry. Small Colombian producers, by contrast, who work closely with
their writers, may be more aware of the sociocultural role played by *fotonovelas*
in Latin American societies (Flora, 1980).

As the impact of *fotonovelas* on the lower classes is well known, they have been
used in campaigns to promote important social functions, as well as entertainment. A newly established Mexican *fotonovela* called *Esporádica* (Sporadic), estab-

lished by two female editors, uses the medium to espouse feminist ideology (Carty, 1989b).

Telenovelas and their radio counterpart, the *radionovelas*, are closely followed. A number of magazines keep readers up to date with the latest *telenovelas* and *radionovelas*. The stories follow standard plots. A rich person falls in love with a poor person, and the families of the couple fight against the love affair (Volsky, 1989). With great emotional content, these programs offer escapism for viewers. When one of the famed TV Globo *telenovelas* in Brazil comes to a climax, streets, stores, movie theaters, and offices empty out (Michaels, 1987). "Brazilians are so gripped by the novela, or nightly soap opera, that the death of a major character is reported on the front page of the country's largest daily, the *Folha de São Paulo*, as if it were real news" (Michaels, 1987, p. 66).

Going hand-in-glove with *telenovelas* are highly successful and popular publications about the programs. Publishers are selling millions of magazines, such as *TV y novelas*, which focus on *novelas'* characters, their relationships, the plot summaries from previously broadcast programs, feature articles on the actors and actresses, and expected new programs.

The biweekly *TV y novelas* circulates in Mexico, Peru, Puerto Rico, and the United States. The magazine is published in separate national editions reflecting television and motion pictures available in the country. Its success is built on articles and photographs about television programs and the actors and actresses of the programs. Also important to the magazine's readers is the film industry. Photographs about new movies and their stars are common. *TV y novelas* does not provide television listings such as found in *TV Guide* in the United States. *TV y novelas'* editors have chosen to focus the majority of content on features, photographs, and other articles rather than listings that are commonly available in newspapers and elsewhere. Although its circulation is about 120,000 in the United States, *TV y novelas* sells about 1.1 million copies in Mexico and Peru (Castany, personal interview, December 27, 1989; Due, 1988; Gill & Smith, 1989).

Comic books are also extremely popular periodicals in Latin America and the Caribbean. Hinds and Tatum (1984) estimate that as many as 70 million copies of comics are published each month in Mexico alone. Romance comic books are on top of the list. For decades, *Lágrimas, risas y amor*, has been the leading romance comic book. *Lágrimas, risas y amor* sells as many as 1.5 million copies a week (Tatum, 1980).

Mafalda is one of the most popular comic strips in Latin America. Named after a little girl, the strip is well known to Argentine readers. The strip was created by Joaquin Salvador Lavado, who is known as Quino. It depicts working-class daily life in Argentina and provides commentary on the "national foibles and pretensions" (Foster, 1980, p. 497). *Mafalda* has been reprinted in at least 10 different books and collections (Foster, 1980; Lindstrom, 1980).

BOOK PUBLISHING

Book publishers in Latin America have some distinct advantages over other developing regions. The media industries are fairly well developed and have relatively strong financial resources. Also, the primary languages are Spanish and Portuguese, which are also major European languages. There is a fairly strong regional distribution network among Spanish-speaking nations that makes trade in books among Latin American nations possible. Portuguese-speaking Brazil has established book trade relations with other Portuguese-speaking nations. Finally, the region has a few geographic publishing centers, notably Colombia, Mexico, Argentina, and Brazil (Altbach & Rathgeber, 1980).

A number of Latin American publishers have added to their revenues by engaging in "pirating," publishing books in violation of international copyright laws. Taiwan is clearly the world leader in this activity, but several Latin American nations, including the Dominican Republic, Peru, Colombia, and Cuba, also engage in the practice (Graham, 1979). Although this practice angers Western publishers, there is generally little they can do because of the difficulties in enforcing international copyright laws.

A major obstacle in Latin America's book industry lies in internal distribution. There are too few bookstores, and most are located in the largest cities. Governments are financially strapped, leading to cutbacks in public libraries. As a result of high newsprint costs, with newsprint supplies limited by governments, and limited circulations, many publishers prefer to print expensive limited publications for the most elite (Segal, 1989).

During the early 1980s, a number of small book publishers in Latin America went out of business as economies weakened. This, however, proved to be a blessing for those that survived and grew stronger with the decreased competition. Many publishers survived with the help of multinational corporations.

The leading non-Latin American publisher in the region is not the United States, but Spain. It produces as many titles and total copies as Brazil. Spain markets its Spanish heritage and leadership in Spanish culture to sell books throughout the Spanish-speaking nations in the region. U.S. firms have a major, but not dominant, influence in the region. Many of the leading U.S. firms operate joint ventures with local publishers. They concentrate on exporting English-language books, and translated textbooks.

BOOK PUBLISHING CENTERS

Latin America lags slightly behind the rest of the world in book titles relative to its population. With 8.1% of the world's population, Latin America produces a little more than 5% of new annual world book titles. By the standards of developing regions, however, Latin America turns out a sizable number of titles

(Segal, 1989). These statistics also disguise the fact that a few leading nations in the region turn out a sizable number of titles.

Brazil is clearly the leading book publishing nation in Latin America, partly because of its large domestic market. In 1984, Brazilian publishers produced 21,184 titles. Brazil exports books to Portuguese-speaking nations, such as Portugal, Angola, and Mozambique. It is followed in number of annual titles by Colombia (15,041 in 1984), Mexico (5,482 in 1985), and Argentina (4,216 in 1983) (Wilkie & Ochoa, 1989).

While Mexico, Brazil, and Argentina turn out a variety of titles, Colombia turns out a number of technical books that are widely used in the region. Almost one third of the titles produced in Colombia in 1984 alone dealt with medical sciences. Colombian publishers also issued about 1,500 titles that were literary texts and criticisms, and over 1,000 titles dealing with law and public administration (Wilkie & Ochoa, 1989).

Cuba has developed a modest book market. The island's book publishing is under the control of the Ministry of Culture. There are 10 publishing houses in Cuba that share printing, editorial, and distribution duties. The most prestigious publisher is Casa de las Américas (Lent, 1985).

Cuba published nearly 50 million copies of 1,500 titles in 1981. Sixty percent are in education, 22% art and literature, 10% in the social sciences, and 8% in science (Lent, 1985). Cuba publishes books by both Cuban writers as well as non-copyrighted international books. Given the political nature of most Cuban mass media, books are surprisingly apolitical. Newspapers, television, and radio are the primary propaganda tools (Nichols, 1982).

Argentina is reasserting itself as a major book publishing center in the region after recuperating from the shock of the brutal military dictatorships that were in power from 1976 to 1983. During the repressive rule of Spain's Generalissimo Francisco Franco, many of Spain's finest book publishers emigrated to Latin America. Buenos Aires, which has a distinctly European culture, was an appealing location to the Spanish publishers. Many re-established their businesses in Buenos Aires. Logos of Argentine publishers appeared on some of the best books distributed throughout Spanish-speaking Latin America (Lottman, 1990).

During the string of dictatorships in Argentina during the 1970s and 1980s, which occurred while Spain was liberalizing, many of the Spanish publishers returned to Spain (Lottman, 1990). Not until censorship was officially lifted by outgoing president Gen. Reynaldo Bignone in 1983 did Argentina gradually begin to become a book publishing center in the region again. Starting in 1983, a number of titles recounting the oppression during the military years went on the market. Many were reprints of works written by Argentine exiles first published abroad. One book, *Malvinas, la trama secreta* (*Malvinas, the Secret Plot*), written by a team of investigative reporters at *El Clarin* was an excellent example of investigative book journalism. It offered a detailed chronology of the generals' mismanaged war with the British over the disputed Malvinas/Falklands Islands.

The book was so popular that there were more than a dozen printings within 6 months after the original release in September 1983.

The biggest surprise in the Latin American and Caribbean book publishing industry may be Haiti. Since the fall of Jean-Claude Duvalier (1971–1986), Haiti's book industry has thrived. The nation of 6 million people, among the poorest in the hemisphere with an illiteracy rate of more than 75%, turns out 500 locally published book titles a year, among the largest number by any Caribbean nation (Norton, 1989). Haiti's leading publisher, Henri Deschamps, asserted that "the information is filtering down to the intellectually alert but non-reading masses by word of mouth and through the radio" (Norton, 1989, p. 2A).

During the rule of Jean-Claude Duvalier, and before that his father, Francois "Papa Doc" Duvalier (1957–1971), book publishing was tightly controlled. Many of its best writers were in exile in North America and Europe (Jonassaint, 1981). Even elementary school textbooks were subject to censorship, resulting in a shortage of school texts. Books and magazines that were delivered to Haiti through the mail had to be checked by censors. The job of sifting through the books was so monumental that stacks of books accumulated in the post offices because officials were unable to keep up with the enormous task (Glass, 1988).

Elsewhere in the Caribbean, Puerto Rico and Jamaica have established leadership in publishing. Puerto Rico and the U.S. Virgin Islands, both territories of the United States, have well-established book production industries. Among the Commonwealth nations of the Caribbean, Jamaica is the clear leader, with its industry centered in Kingston (Bloomfield, 1974).

The Gleaner Company in Kingston, Jamaica, which produces the region's leading daily newspaper, the *Daily Gleaner*, is a large book printer. This is an important distinction because many publishing companies in Latin America and the Caribbean do not actually publish books, but print them.

The Gleaner Company prints textbooks for Jamaican public primary schools after the books have been issued by different publishers in other countries. Reprint rights and a contract from the government are necessary, but the business can be lucrative. The Gleaner Company produces and distributes about 40–50 titles and 3.5 million English-language textbooks a year under contract with the Jamaican government. Although not much original material is currently produced in the Caribbean region, increased efforts are being made to write and edit the books as well as to print them. The most compelling reason for the current printing-only system is low cost. A $12 textbook from outside Jamaica can be produced on newsprint for about $2 in Jamaica (Clarke, personal interview, January 13, 1990).

Other islands in the Caribbean region have gradually increased their book production in the past two decades as publishing became less expensive and more personal computer based. The main reasons for the slow development of the publishing industry in the islands region is their obvious geographic fragmentation (Bloomfield, 1974). Until the 1970s, most Caribbean islands depended on foreign sources for their book publishing needs. Most books came from the United States, Great Britain, South America, and Europe. But the Caribbean basin book publishing industry is changing. As communication means, such as satellite-based telephone systems and computer networking, are used, the industry has begun to grow. Also assisting growth has been political independence, economic expansion, growth of cultural awareness, and expansion of education (Bloomfield, 1974).

* * *

SPOTLIGHT

Chile's *Análisis*: Testing the Limits

Chile's *Análisis* is a small weekly magazine by international circulation standards (about 30,000 each Monday). It tested the limits of press freedom in Gen. Augusto Pinochet's Chile during the 1980s. The clash between the government and *Análisis* came to a head when writer Mónica Gonzalez won the Louis M. Lyon Prize from the Nieman Foundation in the United States for her critical reporting of the regime (Noblet, 1989). For her prize and anti-government views, she endured periodic arrests, two stints in prison, and daily death threats over a 4-year period, 1984–1988. As Chileans described it, she boldly took on the "holy trinity"—Pinochet, his family, and the military (Noblet, 1989).

In late 1984, she wrote the first of a series of investigative articles alleging corruption by Pinochet and his family, noting brutal human rights abuses by the military. She served 6 days in prison before being released. Two of her key sources were found murdered a few months afterward. Gonzalez was jailed again for 22 days in 1987 after publishing an interview with an opposition leader who sharply criticized Pinochet.

In 1988, Juan Pablo Cárdenas, *Análisis*'s editor, was convicted of defaming the president and offending the military. He served a sentence of 541 nights (he was released from prison during the day) in jail. He was arrested and convicted by a military tribunal in connection with a series of articles that appeared in *Análisis* that the government found offensive. Although Cardenas had the decision successfully overturned by another court, the Supreme Court ruled in favor of the military tribunal (Anon., May 27, 1988; Noblet, 1989).

In June 1988, a military court indicted Fernando Paulsen, editor of *Análisis*, and Ivan Badilla, one of the magazine's reporters, for slandering the navy. The article discussed the navy's purchase of eight helicopters, suggesting that the government overpaid for the equipment. Cardenas was also held in jail for 5 days without charges being filed (Anon., June 4, 1988).

In late 1985, *Análisis* was shut down for 4 months by the Pinochet government during a nationwide state of siege along with five other opposition publications. *Análisis* reopened in January 1986. Perhaps the worst of the entire series of events involving *Análisis* was the murder of international section editor Jose "Pepe" Carrasco in September 1986. Carrasco, 46, a director of the journalists union, was found shot 13 times in Santiago after two armed men in civilian clothes forced their way into his house, grabbed him, and took him away (Whitefield, 1986a, 1986b).

Broadcast Media

Broadcasting in Latin America is relatively advanced compared to most developing regions of the world. In most cases, the sophisticated systems were built by private entrepreneurs with varying degrees of government intervention. Television came to Latin America during the early 1950s. Some nations, such as Brazil, Mexico, and Cuba were quick to adopt the new medium. In the cases of Brazil and Mexico, which have the third and fourth largest private television networks in the world, respectively, the governments played a central role in the national expansion of these networks. In the case of pre-Castro Cuba, wealthy entrepreneurs constructed a highly advanced commercial broadcasting system with little direct government intervention. Some large nations with the financial resources to develop television, such as Argentina and Chile, were slow to develop television. As a result of the high cost of operating television systems, television primarily carries profitable entertainment-oriented content. Although print media are the most respected journalistic outlets, most ordinary citizens get their news information from broadcast media. In some nations where literacy rates are low, such as Haiti, radio news broadcasting is popular and influential. As the 1990s begin, some of the broadcast media in the large Latin American nations are adopting sophisticated telecommunications technologies. Their success and financial power have allowed them to produce quality programming rather than rely on imported programming. In the cases of broadcast media in Mexico and Brazil, the media have become significant exporters of television programs. Small nations, particularly Caribbean island nations, still receive substantial amounts of foreign programs.

The print media in Latin America have been associated with serious political affairs since their beginnings. Although there are many fine news and public affairs programs on radio and television, these media primarily serve entertainment and escapist functions. In some nations where literacy rates are low, radio is a popular source for news and public affairs.

145

The less central political role for broadcast media compared to print media is caused by the high financial costs of broadcasting, the limited time for news and public affairs, and the ability of national governments and advertisers to exert pressure on broadcast media with relative ease compared to print media. In addition, broadcast media do not enjoy the journalistic status and tradition that have evolved in the print media. Nevertheless, many Latin Americans rely on broadcast media for much of their knowledge about political affairs, whereas economic factors and literacy rates have tended to make newspapers largely an upper class medium (Alisky, 1981; Boyd, Straubhaar, & Lent, 1989).

An active hemispheric organization has not yet emerged to defend private broadcast media organizations' conflicts with their respective governments and other sectors of society. Latin American print media have a hemispheric organization to protect their interests in the form of the Inter American Press Association (IAPA). The Inter American Association of Broadcasters (IAAB) was created to do for the hemisphere's broadcast media what the IAPA does for print media. In 1984, the IAAB changed its name to the International Association of Broadcasters (IAB) and expanded its interests beyond hemispheric concerns. The IAB is based in Montevideo, Uruguay (Anon., n.d.a).

THE BEGINNINGS OF BROADCASTING

Broadcasting in Latin America essentially began when small radio stations started scheduling programs during the late 1920s and early 1930s (Alisky, 1954). United States networks and electronics firms have been either credited or blamed with developing Latin American broadcasting systems (Deihl, 1977; Fejes, 1986; Howell, 1986). By 1930, radio had arrived in Latin America when two American radio networks, National Broadcasting Company (NBC) and Columbia Broadcasting System (CBS) extended their shortwave broadcast programming to the region. Along with their technologies, the U.S. networks brought their production and business practices with them to Latin America (Deihl, 1977). When television came to Latin America during the early 1950s, several nations with sophisticated radio systems were quick to adopt the new medium of television. Table 8.1 presents the number of AM and FM stations and television stations in the region in 1985.

The influence of U.S. programming in the early days of Latin American radio is illustrated by Latin American radio stations' adaptations of the famous "War of the Worlds" broadcast. The original U.S. broadcast, an adaptation of a novel by British novelist H. G. Wells and set in Great Britain, aired on Halloween day 1938. The U.S. broadcast described a Martian invasion of New Jersey. The broadcast used a format common to radio news at the time with "flashes." Many listeners believed the events described in the story were real. The U.S. broadcast resulted in mass panic in sections of the United States.

TABLE 8.1
Radio and Television Stations in Latin America, 1985

	AM	FM	TV
Argentina	154	45	191
Belize	3	2	1
Brazil	1,485	150	200
Chile	151	81	121
Colombia	375	130	85
Costa Rica	55	46	14
Dominican Republic	122	62	37
El Salvador	76	9	9
Guatemala	98	20	25
Guyana	3	3	0
Honduras	129	32	7
Mexico	630	110	120
Nicaragua	52	11	5
Panama	72	30	14
Paraguay	35	21	73
Peru	212	20	73
Suriname	6	10	6
Uruguay	82	4	22
Venezuela	168	25	57

Source: Anon. (1985b).

A U.S. radio script writer working in Chile in 1944 replicated the famous 1938 radio broadcast for unsuspecting Chilean listeners, resulting in a similar mass panic (Anon., 1944). William Steele, a former writer for the U.S. Mutual Broadcasting network, adapted the "War of the Worlds" for a station in Santiago. Steele, assisted by a Chilean writer, revised the story so the Martians were invading Puente Alto, 15 miles outside Santiago (Anon., 1944). Another adaptation of the story for Peruvian listeners at about the same time resulted in less panic because of the scarcity of radio sets. However, indignant Peruvians who had been angered by the scare burned down the radio station (Koch, 1970; Lowery & De Fleur, 1988).

The U.S. broadcast model of commercial support was influential everywhere in the world during the early days of radio, not just in Latin America. But the U.S. influence was greater in Latin America than elsewhere for three reasons. First, Latin America is geographically close to the United States. Second, the U.S. government long regarded Latin America as part of its political "sphere of influence." Third, and perhaps most important, most Latin American nations subscribed to the concept of private ownership of broadcast media financed through commercial means. This permitted the U.S. networks, long familiar with operating in private enterprise environments, to gain a commercial toehold in the region.

Elizabeth Fox (1988c), a leading scholar of Latin American broadcast media, claimed that the decision by Latin American governments to leave broadcast media in the private sector during the early days of radio broadcasting had a lasting influence on the future development of the broadcast media throughout the region. Attempts by Latin American governments in later years to assert control over the broadcast media—whether for promoting culture and entertainment or for furthering the political aims of the governments or government leaders—was fought by the private media. The broadcast media had evolved into powerful political and economic organizations within their respective nations capable of challenging national governments. In some cases, these powerful broadcast media organizations earned kudos from citizens and the world press community for exposing and criticizing dictatorial leaders; in other cases, the broadcast media were criticized for fighting ostensibly positive efforts to use the broadcast media to promote national culture and education.

The fact that the development of broadcasting was left to private entrepreneurs who ran the medium as businesses had at least two implications. First, the medium was not infused with a strong commitment to news and public affairs. Second, private broadcast entrepreneurs amassed large fortunes, and broadcast media became highly sophisticated enterprises. In pre-Castro Cuba, for instance, radio and television stations were broadcasting powerful signals and producing highly advanced programming. As early as the 1920s, powerful commercial Cuban radio stations could be tuned in as far away as Mexico (Alisky, 1954). Table 8.2 shows the dissemination of radio receivers in Cuba and the rest of Latin America during 1950 and 1982.

Cuban entrepreneurs were quick to adopt television during the 1950s. In October 1950, after Mexico and Brazil officially introduced television, Cuba became the third Latin American nation with television. Pre-Castro Cuba epitomized the best and worst of the ''free-wheeling'' development of broadcast media by private entrepreneurs—with little regulation, heavy doses of advertising, and irresponsible attacks by politically motivated television and radio commentators with their own political agendas and aspirations (Head, 1985; Lent, 1988; Salwen, 1990).

Brothers Goar and Abel Mestre built CMQ-TV into a network of stations that rivaled stations in New York for their technical quality. After the Cuban government took over their $25 million in assets in late 1960, Goar Mestre went on to establish stations or program distribution centers in Argentina, Venezuela, and Peru (White, 1969).

GOAR MESTRE: FATHER OF LATIN AMERICAN TELEVISION

It is difficult to discuss the beginnings of broadcasting in Latin America without describing the career of Goar Mestre and his brother Abel. After leaving Cuba in 1960, Goar Mestre went on to rebuild his broadcasting empire from his base in Argentina, while Abel settled in Miami.

TABLE 8.2
The Growth of Radio Receivers in Latin America, 1950–1982*

	1950	1960	1982
Argentina	128	167	727
Bolivia	50	75	571
Brazil	48	70	355
Chile	92	96	300
Colombia	44	139	122
Costa Rica	29	64	84
Cuba	104	163	317
Dominican Republic	26	34	44
Ecuador	16	41	319
El Salvador	ND**	86	336
Guatemala	10	56	43
(British) Guyana	22	65	352
Haiti	1	6	21
Honduras	18	64	48
Jamaica	16	88	386
Mexico	73	96	292
Netherlands Antilles	210	200	674
Nicaragua	15	51	274
Peru	59	101	161
Suriname	27	50	582
Trinidad & Tobago	41	70	291
Uruguay	148	291	577
Venezuela	44	186	408

*Receivers per 1,000 population.
**No data.
Sources: For 1982 data: Anon. (1986). For other years: Anon. (1963).

The Mestre brothers started a research-oriented advertising business in Cuba in 1941. Goar Mestre (personal interview, May 10, 1990) described radio advertising in Cuba during these days as a shoddy and, at times, dishonest business. Stations frequently tried to cheat advertisers by delivering fewer spots than promised. The clients or the clients' advertising agents had to closely monitor the number of ads they received. Goar described the situation as "very messy." After dealing with radio stations in their capacity as advertisers, the Mestre brothers decided to go into radio themselves. The brothers purchased half the stock of CMQ radio in 1943, the second largest network in Cuba. In 1947, the Mestre brothers founded a 24-hour, all-news station, Radio Relój (Time Clock). The station alternated short commercials with brief news segments in a rapid-paced format. The station announced the time every minute on the minute, calibrated with the National Observatory (Head, 1985).

The Mestre brothers met with so much success in radio that they founded CMQ-TV Channel 6 in 1951. It was the second station on the air in Havana. The first was put on the air several months earlier by a business rival named Gaspar

Pumarejo. Under the Mestre brothers, CMQ-TV witnessed wide popularity and rapid growth.

In 1953, the Mestre brothers scored a major publicity coup when they satiated Cubans' appetites for U.S. baseball by broadcasting the U.S. World Series live in Cuba. CMQ rented a DC-3 airliner and had it fitted with two antennae and an RCA transmitter. The aircraft circled over Key West, Florida, about 90 miles north of Cuba. One antenna picked up the signal of the World Series broadcast and the other transmitted the signal to Matanzas, Cuba, where the signal was then re-broadcast throughout the island. The event was hailed as the first live television intentional broadcast from one nation to another (Sevcec, 1988). According to Abel Mestre (personal interview, March 12, 1990), the event caused a great deal of worry for the CMQ organization because the airplane had limited fuel capacity. If the game went into extra innings, the plane might have had to land, forcing the broadcast off the air, just when interest in the game was at its peak.

In March 1960, more than a year after Fidel Castro came to power, a rapid series of political events led to the downfall of the CMQ empire. Luis Conte Agüero, a leading anti-Communist political commentator, used his CMQ television program to lead a "campaign" against what he viewed as Communist infiltration of Castro's revolutionary government. Pro-Communist students angered by Conte Agüero's remarks over the air demonstrated outside CMQ's 10-story Radiocentro complex and blocked Conte Agüero's entrance into the building. The demonstration turned violent and Conte Agüero was forced to flee and take refuge in the Argentine Embassy. He fled the country in early April. A few days later, Premier Castro devoted 2½ hours of his 4-hour speech denouncing Conte Agüero, and calling anti-Communism a "smokescreen" for being an enemy of the revolution. Goar, who felt his life was in danger, fled Cuba on March 27. Abel appeared on CMQ-TV on March 31, explaining CMQ's decision to broadcast Conte Agüero's speech as Conte Agüero's personal opinion. Abel also used his appearance to denounce other government pressures against CMQ.

Before the month was over, the government had frozen Goar and Abel Mestres' bank accounts. Abel left Cuba in early April. On September 12, the government took over CMQ-TV, the last private broadcast network in Cuba.

The story of Goar Mestre was not over. Goar Mestre (personal interview, May 10, 1990), whose wife was Argentinian, went to Argentina where he found a large South American nation with a highly underdeveloped television system. Although Argentina was the fourth nation in Latin America to introduce television (in 1951), television's development was stunted by political pressure from the previous Peron dictatorship. As late as 1960, Argentina had only one television station, Radio Belgrano-TV, in Buenos Aires. The station was subsidized by the government, and even its transmitters were operated by the Ministry of Public Works (Dizard, 1966).

After establishing a financial arrangement with the U.S. media organizations of CBS and Time-Life, Mestre became 60% owner of the PROARTEL (Producciones Argentinas de Television) programming company. With the assistance of a cadre of exiled management and technical employees from CMQ-TV (so called "Mestre men"), Mestre repeated his formulae for success in Argentina. He took a strong, central management position over the organization's operations and relied on local talent for programming in preference to foreign programming. Because Argentine law prohibited foreign ownership of television, his Argentine wife owned outstanding shares of Channel 13. The station, with PROARTEL programming, quickly became the dominant station in Argentina (Dizard, 1966).

Shortly after Mestre's arrival and success in Argentina, the television world started taking notice of events in Argentina. When U.S. journalism scholar David Manning White traveled to Argentina to interview Mestre in 1969, Channel 13 led the ratings during most time slots. Also by 1969—when two leading U.S. television networks (NBC and ABC) had finally recognized Argentina's potential and established station affiliations in Buenos Aires—more than 14 of 18.5 hours of daily programming on Channel 13 was locally produced.

In 1974 the Isabel Peron government took over Mestre's broadcast empire in Argentina. Although Mestre was credited with having a Midas touch for successful broadcasting business decisions, his acumen failed him in one important respect: He was unable to foresee the potential of Latin American broadcasters to financially penetrate the Spanish-speaking market in the United States. Like other Latin American broadcasters, he believed that it was impossible for Latin American broadcasters to successfully compete against the U.S. television networks in the United States (Sevcec, 1988). Not until the 1980s did Latin American media entrepreneur Emilio Azcarraga, head of the powerful Mexican television conglomerate Televisa, realize the potential of Latin American media to penetrate the large U.S. Spanish-speaking market (discussed later in this chapter).

THE POPULARITY OF TELEVISION

Latin America was the first region outside North America and Europe where television was introduced on a large-scale level. Television arrived in Latin America during the 1950s, at a time when many Latin American nations sought to rapidly modernize and "catch up" with the United States and Europe. In Mexico and Brazil, television was viewed as a symbol of the economic advancement of the nations. Critics charged that television was being introduced too rapidly without adequate policy considerations. These critics added that the U.S. model of reliance on commercial support was adopted as the quickest and most expedient method for widespread development and dissemination of the broadcast medium in Latin America (Fox, 1988a; Lemez, 1974).

Latin America's first television station, XHTV, Channel 4, began broadcasting on August 31, 1950, from Mexico City. With XHTV, Mexico became the sixth nation in the world with television. The station was owned by the newspaper *Novedades*. During its first several months, it aired musical variety programs and government news. By the mid-1960s, Mexican television was well established, producing news and entertainment programming as well as a number of special events (Salinas Quiroga, 1965).

Brazil, Cuba, and Argentina also began television broadcasting on a regular basis during 1950 and 1951. With the exception of Argentina, all four of these "early adopter" nations instituted television as a privately owned medium. Television came to Colombia in 1953 as an official government station under the auspices of the dictator Gen. Rojas Pinilla (de Cardona, 1974). Peru introduced television in 1958 as a government-owned and controlled enterprise (Alisky, 1988).

By 1965, television was an established medium in most of Latin America's largest nations. Mexico had 24 stations, Brazil 33, and Venezuela 6. Argentina, which was slow to develop television until Cuban television entrepreneur Goar Mestre arrived, had 11 stations in 1965. Many nations were expanding television beyond their capitals and largest cities to the rural provinces. Table 8.3 shows the ownership of television receivers in Latin America during 1960 and 1982.

A large South American nation that was a notable exception to the trend of the rapid expansion of television was Chile. Political leaders in Chile sought to introduce television slowly so that the medium could be used for the social good. During the early and mid-1960s the nation began airing television on an experimental basis. In order to keep the medium from becoming a partisan political tool or a crass commercial enterprise, the Chilean government decided to have the nation's universities operate television. This decision turned out to be a failure. Market and political forces transformed Chilean television into both a partisan political tool and crass commercial medium. The Chilean example illustrates how the enormous financial costs of operating television, even for a government, frequently results in the use of the medium for commercial purposes.

CHILE'S UNIVERSITY-RUN TELEVISION SYSTEM

After mounting public pressure, the Chilean government reluctantly agreed to introduce television during the late 1950s. The government carefully formulated policy to introduce television into Chile with the universities as the "gatekeepers" in charge of program content. The choice of the universities as gatekeepers seemed logical at the time. Prior to television's arrival, the Chilean government had undertaken a policy of subsidizing national art and culture through the universities. Each of the universities had state-financed orchestras, ballet companies, and theater groups. It seemed logical to Chilean policymakers that the new cultural medium of television should also be operated by the universities (Dizard, 1966).

TABLE 8.3
The Growth of Television Receivers in Latin America 1960 and 1982*

	1960	1982
Argentina	21	202
Bolivia	ND**	59
Brazil	18	122
Chile	<1***	113
Colombia	11	89
Costa Rica	6	86
Cuba	74	164
Dominican Republic	6	78
Ecuador	<1	61
El Salvador	11	64
Guatemala	9	26
Haiti	<1	4
Honduras	1	13
Jamaica	ND	84
Mexico	19	111
Netherlands Antilles	15	169
Nicaragua	ND	67
Peru	3	50
Trinidad & Tobago	<1	250
Uruguay	9	126
Venezuela	37	126

*Receivers per 1,000 population.
**No data.
***Less than 1 per 1,000 population.
Source: Anon. (1986). Anon. (1963).

However, the decision to have university-controlled television was reached without any consideration as to how the medium would be financially supported. The government was unwilling to provide the nation's universities with money to operate television. As a result, university channels carried imported programming and relied heavily on advertising.

In Santiago, Catholic University's Channel 13 espoused conservative views. The University of Chile's Channel 9 espoused Marxist views. Although Marxist-oriented Channel 9 carried commercials and imported programming, it selected programs such as "Peyton Place" and "The Untouchables" that the university's directors believed portrayed negative aspects of life in the United States. As one expert wrote of early Chilean television: "Between 1965 and 1970 one could say that the 'cold war' was reflected in Santiago with regard to the competition between the two university channels and their interpretations of the purpose of TV in a developing country" (Hurley, 1974, p. 685). Only Channel 4, operated by the University of Valparaiso, kept to the original intent of university television as a nonpolitical medium (Hurley, 1974).

In 1964, Christian Democrat Eduardo Frei won the presidential election. He sought to introduce state-run television into the provinces. Frei correctly argued that the university-run channels strayed from their original goals, carrying political and commercial programming. He was reported to have complained to the U.S. ambassador in Chile about the U.S. programs' reliance on violence and sex. The sympathetic ambassador told Frei that U.S. mass media were privately owned and there was little the U.S. government could do (Hurley, 1974).

Frei's proposal to introduce state-run television was as much a political decision as a well-meaning act to counter the influence of foreign programming. The Christian Democrats expected to be in power for many years, and Frei believed that television could promote the goals of his party (Catalan, 1988). State-run Channel 7, however, wound up being a largely commercial station with imported programming mostly from the United States. Frei, and later President Salvador Allende who succeeded him, learned that the economics of television made it inevitable to rely on commercial support, just as the nation's universities learned earlier. When Allende, the candidate of the Marxist-dominated Unidad Popular party won the presidential election in 1970, state-run television continued to carry programs that Allende's supporters criticized as foreign propaganda (Hurley, 1974).

During Allende's brief presidency (1970–1973), forces on the political right successfully used television to undermine Allende's authority. Catholic University's Channel 13 spearheaded the opposition. The station fueled popular dissent against Allende, calling for strikes and demonstrations against the government. Channel 13's director, the charismatic Father Raúl Hasbun, railed against Allende and Socialism on the air. His vitriolic speeches may have contributed to an atmosphere that allowed the military to swiftly and easily depose Allende during a bloody coup on September 11, 1973 (Hurley, 1974).

U.S. INFLUENCE IN BROADCASTING

Most Latin American governments permitted private entrepreneurs to develop television with few restrictions, just as they did with radio. In fact, the governments frequently intervened to help the growth of the stations and networks. The Brazilian government relaxed restrictions on foreign investments in Brazilian television to stimulate the development of the medium (Blum, 1967). With the assistance of Time-Life Corp. and government incentives, Brazil's TV Globo developed into the fourth largest privately owned television network in the world— behind the three U.S. networks, ABC, CBS, and NBC. Mexico's Televisa developed into the fifth largest network in the world.

U.S. government and private sector interests wanted to stimulate the development of Latin American broadcasting systems. During World War II, the U.S. government actively coordinated efforts with U.S. broadcasting organizations to establish broadcasting in Latin America. The State Department was concerned about the political sympathies of many Latin American governments toward the Axis powers, especially those nations located in South America's southern cone. Through the Office of Inter-American Affairs, the U.S. government arranged short-wave broadcasts to Latin America (Ogilvie, 1945). The U.S. government saw the influence of U.S. broadcasting in the region as a stabilizing force in countering enemy propaganda (Renaud, 1985).

After World War II, U.S. cultural influence in Latin America was firmly established (Fejes, 1986; Read, 1976). Some populist Latin American governments feared the strong U.S. media influence in their countries. In particular, Juan Domingo Peron (1946-1955 and 1973-1974) in Argentina and Gustavo Rojas Pinilla (1953-1957) in Colombia sought to impose strict limits on the amounts of foreign media imports into their nations. These restrictions were clearly unworkable and rarely enforced (Alisky, 1981).

No nation in the region has tried harder to rid itself of foreign cultural influence than Cuba. Years after the Cuban government broke off relations with the United States, foreign visitors were surprised to see the extent of American influence in the island. Some of the most popular television programs were old American films. To justify airing these films on Cuban government television, the government claimed that the films were being broadcast to illustrate problems in capitalist societies. Preceding the airing of the old movies, a Marxist film critic would describe the movies that viewers were about to watch as a "typical product of the exploiting capitalist society at its worst" (Anon., February 20, 1975, p. 3A).

In recent years, many of the larger Latin American nations have witnessed decreased foreign dependence in programming and increased domestic production. Smaller Latin American and Caribbean nations, however, are unable to afford domestic productions. They continue to rely on foreign technology and programming (Demac & Morrison, 1989; Dunn, 1988; Lent, 1989). In addition to the high cost of producing programs, the Caribbean nations' proximity to the United States also contributes to the easy access to inexpensive U.S. programs as well as to the unwillingness by local broadcasters to develop domestic programming (Basdeo, 1989; Lent, 1989). Many private Caribbean broadcasters legally or illegally intercept and carry U.S. domestic satellite signals intended for pay-television in the United States (Weinstein, 1985). A 1987 UNESCO survey of television programming in the English-speaking nations of the Caribbean reported that 87% of the broadcasting content was of foreign origin, primarily U.S. entertainment fare, ranging from 76% in Jamaica to 95%-98% in Monteserrat (Dunn, 1988).

There is a fear that this reliance on foreign broadcasting is subverting traditional Caribbean culture. One recent survey of students in three Kingston, Jamaica, secondary schools about the students' political knowledge illustrated the influence of foreign programming on Caribbean youth. The study reported that 75% of the students could not name the Caribbean political leaders of Barbados and Trinidad and Tobago. By contrast, only 11% were unable to name the president of the United States, and 30% were unable to name the leader of the Soviet Union (Dunn, 1988).

In radio news, the Caribbean also receives sizable quantities of foreign news. In 1984, the successful and respected Caribbean News Agency (CANA), which made a modest impact in providing regionally oriented print news to the Caribbean, established a radio service, Canaradio. Although highly regarded, the service faces stiff competition from the Caribbean service of the Voice of America (VOA) and several European broadcasters (Dunn, 1988).

BROADCASTING GIANTS: TV GLOBO AND TELEVISA

Two of the world's largest broadcasting conglomerates are located in Latin America—Brazil's TV Globo, headquartered in Rio de Janeiro, and Mexico's Televisa, headquartered in Mexico City. Both networks command large audiences. TV Globo's ratings reach as high as 90% during some time slots.

TV Globo's daily installments of *telenovelas*, Latin American-style soap operas, feature slices of real life in Brazil. Instead of simple plots and studio-based production, TV Globo gradually began to go on location with "familiar political and socio-economic situations" (Araujo, 1990, p. 5). These national program genres (formats) cost more than imported programming. This programming by TV Globo has made Brazilian television "unique in developing countries" (Araujo, 1990, p. 5).

TV Globo's initial growth was not left to vacillations of the economy alone. On the contrary, its growth was actively supported by the military dictatorship that governed Brazil from 1964 to 1985. The government viewed the media, particularly the broadcast media, as useful tools for promoting economic development and improving the image of the dictatorship (Guimaraes & Amaral, 1988; Mattos, 1984). To achieve this tremendous growth, the government ignored constitutional amendments prohibiting foreign investment in Brazilian communications media, permitting the U.S. media conglomerate Time-Life Inc. to play a major role in the creation of TV Globo. This put television at the center of a national controversy regarding whether foreigners were influencing Brazilian culture (Blum, 1967). But over the years, TV Globo has come to be viewed as a model illustrating how a developing nation can establish a broadcast system that can provide domestic programming and challenge the large U.S. networks (Straubhaar, 1984).

Today, the Globo organization is a cross-media empire that owns the prestigious daily *O Globo* in Rio de Janeiro (weekday circulation 320,000; Sundays 500,000), Radio Globo, a publishing house, and a record company. TV Globo, however, is the centerpiece of the Globo empire. The Globo organization was established in 1925 by Roberto Marinho, with the publication of *O Globo*. Known as "Citizen Globo," Marinho still presides over the organization that he calls a "family" (Moreau, 1989).

Brazil continues to witness rapid growth in electronic media. The broadcasting revolution has expanded into a full-scale telecommunications revolution. Brazil promises to be a major center for growth in telecommunications if national economic problems can be controlled. The first communications satellite that was entirely Brazilian owned was launched in 1985. By 1989 the nation had two satellites in orbit. The satellites have been used to relay television signals, support data communications systems, and provide telephone service for isolated areas in the Amazon region (Furtado, 1989).

Televisa, the primary source of news for most Mexicans, dominates broadcasting in Mexico (Mahan, 1985; Skinner, 1987). It is the largest television producer in the Spanish-speaking world, producing about 21,000 hours of programming worldwide each year (Molina, 1987). Televisa transmits about 400 hours a week of television, more than any other company in the world (Skinner, 1987). In a decision that proved to be a brilliant stroke of business acumen, Televisa established the Spanish-language Univision television network and extended its reach into the United States. The decision proved that it was possible for Latin American broadcasters to successfully penetrate the U.S. broadcast market in what has been labeled "reverse media imperialism" (Schement, Gonzalez, Lum, & Valencia, 1984, p. 171).

Much of Televisa's growth and success stems from its close connection with the ruling political party. As a result, Televisa's reputation suffers. During the 1988 presidential election, Televisa refrained from reporting campaign "irregularities" involving the ruling Institutional Revolutionary Party (PRI). The widespread fraud by the PRI led to political rallies with chants of "Death to the PRI" and "Death to Televisa" (Moffett, 1989). Recent decisions by Mexican President Carlos Salinas to restructure Mexico's economy have created the possibility that Televisa may face some serious competition. Among Salinas' moves to privatize the Mexican economy, the decision to grant frequency allocations to another network was among the most important. The move was partly the consequence of popular discontent with Televisa's power.

In September 1989, MVS-Multivision went on the air as a private television network to compete with Televisa. Multivision carried eight subscription cable channels to residents of Mexico City and two subscription channels outside of Mexico City. Multivision's management is hoping that popular U.S. Cable News Network (CNN) broadcasts and pay-as-you-view motion pictures will allow Multivision to compete against Televisa (Moffett, 1989).

The Mexican government's official views are frequently broadcast over the government station, Imevision. A 90-minute special broadcast on Imevision during January 1990 was the center of strained U.S.-Mexican relations. The Imevision program charged that a U.S. drug enforcement agent, who was tortured and murdered by Mexican drug traffickers in 1985, was involved in drug trafficking himself. Imevision's director claimed the program was a response to an NBC docudrama televised in the United States on the event. The director added that the program represented "a point of view by a group of professionals," not the government. The program also accused NBC News anchorman Tom Brokaw of harboring "prejudices about the Mexicans."

TELEVISA'S UNIVISION NETWORK

Originally known as the Spanish International Network (SIN), Televisa's Univision television programming network has been broadcasting programs to the Spanish-speaking audiences in the United States since 1961. It has grown into the fourth largest commercial network in the United States, reaching 6 million U.S. households (Coto, 1990).

In 1986, Univision earned about $64 million in national advertising in the United States (Beale, 1986b). Its programming consists of news, sports, entertainment programs, and *telenovelas*, soap operas popular in Latin America. The bulk of programming originates from Televisa.

While SIN/Univision provided programming, the Spanish International Communications Corporation (SICC) owned the stations for the programming. SICC started with U.S. affiliates in San Antonio and Los Angeles. It has expanded to more than 400 stations today. Univision includes cable franchises and nine full-power stations in every major Hispanic market in the United States, including Los Angeles, New York, Miami, and San Antonio. About 75%–90% of the SICC stations' programs were purchased from SIN/Univision (Wilkinson, 1990). For years, Univision was the sole Spanish-language network in the United States. Univision witnessed its first real competition from the Spanish-language Telemundo network, established in 1987. By 1990, Telemundo was reaching 5.2 million households, approximately 78% of the U.S. Hispanic market (Coto, 1990).

In 1987, SICC was purchased by Hallmark Cards. The sale was forced by the Federal Communications Commission (FCC). The FCC limits foreign ownership of television stations to twenty percent. The Azcarraga Vidaurreta family in Mexico owned exactly 20% of SICC's holdings. The Azcarraga family reportedly provided many of the original American SICC stockholders with the cash for their investments and put SICC in a subordinate role to SIN. This led the U.S. government to eventually force the sale (Wilkinson, 1990).

In 1990, Cable Television Nacional (CTN) based in California, announced plans to launch a cable-only Spanish-language network sometime in 1991. CTN, which planned to have 800,000 households, approximately 11% of the U.S. Hispanic market at start time, hoped that a new marketing strategy aimed at high-income households would allow it to find a place in the Hispanic television market. It planned to carry no *telenovelas*, the staple of Spanish-language television, aimed toward the *abuelita* (grandmother) market. By carrying music videos, classic films, and sports, CTN was competing for a chunk of the more than $300 million that U.S. advertisers spent on Spanish-language television in 1989 (Coto, 1990).

JOURNALISM AT TELEVISA

Although much of Televisa's production consists of *telenovelas*, it operates an influential news operation. In 1987, Televisa employed nearly 2,000 persons in 31 different companies in Mexico, ranging from television news to entertainment, film production, radio and television stations, publishing concerns, record production and distribution, night clubs, and even aircraft leasing and food processing (Molina, 1987).

Televisa was formed through a series of mergers and purchases of stations, production companies, and networks over the past 30 years. According to Prof. Gabriel Molina (1987) of the Universidad de las Américas in Pueblo, Mexico, Televisa underwent five distinct stages of growth: (a) an early television start, (b) a nationwide expansion of Telesistema Mexicano, (c) a period of intense commercial competition, (d) a strategic merger between the two competing television rivals, and (e) a period as the world's largest producer of Spanish television programming.

Televisa's flagship news program, "24 Horas," a 60-minute newscast, was launched in 1970. Televisa also broadcasts a morning news magazine, "Hoy Mismo" (Molina, 1987). Despite these important news programs, broadcast journalists working for Televisa and other broadcast companies in Mexico continue to get their training at newspapers or magazines (Alisky, 1988).

As Televisa evolved into a large television consortium, it has lost some of its journalistic luster. Increasingly, news decisions were being made on the basis of profits. Molina (1987) argued:

> In that process of consolidation and diversified expansion, its (Televisa's) television news programming has long ceased to be an area of production primarily governed by individual or journalistic "newsworthiness" and has come under the control of a corporate rationale. (p. 159)

NEW BROADCASTING TECHNOLOGIES

A popular joke going around in Colombia maintains that the nation has a new national flower—the white antenna dish. Colombia is not alone. Satellite dish ownership is becoming common among many of the upper class throughout Latin America, and particularly in the Caribbean, because of the lack of local channels. In Jamaica alone, it was estimated that there were 7,000 privately owned earth stations in 1989 (Demac & Morrison, 1989).

Mexico's Morelos Satellite System represented a major step in the modernization of Mexico's broadcasting system. However, critics say it was created without national goals in mind (Esteinou Madrid, 1988). The Mexican Federal Microwave Network grew out of the need for international broadcasting modernization for the 1968 Summer Olympic Games in Mexico City. The Morelos Satellite System, a direct broadcast satellite system that does not require re-transmission and can be received with a small 1.5-meter dish at home, was created in cooperation with Televisa.

Local officials in Latin America and the Caribbean complain that the influence of television programs, particularly U.S. television programs, is persuading people to spend money for imported U.S. goods at a time when local economies are floundering and the region is experiencing severe debt problems (Oppenheimer, 1989). Meanwhile, during the 1980s, U.S. broadcasters complained about the "piracy" of their programs by Latin American broadcasters (Demac & Morrison, 1989).

Harold Hoyte, former president of the Caribbean Publishing and Broadcasting Association and publisher of the Nation Publishing Co. in the Barbados, attributed the demise of the Barbados garment industry to U.S. television broadcasts. Rather than produce its own clothing, the nation is now importing clothing from Miami. "We used to have a local garment industry," Hoyte said. "Now we don't have one. People want to dress like Don Johnson [star of the once-popular television program 'Miami Vice']" (Oppenheimer, 1989, 1A).

The small Central American Republic of Belize, with about 150,000 people and roughly the size of New Hampshire, also has shown a great interest in receiving the latest U.S. television programs. Belize, which became independent from Great Britain in 1981, had to depend on spillover broadcasts from Mexico until 1982. In 1982, a clever entrepreneur in Belize City established his own earth station and started a rebroadcasting service. Subscribers have to pay a weekly fee. A number of situation comedies, movie channels, and Chicago Cubs baseball games have been particularly popular. It has been said in jest that Belize City has the largest concentration of Cubs fans outside of Illinois (Demac & Morrison, 1989; Johnson, Oliveira, & Barnett, 1989).

THE INFLUENCE OF CABLE NEWS NETWORK

As a result of the rapid growth of broadcast transmission technology, charges of "cultural imperialism" are intensifying (Beltran & Fox, 1980). Although politicians and scholars question the dissemination of U.S. programming into the region, few complaints are heard from the Latin American public.

When Atlanta-based Cable News Network (CNN) began beaming signals to Latin America in 1982, it was believed that the service would only be used by the region's elites who could afford the service and could understand English. But innovative middle-class Latin Americans have developed relatively inexpensive—and not always legal—ways to receive the service. According to Steve Haworth (1990), a company spokesman, CNN knows that its popular service is being pirated on a large-scale level in Latin America. He said CNN writes off the piracy as part of the price to be paid for doing business in the region. As of 1990, CNN maintained two full-time bureaus in the region, one in Managua, Nicaragua, and the other in Santiago, Chile. It also has a bureau in Miami that serves Latin America as needed (Haworth, 1990).

CNN has become an influential regional news force, as evidenced by the fact that it is frequently among the first U.S. news organizations to be expelled by dictatorial regimes during times of political crises. When Panama's opposition leaders staged their first large political rally against strongman Gen. Manuel Antonio Noriega in July 1987, the government immediately expelled the CNN correspondent but took no action against ABC, CBS, and NBC. By September 1987, CNN closed down its Panamá City bureau and moved it to Managua when Noriega demanded that CNN replace Bureau Chief Lucia Newman (Haworth, personal interview, February 5, 1990). Nevertheless, CNN was easily available to Panamanians because it was carried on the U.S. Armed Forces Southern Command television broadcasts directed at U.S. military personnel and canal zone workers (Haworth, personal interview, February 5, 1990).

Today CNN uses its worldwide satellite and cable reach to target Latin America. CNN broadcasts in Spanish in Latin America, as does the Los Angeles-based Univision network. CNN reported that by 1989 its broadcasts were received in 34 Latin American and Caribbean nations. In 1988, CNN began producing Spanish-language newscasts for Telemundo network (Coto, 1989a, 1989b). In early 1990, Cuban state television started broadcasting CNN's "World Report" on a weekly basis. "World Report" consists of reports by broadcasters around the world and is intended to provide an international perspective to world news (Whitefield, 1990a).

THE IMPACT OF SATELLITE BROADCASTING

Satellite technology has had a major impact on Latin American broadcasting. The world's first private international satellite was launched at a cost of $100 million from French Guyana in 1988 by broadcaster Rene Anselmo. Anselmo is the former president of the Spanish International Network (now Univision) and current chairman of Pan American Satellite, which mainly serves Latin America and Europe. Pan American went into service in the fall of 1988. The earth station is strategically based just south of Miami on the Florida mainland (Rowe, 1989). Pan American is in direct competition with the well-established worldwide communications consortium known as Intelsat—the International Telecommunications Satellite Organization. Intelsat is supported by governments and private satellite users from 117 nations. Both Intelsat and Pan American offer telephone and television links to just about every country in the world.

In recent years, Latin American nations have expanded into "informatics"— the interface between computers and communication satellites. Latin American nations and private entrepreneurs hope that this new technology will allow Latin American nations to find a place in the world communication revolution in the 21st century. There are fears in some quarters, however, that Latin America is advancing too quickly into this area with little policy as to how informatics should be used. These critics fear that if informatics technologies fall into private hands, as radio and television did in earlier years, the technologies may not be used for socially beneficial purposes (Gonzalez-Manet, 1988).

GOVERNMENT CONTROLS

More than most regions of the world, Latin American broadcasting systems today are privately owned and operated. Control often rests in the hands of large networks. Most stations, whether privately or publicly owned, depend on advertising revenue for their existence (Howell, 1986). Two-thirds of the region's radio and television stations are private commercial enterprises, and advertising sometimes comprises up to 25% of the air time (Howell, 1986). These statistics tend to underestimate the influence of private broadcast media in the region because the state-run broadcast media often pale in size compared to the private broadcast media. The commercial stations tend to be located in larger markets, with studios and headquarters in national capitals, provincial capitals, and other major cities (Ferreira & Straubhaar, 1988).

Even in cases of private broadcast media ownership, however, governments sometimes institute methods to influence the political content of broadcast media. In Mexico, for instance, the government has the right to access 30 minutes a day from private broadcasters to air public service announcements from government agencies that deal with matters about health, hygiene, birth control, and so forth. This form of government advertising has come to be called *social advertising*.

Broadcast media in Mexico must also make time available to the government for matters considered vital to the president, including emergency bulletins. In addition, as part of the tax law, stations must give 12.5% of their total daily air time for government programming. As a result of the social advertising and fiscal time available to the government, the government may take up to 3.5 hours of broadcast time daily. In practice, the government rarely uses even half of its available time (Alisky, 1982a, 1982b; Head, 1985; Mahan, 1985). All these generalizations about Mexico, however, may change as the government rapidly undertakes plans to privatize the national economy.

Other Latin American governments, including Brazil and Peru, also mandate government air time on broadcast media. University of Miami Prof. Sydney Head (1985), who has written extensively about international broadcast media, claimed that by and large these government efforts to use air time have been unsuccessful:

Though the goals may be laudatory, government broadcasting too often lacks credibility. It tends to leave the "abhorrent vacuum," impelling audiences to turn to
programs from other sources—to spillover services from neighboring countries, private stations, foreign external services, and recordings from abroad. (p. 107)

Even without governmental control casting a pall on the credibility of broadcast media, Latin American journalists traditionally view the print media as a
superior source of political news to broadcast media. During periods of political
change and tumult, the print media are the primary sources of political news and
analyses. This does not mean, however, that the broadcast media have not provided serious political news. In nations such as Haiti, where four out of five Hai-
tians are illiterate and many cannot afford to purchase newspapers, radio has traditionally been in the forefront of political reform and the primary source of news.
As a result, Haitian radio has felt the brunt of government-organized violence
against the news media.

During January 1990, the Haitian government declared an official state of siege
as it prepared for elections in October. Critics took to the airwaves and charged
that with most opposition leaders in hiding or under arrest, it was impossible for
fair elections to be held. To silence these critics, the government of Gen. Prosper
Avril—who resigned office under pressure 2 months later—imposed the tightest
censorship on the nation's news media since President-for-Life Jean-Claude
Duvalier was ousted in 1986. A week before the media clampdown, a leading
late-night radio talk show host, Jean Wilfred Destin, was murdered after he aired
a program containing political satire directed against Avril's policies (Hockstader,
1990).

Directives from the Haitian Ministry of Information imposed prior restraint
on all broadcasts of domestic news and prohibited the broadcast of foreign news
reports about Haiti. The directives banned the airing of "information, declarations, or positions that could cause agitation" (Hockstader, 1990). Haiti's single
commercial television network, Tele-Haiti, comprised of 12 channels, suspended
all broadcasts of the popular U.S.-based Cable News Network (CNN) and French
and Canadian news accounts.

A number of Haitian radio stations, including those run by the Roman Catholic
and Protestant churches, halted all news broadcasts rather than submit to prior
government review. Newspapers, however, were not affected by the restrictions.
With newspaper readership at about 4 in 1,000 people, by far the lowest in the
hemisphere, the Haitian government appeared unconcerned about newspaper
reports about the turmoil (Anon., January 24, 1990).

During the presidency of Augusto Pinochet (1973–1990) in Chile, regarded
as the continent's last 1970s-style military dictatorship, Chileans voiced their desire
against Pinochet's continued rule in an October 1989 plebiscite. Formerly un-
derground, left-of-center publications that opposed Pinochet were openly available at kiosks and were outspoken against the dictatorship (Marash, 1989b).
Although the print media were permitted greater freedom to challenge govern-

ment authority during the plebiscite, Chilean television reported the election with little commentary. The coverage of the plebiscite on the only station that reached the entire nation, the National Television Channel, was described by one observer as "one of the more grotesque aspects of the plebiscite . . ." (Heine, 1989, p. 245).

Although it was true that television did not provide analysis or gavel-to-gavel coverage of the election, Chilean television could be credited with airing both sides of the debate about the plebiscite in the form of regular half-hour broadcasts. Television stations juxtaposed 15-minute "Si" segments in favor of Pinochet's continued rule against 15-minute "No" segments.

The "Si" side lauded Pinochet's conservative economic policies. It credited Pinochet with keeping Chile's inflation under control while much of the continent witnessed rampant inflation. The "No" side stressed Chile's foreign policy failures and human rights abuses. Several well-known Chilean *telenovela* stars spoke against Pinochet in "No" segments. In addition, American entertainers Jane Fonda and Christopher (Superman) Reeves appeared in these segments and urged Chileans to vote against Pinochet's continued rule. Rock star Sting not only appeared for the "No" side, he also provided a rock video entitled "They Dance Alone" about-the hundreds of widows of Chile's "disappeareds" (Marash, 1989b).

Despite the relative openness of Chilean television during the plebiscite, some "blacklisted" television journalists remained banned (Marash, 1989a, 1989b). The best known among the blacklisted journalists was Patricio Banados, known as "Chile's Walter Cronkite." Banados was initially blacklisted in 1979 when, while reporting the funeral of former President Eduardo Frei, he refused to report a line inserted into his script by government censors asserting that Frei "had begun the kind of policies that led this country into communism." Banados reappeared on Chilean television in 1983, only to be blacklisted again after adding a line into his script attacking the government's policy of foreign borrowing (Marash, 1989a, 1990).

* * *

SPOTLIGHT

Brazil's TV Globo and *Abertura*

TV Globo's coverage of the final days of the line of dictators who ruled Brazil for 21 years (1964–1985) provides an example of how the broadcast media can influence political affairs. During the final stages of a political campaign for direct presidential elections, TV Globo broke from its image as a government mouthpiece and called for an end to the dictatorship.

TV Globo's support for direct presidential elections came as something of a surprise. TV Globo was born with the assistance of the dictatorship. The Brazilian dictatorship was obsessed with economic development. The dictatorship subscribed to an ideology that some have called *state-directed capitalism* or *corporatism* (Erickson, 1977; Straubhaar, 1989). According to this ideology, the state actively promoted free enterprise in Brazil by providing major industries with financial resources and favorable legislation for development. In broadcasting, TV Globo was earmarked for growth. The state-owned telecommunication company EMBRATEL provided financing for TV Globo's expansion during the 1960s and 1970s. The government also overlooked legislation prohibiting foreign investments in domestic media industries as a means of providing TV Globo with needed capital for expansion (Harris, 1987; Richeri & Lasagni, 1987). By the early and mid-1980s, TV Globo had grown so big that it was exporting programs to almost ninety nations, principally in Latin America (Mattos, 1984).

In 1974, Brazilian President Gen. Ernesto Geisel announced a policy of gradual liberalization of the military dictatorship. Geisel felt confident that because of the economic health of the nation, the dictatorship could afford to liberalize. Geisel's policy of liberalization came to be known as *abertura* (a political opening).

Abertura was not radical change. For the most part, Brazil's transition to democracy was gradual and peaceful. Not until 1985, after many other Latin American military dictatorships became civilian democracies, did Brazil attain democracy when the Electoral College established by the dictatorship elected a moderate civilian, Tancredo Neves, as president.

Increased press freedom was considered a cornerstone of *abertura* (Dassin, 1982). The dictatorship wanted to maintain an appearance of democracy. It refrained from restricting press freedom, the most visible form of freedom in society. Censorship of the press was relaxed in 1975. It was officially ended in 1978. But most press criticism came from the print media. The *grande imprensa*, or simply *a imprensa*, as the elite print media were known, took advantage of the relaxed political atmosphere created by *abertura*. It called for greater freedom, political reform, and an end to the dictatorship (Dassin, 1984). The broadcast media, especially TV Globo, refrained from criticizing the government.

There were limits to press freedom under *abertura*. In February 1979, *Veja* magazine ran a controversial investigative report on government torture camps. The story so infuriated the military that the journalist who wrote the story was prosecuted. Two years later, *Jornal de Brasil* reported a confidential memo exposing the participation of the military in terrorist acts. The publication was denounced by military leaders who charged that the newspaper was "infiltrated by elements of the left" (Samper, 1982, p. 9). During these early years of *abertura*, when the print media dared to criticize the government, TV Globo and other broadcast media not only refrained from criticizing government policies, they often came to the support of the government and challenged the government's critics (Guimaraes & Amarel, 1988).

Although *abertura* was a slow process, when political change finally came to Brazil in 1984, it came rapidly. During the last years of President Joao Baptista Figueirdo's (1979–1985) administration, the middle-class coalition that had tolerated the dictatorships for so long broke apart. Throughout Brazil, there were a number of public demonstrations calling for direct presidential elections. Although *a imprensa* reported these demonstrations, TV Globo avoided publicizing the issue of direct elections. A number of leading daily newspapers openly criticized the network for its deference to the regime. When demonstrators marched against the government, they not only shouted "Down with the dictatorship!" they also shouted "Down with Globo!" (Aufderheide, 1984). Only much later, after it was apparent that there was wide public support for direct presidential elections, did TV Globo report the demonstrations and support direct elections.

Since 1974, the Electoral College selected Brazil's presidents. Each year it selected leaders from the military. The campaign for direct elections reached its zenith from February through June 1984. At this stage, TV Globo covered the rallies. When the government attempted to impose censorship on TV Globo's coverage of the rallies, its leading news anchor remained silent on the air rather than read government accounts (Guimaraes & Amaral, 1988).

Despite wide support for direct elections, most members of parliament, who had to vote on whether to continue the Electoral College or permit direct elections, remained loyal to the government. They refused to permit direct presidential elections. As a result, opponents of the government channeled their energies to having the Electoral College select a civilian successor instead of a member of the military. Demonstrators now called on the Electoral College to select the civilian team of Tancredo Neves and his vice presidential candidate Jose Sarney. None other than former President Geisel himself, who started the process of *abertura*, joined the call for the selection of the Neves-Sarney team. At this point, TV Globo jumped on the bandwagon and called on the Electoral College to pick the Neves-Sarney team.

The popular public support for Neves, combined with TV Globo's coverage, resulted in success. On January 15, 1985, the Electoral College selected the 74-year-old Neves, a moderate career politician, as president. TV Globo accounts portrayed Neves as a democrat, a sage, and a statesman (Guimaraes & Amaral, 1988). But Neves died before his swearing into office and Sarney was sworn into office on March 15, bringing an end to 21 years of military rule.

The election of Neves ushered in an era of democracy in Brazil that was still in place when the next decade began. In December 1989, Brazil held a direct presidential election, its first in almost 30 years. Conservative Fernando de Mello defeated socialist Labor candidate Inacio Lula da Silva.

Advertising and Public Relations

United States advertising agencies expanded into Latin America at the conclusion of World War II to serve their large U.S. clients who had decided to "go international." U.S. advertising agencies still remain the largest agencies in Latin America. However, several Latin American agencies, particularly those in Brazil, have become potent forces. National economic problems slowed advertising growth throughout the region during the 1980s. As a result of numerous complaints over false and misleading advertising, Argentina and Brazil have developed self-regulatory bodies so advertisers can police themselves. Self-regulatory bodies were created to improve the public image of advertising and head off possible government attempts to regulate advertising. The practice of public relations is not very sophisticated in Latin America. Several Latin America nations—both from the political right and left—have contracted with U.S. public relations firms (so-called "public relations counselors") to improve the national and international images of governments. Little is known about the dealings of these public relations counselors because much of their activities is proprietary.

After World War II, the fields of advertising and public relations were viewed throughout the world as uniquely American professions. U.S. advertising agencies started expanding offices into Latin America after the war in an effort to follow their largest clients who had decided to "go international." During this time, the agencies did not expect to profit by expanding into the region. They simply wanted to maintain connections with their largest clients. It was inevitable, however, that while in Latin America they would expand to serve Latin American clients and to influence Latin American advertising agencies and advertising practices. A number of Latin American agencies were formed in the region, particularly in Brazil, that became immensely powerful within their own countries and offered the U.S. agencies serious competition.

The expansion of North American and European industries overseas traces its roots to the late 19th and early 20th centuries. During this time, the United States and Great Britain vied for the largest economic investments in Latin America. U.S. industries took advantage of Great Britain's involvement in World War I to extend its grip into the region and overtake British investments (Fejes, 1980). By 1929, U.S. companies had acquired about 40% ($3.5 billion) of foreign investments in Latin America (Fejes, 1980). The post-World War II era experienced yet another U.S. expansion into the region. This time, many U.S. industries did more than simply invest in the region's industries—this time they established divisions in the region (Lee, 1990).

U.S. economic investments in the region became so important during the 20th century that many U.S. government military interventions in the region were undertaken to protect the interests of large U.S. corporations (Fejas, 1980, 1983, 1986; McCann, 1976). The U.S.-supported military coup in Guatemala during the 1950s on behalf of United Fruit Company, whose name is synonymous with what has been called "Banana Imperialism," was perhaps the most egregious example of the U.S. government's attempts to protect U.S. economic investments in the region.

Thomas P. McCann (1976), former vice president of public relations for the United Fruit Company, figured prominently in organizing the covert U.S. overthrow of the elected government of Guatemala. During the 1950s, the elected reform-minded Guatemalan president, Jacobo Arbenz Guzman, began expropriating large land holdings for distribution to homeless peasants. In 1953, Arbenz sought to expropriate land owned by United Fruit. McCann, with the help of U.S. Secretary of State John Foster Dulles, a former member of a law firm that represented United Fruit, led a campaign to persuade U.S. journalists and the public that the Guatemalan government was infiltrated by communists.

United Fruit retained the services of Edward L. Bernays, "the father of public relations," to help United Fruit discredit Arbenz. Bernays worked closely with the most influential news media in the United States, bringing the Guatemalan situation to the attention of *The New York Times* and other media, and arranging fact-finding tours to the region (McCann, 1976).

EARLY DOMINANCE OF U.S. ADVERTISING

U.S. economic dominance in Latin America inspired a combination of awe and fear among Latin Americans. U.S. advertising practices seemed appealing to Latin Americans who copied American practices. U.S. advertising agencies had reputations for advertising acumen. The U.S. advertising agencies claimed to adhere to "professional" standards that, among other things, precluded offering bribes to secure accounts (Tunstall, 1977).

The number of U.S. advertising offices in Latin America, most in Mexico and

Brazil, grew from 18 in 1960 to 49 in 1964 to 69 in 1970. Two agencies, J. Walter Thompson (JWT) and McCann–Erikson, account for most of the offices (Fejes, 1980). As a result of JWT's and McCann–Erikson's early entry into the region, they maintain their dominance in Latin America today.

The results of a 1989 survey by the trade publication *Advertising Age* of the leading advertising agencies in Latin America show JWT and McCann–Erikson ranked Numbers 1 and 2, respectively. Of the largest 11 agencies in the region, 3 are Brazilian agencies (MPM Propaganda, Salles/Iter-Americana de Publicidad, and Duailibi, Petit, Zaragoza Propaganda). Seven have their bases in the United States, whereas 1 is from the United Kingdom (Anon., "Top advertising agencies," July 24, 1989).

By the late 1930s, advertising revenues from U.S. exports to the region were enough for some Cuban and Argentine radio stations to maintain permanent sales representatives in New York (Fejes, 1980). During the 1960s, after America's post-war boom began declining, U.S. advertising agencies redoubled their efforts to penetrate the region. The relatively rapid introduction of television into Latin America, compared to other developing regions, helped U.S. advertising agencies attract large Latin American audiences (Wells, 1972).

The U.S. broadcast networks immediately sensed the value of Latin American markets to U.S. advertisers. During the early years of television in Latin America, the U.S. networks had grandiose plans to establish a large, centralized hemispheric broadcasting network. Although these plans never fully materialized, U.S. network connections in the region helped the networks establish contacts with Latin American television stations and networks that resulted in the profitable distribution of network programs in the region (Fejes, 1980). Although these revenues never accounted for large revenues to the U.S. networks, the programs were already produced for U.S. affiliates. Whatever extra revenues the networks could make by selling the programs in Latin America would be largely pure profit.

During the early and mid-1980s, some observers suggested a trend for Latin American nations to produce more and import fewer television programs (Antola & Rogers, 1984; Wert & Stevenson, 1988). Latin America's emerging cultural centers for television production appear to be Mexico and Brazil, and to a lesser extent Argentina and Venezuela (Antola & Rogers, 1984).

Advertisers have sought to court the newly emerging middle classes in Latin America with their advertising messages. Leo Bogart, then director of research for Revlon, Inc., observed in 1959 that many U.S. advertisers hoped to break into Latin American markets by appealing exclusively to middle-class interests. Since then, however, U.S. advertisers have sought to expand their appeals to lower classes as more and more Latin Americans desire consumer goods. Brazil's alluring advertising market witnessed 5% real growth in 1980, despite an economic downturn. Total expenditures for advertising in Brazil increased from $395 million (U.S.) in 1970 to almost $1 billion in 1975 to nearly $2 billion in 1985.

Unstable economic conditions in Brazil and elsewhere in Latin America have resulted in sometimes confusing situations for advertisers. For instance, in February 1986 the Brazilian government instituted a wage-and-price freeze to cope with rampant inflation. This only encouraged consumers to go on a spending binge for consumer goods ranging from cigarettes and clothing to appliances and automobiles because they knew that prices would only skyrocket after the freeze was lifted. Normally, advertisers would expect to profit when there are so many consumers in the market. But with an artificially created sellers' market as a result of the price freeze, producers did not feel any need to advertise. Both advertising agencies and media suffered (Michaels & Downer, 1986).

Despite these unexpected developments in national economies, most advertising agencies in Brazil saw rapid growth. Not only did U.S. advertising agencies profit, Brazilian agencies did too. In 1972, not even one Brazilian advertising agency was rated among the world's 50 largest agencies. In contrast, by the early 1980s, three of the world's 50 largest advertising agencies were Brazilian agencies. Despite this rapid growth, Brazil still lagged far behind the two advertising giants, the United States and Japan. In 1981, 31 U.S. advertising agencies were among the world's top 50, with $25.5 billion (U.S.) in billings. Ten Japanese agencies with $6.6 billion were on the top 50 list. The 3 Brazilian agencies on the list reported $280 million in billings (Aydin, Terpstra, & Yaprak, 1984).

With this advertising growth in Latin America, advertisers paid more attention to the importance of producing high quality advertisements in Latin America. During the 1970s and 1980s, not all agencies were content with directly translating English-language advertisements into Spanish. More attempts were made to carefully translate advertisements for subtle linguistic meanings and even devise original advertisements for local cultures.

Literal translations from English to Spanish resulted in several embarrassments. The Chevrolet Nova ("no va" means "no go" in Spanish) debacle is perhaps the most well-known embarrassment. Frank Perdue of Perdue chicken fame, appeared on South American television in a dubbed translation of an English-language advertisement telling viewers: "It takes a sexually excited man to make a chick affectionate." The original English-language advertisement originally had Purdue saying: "It takes a tough man to make a tender chicken" (Baker, 1988, p. 219).

ADVERTISING AND CULTURAL IMPERIALISM

Critics of advertising in Latin America charge that advertising nurtures tastes for consumer goods, a charge that could be leveled against advertising anywhere. In fact, the stated purpose of advertising is to create consumer demand. Critics of advertising in Latin America, however, charge that much of the created demand is for foreign, "nontraditional" goods. This, they assert, subverts local culture and tradition and cultivates consumer tastes to Western lifestyles. These have resulted in charges of "Coca-Colonialism." The charges of "media imperialism" and "cultural imperialism," which are also discussed in chapter 4, leveled against Western mass media in Latin American nations may be particularly apropos in regard to advertising (Cordoso & Falleto, 1979; Fejes, 1980; Frank, 1979; Janus, 1986; Mosco & Herman, 1981; Oliveira, 1988).

Many of the claims of the adverse cultural effects of advertising are "anecdotal and circumstantial" (Lealand, 1984), made with little empirical support. For instance, critics claim that television ads in Mexico feature beautiful blonds, setting a European standard of beauty in a country where there are few blonds (Walsh, 1987). A rare empirical study of the effects of advertising in Latin America that was firmly grounded in dependency theory was conducted by Oliveira (1988a).

Oliveira sampled 198 residents in the capital city of Brazil's second largest state. Two hypotheses were tested: (a) mass media usage would be positively associated with consumption of consumer goods, and (b) mass media usage would be positively associated with preferences for industrialized goods.

Oliveira measured preference for industrialized goods using a scale on which respondents expressed their preferences for either a "traditional technology product" or an "industrialized product." For example, the respondent could choose between preferring a regular shaving razor (traditional) or a disposable razor (industrialized), a cloth napkin or a paper napkin, *feijao trapeiro* (regional beans) or a hamburger, fresh food or canned food, regular trousers or blue jeans, and so forth.

Partial support for the first hypothesis was found. Time spent with newspapers, magazines, and FM radio was associated with consumption of industrialized goods (i.e., food consumption and ownership of appliances and luxury goods). However, time spent with television and AM radio was not associated with consumption of industrialized goods. Oliveira also found partial support for his second hypothesis. Television and newspapers were associated with preferences for industrialized goods, but AM and FM radio and magazines were not associated with preferences for industrialized goods.

Overall, Oliveira's findings lent mixed support for the cultural imperialism effects of advertising. Some media usage variables were correlated with consumption of goods and preferences for industrialized goods. In addition, as Oliveira noted, key variables such as education and income were associated with media usage, raising questions of causality, always a concern in correlation studies. The question, of course, was whether media usage was a *cause* of preferences for industrialized goods or whether media use was simply associated with other variables related to preferences.

Despite the criticisms of advertising in Latin America, there is no question that modernization, accompanied by advertising, have helped Latin American economies expand and have provided needed revenues for the growth of indigenous mass media industries. Argentina, Brazil, and Mexico are the best examples of Latin American nations that have reached the status of industrialized nations with sophisticated media systems, and have even developed small-scale multinational industries (Lall, 1983). Their rapid growth, at least in part, can be attributed to advertising, which spurred the growth of national economies.

ADVERTISING EXPENDITURES
IN THE LARGEST NATIONS

Use of advertising as an indicator of national development suffers the same problems as use of gross national product (GNP). Advertising expenditures reflect on total economic wealth, but not the distribution of national wealth.

As was already noted, Latin American critics of advertising claim that advertising cultivates foreign values. Supporters of the beneficial role of advertising in society, however, assert that advertising "is necessary in a free enterprise system of production and consumption where the customer decides what he wants to spend his money on from a wide field of choices rather than have someone else make up his mind about what is good for him" (Marston, 1973, p. 21).

National advertising expenditures both reflect and affect economic and media growth. Table 9.1 reports recent statistics on total and per capita advertising expenditures in Latin American nations. Table 9.2 reports how the various nations

TABLE 9.1
Total Expenditures and Per Capita Expenditures on Advertising*

	Total Expenditures on Advertising (in millions of U.S. $)	Per Capita Expenditures (in U.S. $)	Advertising as Percentage of Gross National Product
Argentina	$ 900.22	$28.87	1.18%
Bolivia	43.58	6.85	1.12
Brazil	1,958.40	13.67	.69
Chile	144.23	11.76	.94
Colombia	315.00	10.52	1.00
Costa Rica	48.17	17.75	1.28
Dominican Republic	64.17	9.46	1.26
El Salvador	23.80	4.66	.44
Guatemala	88.57	10.29	.58
Jamaica	18.36	8.03	.93
Mexico	382.79	4.68	.32
Panama	49.50	22.30	1.03
Peru	206.21	10.20	.84
Trinidad & Tobago	32.68	27.14	.45
Venezuela	252.57	14.20	1.27
United States**	102,140.00	424.07	2.43

*Source: Anon. (1987). All data are 1986 figures.
**Included for comparison.
Reprinted with permission of Starch/NRA Hooper.

TABLE 9.2
Percentage of Advertising Spent on Print, TV, and Radio

	Print	Television	Radio
Argentina	38.2	36.9	12.1
Bolivia	16.9	19.3	5.8
Brazil	33.6	56.4	7.7
Chile	40.9	44.0	10.8
Colombia	23.5	54.0	22.4
Costa Rica	3.6	77.6	18.6
Dominican Republic	20.0	60.0	19.0
El Salvador	35.7	47.6	16.7
Guatemala	28.2	54.5	16.9
Jamaica	50.7	19.7	33.7
Mexico	17.0	51.7	20.9
Panama	29.2	55.0	11.2
Peru	4.6	88.0	7.5
Trinidad & Tobago	34.2	38.2	26.3
Venezuela	27.4	64.5	5.1
United States**	51.6	35.8	11.0

Source: Anon. (1987). All data are 1986 figures.
**Included for comparison.
Reprinted with permission of Starch INRA Hooper.

divide their advertising by various media. The United States is included in this list for comparison. As is immediately apparent, Latin American nations spend smaller proportions on print media than the United States.

A longitudinal study of advertising expenditure trends in 29 nations, reported in the *International Journal of Advertising* (Anon., 1984), is considered one of the more reliable studies. It was conducted by advertising professionals at the J. Walter Thompson Company, among the largest multinational advertising agencies.

One of the best comparative measures of advertising in the report was advertising expenditures as a percentage of the GNP. The measure is an indicator of the relative importance of advertising within the context of the entire national economy. According to the report, the commonwealth of Puerto Rico is believed to have the highest advertising expenditure as a percentage of the GNP in the world, 2.32% in 1982, even more than the United States.

Mexico experienced serious economic problems during the late 1970s and early 1980s. In 1982, foreign debt reached $85 billion (U.S.), second only to Brazil ($90 billion) in the region. To deal with the crisis, the peso was devalued by 500%, resulting in far less buying power and imports. Under these conditions, advertising expenditures plunged. In 1973, advertising expenditures as a percentage of the GNP were 0.73%. By 1975, expenditures were 0.56%. By 1980, expenditures fell to 0.29%. As the decade drew to a close, the government was planning to privatize the economy to improve the economic situation. As the Mexican government carries out its plans of privatization of the economy, it is reasonable to assume that advertising expenditures will increase as more sellers attempt to enter the marketplace.

In Chile, commercial advertising was virtually nonexistent in the early 1970s. After the overthrow of the elected Marxist government of Salvador Allende, the military dictatorship that succeeded Allende promoted free enterprise. As a result, advertising expenditures as a percentage of GNP reached 0.70% in 1977 and surpassed 1% in 1981.

Peru witnessed the collapse of a reform-minded military dictatorship in the early 1980s. As a result, previously nationalized media organizations were returned to private ownership. As in Chile after the collapse of Allende, the new government sought to stimulate economic growth by opening the nation to imported products. This increased the demand for advertising. Although advertising accounted for an almost negligible 0.06% of the GNP in 1970 and 0.18% in 1975, it increased to 0.43% in 1980. Advertising expenditures increased to 0.98% of the GNP in 1981 and 1.16% in 1982. Peruvian newspapers, in particular, witnessed increased advertising revenues during the 1980s. During 1977, when many newspapers were nationalized, newspapers accounted for 7.4% of advertising expenditures. That fell to 3.8% in 1978. In 1981, newspapers received 29.8% of national advertising expenditures.

There are many reasons for the erratic fluctuations in advertising expenditures in various Latin American nations. In some cases, governments are actively involved in stimulating national economies by promoting the growth of private industries. This would tend to stimulate advertising growth. The unstable economic environments of high inflation—and in some cases hyperinflation—also account for the fluctuations. In response to hard economic times, advertisers have reduced their expenditures on advertising. This has caused serious problems for media organizations. According to Jorge Fascetto, publisher of *El Diario Popular* of Buenos Aires: "If you keep your normal ratio of editorial to advertising, you'd end up with a paper of ten pages, which is hardly enough for anyone to want to buy. If you go up to 14 (pages), with more editorial, you end up losing money" (Bogart, 1990, p. 9).

BRAZIL: A SUCCESS STORY?

Brazil is the economic and advertising center in Latin America, with total advertising expenditures approaching $2 billion (U.S.) in 1986, about $13.50 per capita. No other Latin American nation comes close to Brazil in total advertising expenditures. Advertising expenditures as a percentage of GNP between 1971 and 1982 has not displayed the fluctuations so common as in other nations, hovering about 1% a year. As a result of economic troubles, advertising expenditures dipped about 10% in 1987 (Anon., March 28, 1988). Argentina, with $900 million (about

$29 per capita) total advertising expenditures in 1986, ranks behind Brazil in to-
tal advertising expenditures. Argentina is followed by Mexico with $383 million
(less than $5 per capita; see Table 9.1).

In all of Latin America, only Brazil has witnessed total advertising expenditure that puts it on par with some European nations (Smith, 1980). Modernization and economic development have contributed to the growth of some of Latin
America's largest broadcast networks. Brazil's commercial TV Globo network
witnessed rapid growth under a "bureaucratic authoritarian" military dictatorship (1964–1985). The Brazilian dictatorship took an active role in promoting
the rapid economic development and modernization of the nation. That meant
expanding internal markets as increased advertising revenues contributed to the
growth of national media. Under such an economic environment, TV Globo's
growth was assured. During the early years of the Brazilian "economic miracle,"
critics claimed that growth was achieved at a heavy cost of accepting foreign investments, programming, and advertising, and thereby subverting local cultural
values (Mattos, 1984).

Several other observers, however, have argued that over the years Brazil has
largely freed itself from its dependence on foreign programming and advertising
and has become a media exporter, not only of media technologies but of cultural
programming as well (Straubhaar, 1984). After studying the TV flow in Brazil's
30-year history with television, Straubhaar (1984) concluded that American cultural programming influence in Brazil is on the decline. Brazil has entered the
small club of nations whose creativity in advertising has advanced so far that U.S.
advertising agencies keep a close watch on Brazilian techniques to see what can
be borrowed (Stern, 1985).

Brazil's success in advertising is the result of at least four factors:

1. active government involvement in mass media growth,
2. the large population of nearly 140 million that can support indigenous mass
   media systems and national production centers,
3. a reliance on market research to improve advertising and programming (de
   Andrade, 1987), and
4. a reputation for creative advertising and marketing techniques (Stern, 1985).

In market research, de Andrade (1987) reported that Brazil has more than 50
agencies actively involved in conducting market research. It is one of the few nations in the region where multinational companies feel comfortable relying on local agencies for their market research needs instead of exclusively relying on U.S.
research firms.

As far as creativity is concerned, Brazilian advertisements are now considered
on a par equal to European advertisements. TV Globo claims to have pioneered
the technique of "plugging" (or as it is known in Brazil, "merchandising")
products within program story plots. For years, American motion picture pro-

ducers have plugged products such as McDonalds hamburgers and Ford automobiles by charging advertisers to prominently display brand products in films. TV Globo has been merchandising brand name products in soap operas known as *telenovelas* on a regular basis since the early 1980s. Although such a practice may face consumer resistance if it were adopted in the United States, the practice is accepted in Brazil. The Brazilian advertising agency MPM Propaganda surveyed television viewers and found that even viewers ordinarily critical of advertising accepted merchandising because it is "part of everyday life" (Stern, 1985).

ADVERTISING AS A MEANS OF PRESS CONTROL

Because a relatively small number of advertisers account for large proportions of newspaper advertising in some small Latin American nations, particularly in some parts of Central America, advertisers have sometimes been effective in manipulating media content by threatening to withdraw advertising (Goldman, 1988; Janus, 1986). In some nations, governments own and operate sectors of the economy. This provides governments with the ability to reward or punish media by awarding or withholding advertising revenue.

The Mexican government has practically institutionalized the manipulation of the press by means of state domination of advertising. Until recently, the Mexican government owned and operated major sectors of the economy, including the national airlines, the national bank, the lottery, and movie theaters. As a result, the Mexican government was a primary source of advertising revenue for the media (Pierce, 1979). The Mexican situation may change. In 1982, the state controlled 1,200 companies. By the end of 1989, the government had sold almost 500 of those companies to the private sector and targeted hundreds more for sale to the private sector (D'Alimonte, 1989).

Mexico is only the most notable example of a growing trend of privatization of national economies spreading throughout Latin America. The trend is occurring elsewhere, including Brazil, Chile, Argentina, and parts of the Caribbean and Central America. Even socialist Guyana has joined the privatization trend (Schroeder, 1989).

According to Mexican President Carlos Salinas de Gortari, who is in the forefront of this trend, the move toward greater privatization of the economy represents a "redefinition of the role of the state." As of late 1989, Salinas was attempting to unsaddle the government of the heavy economic burdens of the telephone company, airlines, mines, electric projects, the newsprint industry, and even highways. Salinas' attempts to privatize the economy, which includes making it easier for foreigners to invest in Mexico, was aimed at bringing needed capital into the state's ailing government industries. If successful, the denationalization of the economy could weaken the ability of the government to control the press (Work & Bussey, 1989).

Salinas' denationalization policies are having an effect on Mexican's perceptions of entrepreneurs. Hundreds of thousands of Mexicans died during the 1910s to fight a dictatorship closely associated with the wealthy landowners. The framers of the constitution were wary of the private sector and made sure that the state maintained control over important sectors of the economy. During the 1970s, Mexican presidents expropriated a number of private holdings in banking, farming, and timber, invoking the "Revolution" as their justification. Even before Salinas took office, the private sector purchased a number of radio and television advertisements to promote the image of entrepreneurs as serving the commonweal.

Government control of the economy does not have to lead to government control over the press. In Venezuela, regarded as one of the most democratic nations in Latin America, the percentage of government advertising has ranged from 25% to 40% (Fejes, 1979, 1980). One author contends that Venezuela's media system would probably collapse without government advertising (Capriles, 1976). In Argentina, the official news service TELAM serves as the exclusive agent for all government advertising. Because the government controls about 40% of the national economy, the potential for the formidable exercise of government power over the press exists. However, during the recent democratic administrations, few attempts to manipulate the Argentine press by this means have been documented (Anon., February 1990).

Advertising's influence on Latin American journalism is not only limited to distributing or withholding advertising revenues. As journalism history scholars have observed, a system's increasing reliance on advertising support tends to diminish partisan political journalism. This has been particularly true of the press in the United States, where "objectivity" has become enshrined (Altschull, 1984; Schiller, 1979; Schudson, 1967).

In the United States, the media's reliance on advertising support meant that publishers were reluctant to take strong political positions. Advertisers preferred selling their wares in nonpolitical publications that did not offend the political senses of the public. As a result, these historians argue, the concepts of "objectivity" and political neutrality in U.S. journalism took hold. Objectivity and neutrality took hold so gradually over a long period that journalists were not even aware that their "nonpolitics" was a philosophy (Altschull, 1984). Altschull argued that journalists never consciously compromised their commitment to journalism when they adopted objectivity. They still claimed to adhere to the noble role of "watchdogs" of the government and industry. The process was a subtle one that took place over a period of years.

The increasing reliance of the Latin American press on advertising revenue may have a similar effect on Latin American journalism as it had on U.S. journalism. Mexican press scholar Fernando Reyes Matta (1977, 1979a, 1979b) asserted that the Latin American "concept of news" originally involved the press taking strong political stands on issues and contributing to national political debate. But with the coming of Western news agencies to Latin American in the late 19th and early 20th centuries and changing economic structures, Latin American journalism changed:

> New factors—an eager market, the need for information with impact, and an interest in the immediacy of information—then gradually affected the concept of news. . . .The result was a concept of news which moved from the task of interpreting events and presenting opinion to the daily process of selecting events deemed "newsworthy" and commercially interesting. (Reyes Matta, 1979b, p. 164)

ADVERTISING SELF-REGULATION

In the early years of broadcast media development in many Latin American nations, the media were operated by entrepreneurs in an atmosphere of little government regulation. In Cuba, broadcasting "had become notorious for its freewheeling commercialism" (Head, 1985, p. 27). Head described a situation in pre-Castro Cuba where there was so little government involvement in media that advertisers often made unsubstantiated and often outrageous product claims. In addition, the advertising was just downright grating. As a *New York Times* reporter in 1959 observed:

> Cuban commercials have some originality but are merciless in their devastation of the viewer's nervous system. Lengthy, repetitious, noisy and often in bad taste, they blare out a speil that would make even a Madison Avenue man shudder. The accent on sex stems from customs firmly entrenched on the island. (Friedman, 1959, p. 10)

It remains a fact of consummate irony to some Latin Americans that even though the United States is usually portrayed as a model of press freedom—in terms of an independent press with little or no government intervention—advertising in the United States is directly regulated by a government agency. Advertising in the United States is monitored by the Federal Trade Commission (FTC) and indirectly regulated by other government agencies such as the Food and Drug Administration and the Federal Communications Commission (FCC). Regulation of advertising messages exists in the United States even though the First Amendment of the U.S. Constitution, which broadly grants freedom of the press, makes no distinction between "commercial speech" and "political speech."

The FTC, which is empowered to regulate "truth in advertising," sets regulations for advertising claims that can be legally enforced. Advertisers found to engage in "false or misleading" claims can be prohibited from continued use of the objectionable advertisements. In extreme cases, the offending advertisers may be required to correct the offending ads by running "corrective advertising" or may even have misdemeanor charges brought against them.

What advertising-related laws exist in most Latin American nations must be enforced indirectly through laws dealing with contracts, fraud, and obscenity (Boddewyn & Merton, 1978). Caribbean nations also have only indirect laws that deal with regulation of advertising (Boddewyn & Merton, 1978). Part of the reason for the lack of direct government regulation of advertising stems from national policies to achieve rapid economic advancement and modernization. The growth of mass media and advertising are seen to contribute to modernization. Advertising is viewed as a means of giving ''a shot in the arm'' to the economy by stimulating demand for consumer goods. Government intervention, therefore, could stifle development.

During the 1970s and early 1980s, however, a number of Latin Americans called for increased governmental regulation of advertising. As a result, a number of advertisers responded by developing self-regulatory procedures to offset the possibility of government regulation, with Argentina and Brazil in the forefront of this trend (Boddewyn, 1981). Latin American industries developed regulations and organizations to police themselves, address consumer complaints, and obtain the goodwill of consumers and governments. To the extent that self-regulation involved attempts to foster goodwill among consumers, advertising self-regulation had as much do with public relations as advertising.

Prof. Jean J. Boddewyn (1989), who has written extensively about self-regulation of advertising in various nations, claimed that industry self-regulation of advertising offers a reasonable alternative to government regulation of advertising. By means of self-regulation, industry serves as a form of ''private government'' to the extent that peers impose voluntarily accepted rules of behavior on the industry.

Two Latin American nations, Argentina and particularly Brazil, have developed extraordinary degrees of advertising self-regulation. Argentina was one of the first nations in Latin America to establish advertising self-regulation in 1969. For many years, self-regulation was not enforced because of a lack of industry participation. In 1976, however, the Argentine advertisers formed the Intersociety Committee of Advertising Self-Regulation (CIAP). The CIAP has publicly criticized advertisers who do not adhere to the CIAP's ethical codes.

Brazilian advertising self-regulation is viewed as a model for developing nations (Boddewyn, 1984, 1988). Brazil's self-regulatory system dates to the late 1950s. However, the most important aspects of Brazil's system developed during the late 1970s when Brazil was run by a military government. The military government promoted rapid modernization of the nation through state-directed capitalism and gave little priority to consumer concerns. As a result of the public outcry against false and exaggerated advertising claims, and the unwillingness of the government to take actions against these claims, industry and media leaders strengthened self-enforcement procedures against advertising abuses. Argentine self-regulation also was established during a military government.

In Brazil, an advertising code of ethics was promulgated in 1957 with no enforcement procedures. In 1978, several organizations were established that approved bylaws and investigated cases of unethical advertising. There has been a trend toward greater consumer participation over the years (Neelankavil & Stridsberg, 1980). The code called for the establishment of a National Council for Advertising Self-Regulation (CONAR), which went into operation in 1980.

Although the code lacks legal enforcement, an Ethics Council was established that could penalize offenders in the following ways:

- issuing a warning,
- requesting that the offending advertisement be corrected,
- calling on the mass media to refuse to publish or air the offending advertisement,
- publicizing the offending advertiser's noncompliance with the code, and
- expelling a noncomplying advertiser from CONAR's ranks (Boddewyn, 1988, p. 93).

CONAR is considered a strong self-regulatory body (Boddewyn, 1988). Complaints about offending advertisements can be brought to CONAR's attention by anyone—citizens, government officials, competitors, and so forth. In addition, the Ethics Council can investigate advertisements even without complaints.

A number of complaints against advertisers have dealt with issues of morality and public taste. CONAR has been reluctant to censor advertisers in matters of morality. CONAR claims, with some justification, that Brazilians are tolerant of risqué advertisements, and even nudity (Boddewyn, 1988).

Part of CONAR's success stems from the active support of the Globo organization, which owns the TV Globo television network and several other large media enterprises. Globo pressures its advertisers to adhere to CONAR's rules. CONAR has also run ad campaigns to make the public aware of its existence and that Brazilians have consumer rights that they can exercise through CONAR (Duailibi, 1988).

PUBLIC RELATIONS FOR NATIONS:
A CONCERN WITH IMAGES

The practice of public relations is advancing in Latin America, but still has a long way to go. For instance, the Public Relations Association of Trinidad and Tobago (PRATT) was technically in existence since the 1970s, but during its early years it was largely nonfunctional (Rivas, personal communication, December 11, 1989). During an international public relations symposium in Trinidad and Tobago in 1984, a number of local public relations practitioners worked to make PRATT an active organization. Since then, PRATT has tried to educate the public about the role of public relations in society. As PRATT's president, Maria Rivas (personal communication, December 11, 1989), said: "We also realized that the public as a rule had no idea of what the practice of public relations entailed and considered it a profession for beauty queens."

As North American and European companies began moving overseas during the 1960s, they quickly came to see advantages in maintaining the goodwill of the publics and governments they served (Lusterman, 1985). This created a need for North American and European industries based in Latin America to contract with public relations firms—so called "public relations counselors."

Public relations counselors for nations can either do one-shot projects, such as lobbying on their behalf before U.S. political bodies, or arranging long-term campaigns. The activities of public relations include: scheduling tours, shows, and presentations; working on newsletters; providing advice; working with the national and foreign press; providing assistance for marketing exports; staging special marketing events; and providing advice for cultivating a positive image abroad.

Well before governments formally understood the value of contracting with public relations firms, several Latin American governments recognized the value of obtaining positive media portrayals. In 1943, Argentine dictator Juan Domingo Peron established a state monopoly on broadcast media under the Secretary of Press and Information of the Presidency. The organization had 1,600 journalists committed to promoting Peron's policies and his image. His wife, Evita, purchased the daily *Democracia* in 1947 as her personal political organ. Peronist media contained heavy doses of sex, sports, and crime (Fox, 1988c). Peron is reported to have advised his military government: "We are being attacked on all sides. I suggest we try advertising. Propaganda is a powerful arm, especially when one has control over the media. It is time to think how we are going to advertise" (cited in Fox, 1988c, p. 39).

The military dictatorship that ruled Uruguay from 1973 to 1984 established the National Office of Public Relations (NOPR) to coordinate the regime's propaganda. The combination of media censorship and coordinated propaganda carried out by the government through the NOPR was meant to limit the dissemination of negative news about the government and promote positive news. The NOPR was responsible for official news bulletins about the regime's successes and even was responsible for the creation of anti-protest songs (such as "*Disculpe*" and "*Yo Creo en ti*"), which were disseminated to radio and television stations (Faraone & Fox, 1988).

During the late 1970s, the Cuban government reversed its closed-door policy toward the international press and engaged in vigorous international public relations efforts. Plagued by reports of human rights abuses, the Castro government gave an unprecedented number of interviews to U.S. and European journalists. International journalists were given the VIP treatment, and the *Wall Street Journal* commented that "the hospitality is tremendous—overpowering, in fact, if one doesn't have a strong stomach for rum, lobsters and big, black Cuban cigars" (cited in Nichols, 1980, pp. 1-2).

*   *   *

SPOTLIGHT

Public Relations Efforts of Governments

Although these examples in Argentina, Uruguay, and Cuba illustrate an interest in nations obtaining the goodwill of citizens at home and abroad, they were not well-planned, formally coordinated public relations campaigns. Some critics of the Western press claimed that developing nations engage in media manipulation through subtle or blatant means to counter negative images in the Western press. During the height of UNESCO calls for a New World Information and Communication Order in the 1970s, some developing nations took an active role in controlling their images in the Western press—by means of press control and censorship; a few others more cleverly contracted with Western public relations firms to improve their images (Booth, 1986; Lobsenz, 1984; Manheim & Albritton, 1984; Tedlow & Quelch, 1981). Many public relations practitioners assert that governments have a right to communicate with the U.S. public and foreign publics through public relations counselors. As two Harvard Business School faculty members wrote:

> A censorship strategy (to control national images), which some nations support, will quickly prove unworkable and counterproductive. These nations will soon understand that they cannot command the tide to go out. They must educate themselves to the needs of the Western news agencies and understand the market for information in the United States. Armed with this understanding, they must manage the news process rather than attempt arbitrarily to shut it down. To learn how to do this, they could do well to turn for assistance to U.S. public relations counselors. (Tedlow & Quelch, 1981, p. 22)

Still, the practice of foreign governments contracting with U.S. public relations firms often evokes suspicion in the United States. The U.S. Congress passed the Foreign Agents Act in 1938 when it discovered that several well-known U.S. public relations firms established contracts with Nazi Germany. The Congress feared that the trend of governments contracting with U.S. public relations firms would permit foreign governments to disseminate "pernicious propaganda" into the United States. The act stipulated that Americans employed by foreign governments be registered as "foreign agents." The information on registered foreign agents must be open to the public (Cutlip, 1987).

Despite the fear that public relations firms employed by foreign governments would lead to political propaganda and the subversion of the democratic process, most Latin American nations have not hired U.S. agents to disseminate political propaganda. Most agents have been hired by governments to promote trade and tourism (Lobsenz, 1984). For instance, some small Caribbean islands spend large sums of money hiring agents in the United States to promote tourism. Jamaica,

TABLE 9.3
Latin American Nations Expenditures
on Foreign Agents in the United States, 1983

Country	Expenditures (U.S. $)
Antigua & Barbuda	686,000
Argentina	465,000
Bahamas	13,179,000
Barbados	1,954,000
Belize	5,100
Bolivia	——
Brazil	696,000
Chile	1,644,000
Colombia	20,044,000
Costa Rica	1,635,000
Dominican Republic	458,000
El Salvador	277,000
Grenada	782,000
Guatemala	1,100,000
Guyana	81,000
Haiti	411,000
Honduras	21,000
Jamaica	18,135,000
Mexico	6,695,000
Netherlands Antilles	959,000
Nicaragua	170,000
Panama	199,000
Paraguay	——
Peru	1,404,000
St. Kitts-Nevis	37,000
St. Lucia	152,000
Suriname	——
Trinidad & Tobago	7,744,000
Uruguay	——
Venezuela	280,000

Source: Anon. (1984).

Bahamas, and Trinidad and Tobago are perhaps the best examples. Table 9.3 reports the expenditures of Latin American nations on foreign agents in the United States.

After a September 1985 earthquake in Mexico that devastated Mexico City, the Mexican government launched a $10 million public relations campaign to lure U.S. tourists back to Mexico. Colombia spends large sums promoting Colombian coffee in the United States. In 1989, it was estimated that the national Federation of Coffee Growers in Colombia spent $36 million (U.S.) annually to promote coffee consumption in the United States and elsewhere (Whitefield, 1988). During 1989 and 1990, the Mexican and Colombian governments individually launched public relations campaigns in the United States with the goal of convincing the American people that the Mexican and Colombian governments were trying to curb their drug problems.

One rare example of a Latin American nation relying on public relations counsel to improve a negative political image occurred during the Argentine military dictatorship of Gen. Jorge Videla, who came to power during a 1976 coup. As most of the dealings of public relations counselors are proprietary, not much is known about their advice to their clients (Manheim & Albritton, 1984).

The dictatorship contracted with the New York-based public relations firm of Burston-Marsteller (Alisky, 1981; Dassin, 1982). The firm reportedly received $1.2 million from the Ministry of Foreign Relations to conduct extensive studies and to carry out an image-building program for the government. Alisky claimed that foreign journalists were not fooled by these activities and the government's public relations actions had little effect.

However, a study of U.S. press coverage of Argentina before and after contracting with public relations counsel suggests that U.S. press may have been influenced by the public relations campaign. The study by Albritton and Manheim (1985) analyzed how Argentina was portrayed in the prestigious *New York Times* before and after contracting with a public relations counsel (the study also included the portrayal of several other nations that had contracted with firms).

The researchers reported that before Argentina actively sought to improve its image by contracting with a public relations counselor, it was portrayed in *The Times* as a brutal dictatorship that wantonly violated human rights. Political murders and kidnapping were commonplace. Coverage of Argentina was analyzed for 2 one-year periods, 12 months before contracting with counsel and 12 months after. The study reported that Argentina received quantitatively less press coverage and qualitatively somewhat better coverage after contracting with the firm. The amount of coverage dropped almost 50% after contracting with the firm. Albritton and Manheim concluded that public relations counselors could, in some instances, improve the tarnished images of nations. However, they conceded that other factors could have accounted for their findings.

When the Sandinistas were in power in Nicaragua, they retained the services of Agendas International, a New York-based firm. The firm undertook a number of activities to arrange favorable publicity for then President Daniel Ortega during his U.S. visit. It also coordinated Sandinista officials' appearances on U.S. news programs to respond to U.S. government allegations of Nicaraguan government human rights violations (Gupte, 1988).

Chapter 10

Into the Next Century:
Conclusions

The 1990s are an era of opportunity for the news media in Latin America and the Caribbean. The wave of democratic reforms promises new growth and progress. In an earlier era, government–press relations would, and perhaps should, have been the central focus of a book such as this. But with the trend toward democratization, we chose to examine how Latin American media are faring in their new sociopolitical environments without the central focus on government–press relations. With political control in the hands of the electorate, the news media have claimed, or reclaimed, freedoms that are attendant to functioning democracies. However, the economic troubles of the region place a question mark on the future of the region's news media.

The worldwide trend toward democracy in the late 1980s and early 1990s had its impact in Latin America. But significant political changes in countries such as Peru, Uruguay, Paraguay, Chile, and Brazil were not as widely noted as were similar moves toward democracy in other parts of the world such as the Soviet Union and Eastern Europe.

Why was democratization in Latin America overlooked by the Western news media during the 1980s while world and press attention focused on Eastern Europe and the Soviet Union?

Lawrence Weschler (1990), a staff reporter for *The New Yorker*, has covered both Eastern Europe and Latin America as a journalist. With the help of the prestigious *Columbia Journalism Review*, he conducted an impressionistic study of how democratization in the two regions was reported in the U.S. news organizations of *Newsweek, Time, The New York Times, The Washington Post*, the *Los Angeles Times*, and the evening television newscasts of ABC, CBS, and NBC.

As expected, Weschler reported that democratization in Eastern Europe re-

ceived more news coverage than democratization in Latin America. Nevertheless, the difference in the U.S. news coverage of the two regions was even more
striking than what might have been expected. For instance, Weschler reported
that *Newsweek* devoted 90 pages to democratization in Eastern Europe at a time
when Chile and Brazil held their first free direct presidential elections in 16 and
25 years, respectively. During the same period, the coverage of Chile and Brazil
did not even total 1 page. *Time* did somewhat better. During the same period,
Time devoted 98 pages to Eastern Europe and a bit more than 6½ pages to Latin America. The results in the other news media that Weschler examined were
similar.

Why these differences? Is this a classic case of the Eurocentric focus of the U.S.
news media? The U.S. news media have long been interested in events in Europe, believing that events in Europe are of interest to American readers. But
surely the news media could not have overlooked the demographic changes over
the years as Hispanics have become a political and economic force in the United
States. In all fairness, Weschler suggested that the results could not be explained
by ethnocentrism alone. The themes of the fall of communism and success of
capitalism had a lot to do with the focus on Europe.

Students being introduced to Latin American media still cling to the stereotype of the boot-in-the-groin dictatorships that dominated the region not so long
ago. Even those aware of the remarkable changes still have a difficult time ap-
preciating the full implications of democratic change in the region. As we mentioned in chapter 2, the Inter American Press Association (IAPA), the hemisphere's
privately supported media ''watchdog'' association, is redefining its mission in
the 1990s as economic problems and narco-terrorism supersede government–press
problems. Whether the changes in Latin America were noticed or not, like the
changes in the Soviet Union and Eastern Europe, Latin America's changes have
been so extensive and rapid that a full understanding of their meaning and impact will take time.

Although we can only speculate about the Latin American media during this
period of change, one thing is certain: The problems facing the Latin American
press in the post-democratic era will be far more complex than the problems faced
by the region's press during the boot-in-the-groin days. Our broad-brush overview of Latin American media in the 1990s pointed to several important issues
that need to be addressed: press control and intervention, unstable economic conditions, large media organizations, the function of press freedom in society, and
technology and production.

PRESS CONTROL AND INTERVENTION

Even in the 1990s, the Latin American press still faces press freedom problems.
The worse problems, however, in the form of violence and other direct intimidation against journalists, come from non- and pseudo-governmental forces, such

as narco-terrorists and death squads. Even in democracies, governments still have the "potential" to control the press by legal means if they wish. But so long as these potential controls are exercised by democratic governments, which grant the media legal recourse to challenge these controls, the probability that these potential controls will be abused decreases.

This raises the question why potential controls over the press should exist at all. As we noted in several chapters, Latin American governments generally subscribe to the notion of privately operated mass media without government interference. In practice, however, the governments have frequently implemented various degrees of government intervention in the press. Quite often these interventions were instituted to silence a critical press. But in numerous instances these interventions were taken to assist the press as part of larger efforts to spur economic growth. For instance, a few of Latin America's large television networks could never have become the giants that they are today without the intervention of their respective governments.

According to traditional Western press theory, the proper role for the press in society is to inform the public by being critical and independent of the government. The terms *critical* and *independent* go hand in hand. From this perspective, it is impossible for the press to be critical without being independent, private enterprises. Even without evidence of government manipulation, supporters of this theory charge, the "potential" for government control and manipulation over the press is a cause for concern because these controls may someday be used to control the press.

But simply eliminating all potential government controls over the press overlooks the potential benefits of various forms of government intervention in the press for the press and society. Ironically, although Western journalists criticize economic and political mechanisms that can be used by governments to control the press, these same mechanisms can also be used to enhance press freedom and contribute to the marketplace of ideas. We are not making a case here for government intervention in the press; rather, we are pointing to the complexity of the problems facing the Latin American press today.

As we noted in chapter 2, as Latin American governments sell their newsprint industries as part of wider plans to unbridle themselves of unprofitable industries and privatize their economies, many newspapers will no longer receive subsidized newsprint. It is quite possible that smaller newspapers unable to compete against large newspapers without subsidized newsprint may go out of business. Not all newspapers are happy about this new-found freedom of having to pay more for newsprint and other essential goods. Similarly, as we noted in chapter 3, many Latin American journalists are satisfied with their nations' legally enforced *colégio* laws. Many journalistic organizations lobbied for the laws and urged their governments to enforce the laws. If these potential government controls over the press are removed, it must be understood that many of the associated benefits that come with these potential controls will also be eliminated.

UNSTABLE ECONOMIC CONDITIONS

The rapidly changing economic conditions in Latin America have led to some uncertainty about the future of the region's mass media. The worst imaginable consequence of the out-of-control inflation that plagues much of the region is the possibility that nations that only recently broke from authoritarian pasts may opt for a return to dictatorships and their boot-in-the-groin solutions for solving economic problems. Dictatorships have rarely shown an understanding for the important social role of the press in society.

The countries in the region should continue a democratic path during economic hard times. However, without a strong economic base, press freedom becomes meaningless. And as governments privatize their economies and withdraw subsidies to the press, things may get worse before they get better. Economic success or failure could become as significant an issue to the Latin American media during the 1990s as freedom of the press was in the past.

LARGE MEDIA ORGANIZATIONS

One thing that is immediately obvious from our review of Latin American journalism, Latin America has a number of large media organizations. Despite the region's poverty, the region also has a number of wealthy entrepreneurs, a sufficiently developed middle class, and a number of advertisers from both the public and private sectors to support print and broadcast media systems.

Large media organizations, however, pose their own problems. For one thing, they may become such large economic enterprises that they identify with wealthy economic interests and become defenders of the status quo. For another, there is something to be said in favor of having a number of small media voices representing minority views instead of a few, large powerful voices. Finally, large media organizations may be so concerned with profits that they may focus their energies on entertainment programming and give short shrift to news and public affairs programming.

THE FUNCTION OF PRESS FREEDOM IN SOCIETY

As we noted in chapter 2, just about every nation in Latin America promises freedom of the press. But, we must ask, freedom for whom? And for what purpose?

Certainly we can't expect all nations to follow the same concept of press freedom. On the other hand, there must be some universals. The very fact that all nations claim to have freedom of the press is of no small import.

Therefore, we must ask to what extent press freedom is a human right and to what extent it is a social right? Latin American nations are torn between viewing press freedom as an individual's human right and society's social right.

As a human right, press freedom is an individual's right to express him or herself in the news media. As a social right, press freedom stresses the role that the press performs for the greater society. The two rights are inseparable. Press freedom as a human right has come under attack because commercial enterprises have claimed press freedom to what—from an outsider's point of view—appears the right to use the news media with few or no restrictions to make money. Even the United States views press freedom—at least broadcast media press freedom—as a social right to some extent by creating regulatory bodies and setting standards for broadcast media.

It may appear in chapter 3 that we sarcastically concluded that *colégios* involve labor–management disputes, in which rank-and-file journalists want *colégios* for the purpose of limiting the market for journalists and thereby keeping journalists' salaries high, whereas management is against *colégios* to keep salaries low. We want to emphasize, however, that this is what we believe the *colégio* dispute has "evolved" into. There is a certain logic underlying *colégio* laws that reflects the region's commitment to the social right of freedom of the press over the individual right. The social right asserts that because journalists have freedom of the press for society, society has a right to set standards to see that journalists meet minimum qualifications to exercise that right.

Even if one accepts this social right of freedom of the press, press freedom as a human right cannot be given short shrift simply because some people abuse the right or some people are somehow deemed unqualified to practice the right. If we permit a society to grant a license to use the mass media—ostensibly to see that the right is practiced for the social good—this causes all sorts of problems for press freedom as a human right. It is difficult to imagine the licensing requirement of any other human right. What if a nation licensed freedom of speech or freedom of religion? The freedoms would be meaningless grants indeed.

TECHNOLOGY AND PRODUCTION

We have noted the rapid spread and adoption of mass media and other communications technologies in all areas: newspapers, magazines, books, radio and television, and so forth. Today, a good deal of the region enjoys creative programming and advertising that originates from within. A young industry, public relations still lags behind the other media enterprises, but there is optimism that it may develop.

Less and less in the 1990s, political boundaries will set the limits of mass media enterprises in Latin America. With growing satellite, facsimile, personal computer, and other communications technology for distribution of television and publishing efforts, *international*, or *transnational*, mass media will be more the rule than the exception as Latin America enters the 21st century. In chapter 6, we observed that Latin America's magazine industry has already developed into a transnational medium.

The old foundations for cultural imperialism remain. The influence of the U.S. mass media worldwide is significant, but Latin Americans seem to feel the influence perhaps a bit more than other parts of the developing world because of their proximity to the United States. However, the scope and breadth of *O Globo* in Brazil is worldwide. Media owners of the print news media and broadcast networks do not feel a kinship with the "Third World." Indeed, our interviews with leading Latin American publishers indicated conservative and sometimes far right views. These industry leaders feel no need for a new world information and communication order. Increasingly, it seems, Latin American news media are successfully penetrating U.S. media markets. As a result of the growing Spanish-speaking market in the United States, it is not only the technologies, but Latin American culture that is penetrating the U.S. market.

Increasingly, we see the potential for a hemispheric media market to tear down political and cultural barriers. The spread of Ted Turner's Cable News Network to a cutting edge worldwide enterprise in just 10 years not only shocked media experts who forecast its doom in 1980, but has amazed governments and consumers alike in its phenomenal spread and influence. The case of CNN demonstrates the influence of television in the Western hemisphere. CNN is now seldom discussed in terms of financial success. When it celebrated its 10th birthday in 1990, numerous media observers talked about CNN in terms of its saturation throughout the world. Its impact during the Persian Gulf crisis in 1990–1991 only underlined its worldwide role.

In chapter 8, we drew on this history of the introduction of television into Latin America during the 1950s to illustrate how a new media technology influenced the region. The new medium had vast social, economic, and political implications. Television posed a number of policy problems for governments. Many were awed by the implications. Many were frightened. Many saw great possibilities. The introduction of new media technologies into the region during the 1990s will also pose a number of problems—as well as promises.

As Latin America enters the 21st century, it faces a host of problems as well as opportunities. The problems posed by the old boot-in-the-groin dictatorships, although serious, were relatively simple compared to the complex problems faced by the region's media today. Few could justify the dictatorships, including the dictators themselves. All the dictators and their supporters could do was rationalize the "necessity" of their harsh methods to deal with the social chaos to achieve stability. The fact that today this rationalization seems lame in Latin America suggests that great progress has been made.

References

BOOKS AND PERIODICALS

Abreu, J. (1986, Winter). La Prensa Asociada: On the move. *AP World*, pp. 12-17.

Aggarwala, N. (1978). News with Third World perspectives: A practical suggestion. In P. C. Horton (Ed.), *The Third World and press freedom* (pp. 197-209). New York: Praeger.

Aggarwala, N. (1979). What is development news? *Journal of Communication, 29*(2), 181-182.

Albritton, R. B., & Manheim, J. B. (1985). Public relations efforts for the Third World. *Journal of Communication, 35*(1), 43-59.

Alisky, M. (1954). Early Mexican broadcasting. *Hispanic American Historical Review, 34*, 513-526.

Alisky, M. A. (1960). Growth of newspapers in Mexico's provinces. *Journalism Quarterly, 37*, 75-82.

Alisky, M. (1976). Government-press relations in Peru. *Journalism Quarterly, 53*, 661-665.

Alisky, M. (1979). Governmental mechanisms of mass media control in Mexico. In J. Herd (Ed.), *Mass media in Cuba and the Caribbean area: The role of television, radio, and the press* (Latin American monograph series, No. 10, pp. 63-77. Mercyhurst College: The Northwestern Pennsylvania Institute for Latin American Studies.

Alisky, M. (1981). *Latin American media: Guidance and censorship*. Ames, IA: The Iowa State University Press.

Alisky, M. (1982a). Government and the news media: Mexico. In D. Nimmo & M. W. Mansfield (Eds.), *Government and the news media: Comparative dimensions* (pp. 219-241). Waco, TX: Baylor University Press.

Alisky, M. (1982b). Mexico. In G. T. Kurian (Ed.), *World press encyclopedia* (pp. 627-639). London: Mansell Publishing.

Alisky, M. (1983). Latin America. In J. C. Merrill (Ed.), *Global journalism* (1st ed., pp. 249-301). New York: Longman.

Alisky, M. A. (1988). Mexico. In P. T. Rosen (Ed.), *International handbook on broadcasting systems* (pp. 215-224). New York: Greenwood Press.

Alisky, M. (1989, August 23). Glasnost has not changed Latin America. *The Times of the Americas*, p. 14.

Altbach, P. G., & Rathgeber, E. (1980). *Publishing in the Third World: Trend report and bibliography*. New York: Praeger.

Alter, J., Contreras, J., & Kreimerman, J. (1986, November 17). Reporters under the gun. *Newsweek*, p. 62.

Altschull, J. H. (1984). *Agents of power: The role of the news media in human affairs.* New York: Longman.

Anderson, M. H. (1981). Emerging patterns of global news cooperation. In J. Richstad & M. H. Anderson (Eds.), *Crisis in international news: Policies and prospects* (pp. 317–343). New York: Columbia University Press.

Antola, L., & Rogers, E. M. (1984). Television flows in Latin America. *Communication Research, 11*, 183–202.

Araujo, A. R. (1990, February). *A differentiation of fictional programming content at Brazil's TV Globo and American network programming.* Paper presented at the Intercultural Communication Conference, Miami, FL.

Asman, D. (1988, October 5). Le Perestroika Mexicana. *Wall Street Journal*, p. A13.

Atwood, R. (1986). Assessing critical mass communication scholarship in the Americas: The relationship of theory and practice. In R. A. Atwood & E. G. McAnany (Eds.), *Communication and Latin American society* (pp. 11–27). Madison: The University of Wisconsin Press.

Aufderheide, P. (1984, May–June). Tuned out in Brazil. *Columbia Journalism Review*, pp. 6–8.

Aydin, N., Terpstra, V., & Yaprak, A. (1984). The American challenge in international advertising. *Journal of Advertising, 13*(4), 49–59.

Bailey, H. M., & Nastir, A. P. (1968). *Latin America: The development of its civilization* (2nd ed.). Englewood Cliffs, NJ: Prentice-Hall.

Bailey, J. J. (1988). *Governing Mexico: The statecraft of crisis management.* New York: St. Martin's Press.

Baker, S. (1988). *The advertiser's manual.* New York: Wiley.

Balmaseda, L. (1989, December 25). "Public enemy" set to return. *The Miami Herald*, pp. 1E, 2E.

Bamrud, J. (1988, October). Free elections, unfree press. *Index on Censorship*, pp. 10–11.

Banks, A. S. (1988). *Political handbook of the world: 1988.* Binghamton, NY: CSA Publications.

Barnes, P. (1964, March). The wire services in Latin America. *Nieman Reports*, pp. 3–9.

Basdeo, S. (1989). Caribbean media and telecommunications in the information age. *Caribbean Affairs, 2*(2), 44–52.

Beale, S. (1986a, October). Off to a shaky start. *Hispanic Business*, pp. 11–12, 54.

Beale, S. (1986b, December). Turmoil and growth: New ownership transforms Spanish-language TV. *Hispanic Business*, pp. 48–52, 89–91.

Beltrán, L. R. (1978). Communication and cultural domination: USA–Latin America case. *Media Asia, 5*(4), 183–192.

Beltrán, L. R. (1988). Foreword. In E. Fox (Ed.), *Media and politics in Latin America: The struggle for democracy* (pp. 1–5). Newbury Park, CA: Sage.

Beltrán, L. R., & Fox, E. (1980). *Comunicacion dominada: Estados Unidos en los medios de America Latina.* Mexico City: Nueva Imagen.

Bibliowiecz, A. (1980, Winter). Be happy because your father isn't your father: An analysis of Colombian telenovelas. *Journal of Popular Culture, 14*, 476–485.

Blaustein, A. P. (1989). *Constitutions of countries of the world.* Dobbs Ferry, NY: Oceana Publications.

Bloomfield, V. (1974). Caribbean acquisitions. *Caribbean Studies, 13*, 86–110.

Blum, E. (1967, May 29). Brazil's Yankee network. *Nation*, pp. 678–681.

Boddewyn, J. J. (1981, Spring). The global spread of advertising regulation. *MSU Business Topic, 24*(2), 5–13.

Boddewyn, J. J. (1984). Developed advertising self-regulation in a developing country: The case of Brazil's CONAIR. *Inter-American Economic Affairs, 38*(3), 75–93.

Boddewyn, J. J. (1988). *Advertising self-regulation and outside participation: A multinational comparison.* New York: Quorum Books.

Boddewyn, J. J. (1989). Advertising self-regulation: True purpose and limits. *Journal of Advertising, 18*(2), 19–27.

Boddewyn, J. J., & Merton, K. (1978). *Comparison advertising: A worldwide survey.* New York: Hastings House.

Bogart, L. (1990, April). Latin American press sets sail. *presstime*, 8–11.

Bohning, D. (1990, June 22). Free-wheeling tabloid is making Friday a fun day. *The Miami Herald*, p. 11A.

Bollinger, W. (1990, January). Pollsters invade Nicaragua. *Interamerican Public Opinion Report, 1*, 4.

Booth, A. L. (1986, February). Going global. *Public Relations Journal, 42*, 22–27.

Boyd, D. A., Straubhaar, J. D., & Lent, J. A. (1989). *Videocassette recorders in the Third World*. New York: Longman.

Boyd-Barrett, O. (1980). *The international news agencies*. Beverly Hills: Sage.

Boyle, K. (1988). *Article 19: Information, freedom and censorship world report 1988*. New York: New York Times Books.

Bradley, E. (1988). *From lapdog to watchdog: Editorials in Buenos Aires's La Prensa during dictatorship and democracy, 1977–84*. Unpublished master's thesis, University of North Carolina at Chapel Hill, NC.

Brotherson, F., Jr. (1989). The foreign policy of Guyana, 1970–1985: Forbes Burnham's search for legitimacy. *Journal of Interamerican Studies and World Affairs, 31*, 9–35.

Brown, A. (1976). The mass media of communications and socialist change in the Caribbean: A case study. *Caribbean Quarterly, 22*(4), 43–49.

Brown, R. U. (1962, November 3). IAPA attacks Communists infiltration of press. *Editor & Publisher*, pp. 62–63.

Brown, R. U. (1974, April 13). Freedom under assault. *Editor & Publisher*, p. 56.

Brownlee, B. (1984). The Nicaraguan press: Revolutionary, developmental, or socially responsible? *Gazette, 33*, 155–172.

Bryan, A. T. (1989). A tropical perestroika? Cuba, the Soviet Union and the Caribbean. *Caribbean Affairs, 2*(2), 92–103.

Buckman, R. T. (1990a). *Conflict between young democracy and press freedom in the Third World: A case study of Guatemala*. Paper presented to the Intercultural Conference, Miami, FL.

Buckman, R. T. (1990b). Cultural agenda of Latin American newspapers and magazines: Is U.S. domination a myth? *Latin American Research Review, 25*(2), 134–155.

Buckman, R. T. (1990c). Free at last. *The Quill*, 24–27.

Burns, E. B. (1986). *Latin America: A concise interpretive history* (4th ed.). Englewood Cliffs, NJ: Prentice-Hall.

Bussey, J. (1989, September 21). Mexico's leftists are losing their "reverence" for Castro. *The Miami Herald*, p. 16A.

Cambridge, V. C., & Hazzard, M. L. (1988, February). *Resistance and counter resistance: The Guyanese audience's reaction to the government of Guyana's official policy of resistance to mediated cultural aggression, imperialism and homogenization, 1964–1985*. Paper presented to the Intercultural Conference on Latin America and the Caribbean, Miami, FL.

Camp, R. A. (1985). *Intellectuals and the state in twentieth-century Mexico*. Austin: University of Texas Press.

Camp, R. A. (1989). *Entrepreneurs and politics in twentieth-century Mexico*. New York: Oxford University Press.

Campbell, M. V. (1962). The Chilean press: 1823–1842. *Journal of Inter American Studies, 4*, 545–555.

Cano, L. G. (1989, November 1). Colombian editors speak out: mafia imposed censorship. *Times of the Americas*, 18.

Capriles, O. (1976). *El estado y los medios comunicacion en Venezuela* [The state and the communication media]. Caracas: Foto-Impre.

Cardenas, H. J. (1980, April-May). The experience of *El Comercio* in Lima. *IDOC Bulletin*, pp. 11–16.

Carty, J. W., Jr. (1976). Cuban communicators. *Caribbean Quarterly, 22*(4), 59–67.

Carty, J. W., Jr. (1981). Prensa Latina and Noticias Alidas: Different models. *Media Development, 28*(1), 25–27.

Carty, J. W., Jr. (1989, October 19). Cuban daily improves, but circulation falling. *The Times of the Americas*, p. 14.

Chaffee, S. H., Gomez-Palacio, C., & Rogers, E. M. (1990). *Mass communication research in Latin America: Views from here and there.* Paper presented to the International Communication Association, Dublin, Ireland.

Chandisingh, R. (1983). The state, the economy, and type of rule in Guyana: An assessment of Guyana's "socialist revolution". *Latin American Perspectives, 10*, 59–74.

Chaudhary, A. (1974). Comparative news judgments of Indian and American journalists. *Gazette, 20*(4), 233–247.

Christian, S. (1985). *Nicaragua: Revolution in the family.* New York: Random House.

Cifrino, D. A. (1989). Press freedom in Latin America and the emerging international right to communicate. *Boston College Third World Law Review, 9*, 117–142.

Cole, R. R. (1975). The Mexican press system: Aspects of growth, control and ownership. *Gazette, 21*, 65–81.

Collett, M. (1988, November/December). The voice of the Shining Path. *Columbia Journalism Review*, pp. 16–18.

Cooper, D. R. (1987). *Basic training for Third World journalists.* Unpublished doctoral dissertation, The University of Tennessee, Knoxville, TN.

Cordosa, F. H., & Falleto, E. (1979). *Dependency and development in Latin America.* Berkeley: University of California Press.

Coto, J. C. (1989a, April 2). Spanish TV upgrading its image. *The Miami Herald*, p. 1K.

Coto, J. C. (1989b, July 9). Spanish news gives CNN ratings lesson. *The Miami Herald*, p. 1K.

Coto, J. C. (1990, June 22). New battle for Hispanic viewers. *The Miami Herald*, pp. 1C, 2C.

Cuthbert, M. (1976). Some observations on the role of mass media in the recent socio-political development of Jamaica. *Caribbean Quarterly, 22*(4), 50–58.

Cuthbert, M. (1979). *The Caribbean News Agency: Genesis of an indigenous news agency in a developing nation.* Unpublished doctoral dissertation, Syracuse University, Syracuse, NY.

Cuthbert, M. (1980). Reaction to international news agencies: 1930s and 1970s compared. *Gazette, 26*, 99–110.

Cuthbert, M. (1981a). The Caribbean News Agency: Third World model. Lexington, KY: *Journalism Monographs*, No. 71.

Cuthbert, M. (1981b). The first five years of the Caribbean News Agency. *Gazette, 28*, 3–15.

Cuthbert, M. (1985). *Evolution of communication training in the Caribbean.* New York: UNESCO report.

Cuthbert, M., & Sparkes, V. (1978). Coverage of Jamaica in the U.S. and Canadian press in 1976. *Social and Economic Studies, 27*, 204–216.

Cutlip, S. M. (1987, Spring). Pioneering public relations for foreign governments. *Public Relations Review, 13*(1), 13–34.

D'Alimonte, C. (1989, October 4). Mexico: Is Salinas moving too fast in privatizing state industries? *The Times of the Americas*, p. 13.

Dassin, J. R. (1982). Press censorship and the military state in Brazil. In J. L. Curry & J. A. Dassin (Eds.), *Press control around the world* (pp. 149–186). New York: Praeger.

Dassin, J. R. (1984). The Brazilian press and the politics of abertura. *Journal of Interamerican Studies and World Affairs, 26*(3), 385–414.

Day, J. L. (1966). How CIESPAL seeks to improve Latin American journalism. *Journalism Quarterly, 43*, 525–531.

Day, J. L. (1968). The Latin American journalist: A tentative profile. *Journalism Quarterly, 45*, 509–515.

de Andrade, P. P. (1987, August). Market research in Brazil. *European Research, 15*, 188–196.

de Cardona, E. (1974). Multinational television. *Journal of Communication, 25*(2), 122–127.

Deihl, E. R. (1977). South of the border: The NBC and CBS radio networks and the Latin American venture, 1930–1942. *Communication Quarterly, 25*(4), 2–12.

Demac, D. A., & Morrison, R. J. (1989, March). US–Caribbean telecommunications. *Telecommunications Policy, 13*(1), 51–58.

de Melo, J. M. (1988). Communication theory and research in Latin America: A preliminary balance of the past twenty-five years. *Media, Culture and Society, 10*, 405–418.

de Noriega, L. A., & Leach, L. (1982). *Broadcasting in Mexico.* London: Routledge & Kegan Paul.

de Onis, J. (1976, April 4). Argentine junta makes basic changes. *The New York Times*, p. 10.

Deutsch, E. P. (1957, July). "Desacato": Old Spanish penal law flaunts press freedom in Latin America. *Nieman Reports*, pp. 7–9.

Diaz-Rangel, E. (1967). *Pueblos subinformados: las agencias de noticias y America Latina* [Underinformed people: The news agencies and Latin America]. Caracas: Universidad de Venezuela.

Dizard, W. P. (1966). *Television: A world view.* Syracuse, NY: Syracuse University Press.

Duailibi, R. (1988, May-June). The Brazilian experience. *International Advertiser*, p. 26.

Due, T. (1988, September 29). Hispanic magazines growing. *The Miami Herald* (Neighbors Northwest Ed.), pp. 15–16.

Dunn, H. (1988, May). Broadcasting in the Caribbean. *InterMedia, 16*(3), 39–41.

Dyer, R. (1988, September-October). Costa Rica's colegio at work. *IAPA News*, p. 6.

Dyer, R. (1989a, April). Licensing: Flagrant violation of press freedom. *IAPA News*, p. 22.

Dyer, R. (1989b, September). Colegiatura obligatoria y derechos humanos [Obligatory journalism colleges and human rights]. *Cumbre, 9*, 30–33.

Dyer, R. (1989c, October). Vargas handed 7-month sentence. *IAPA News*, p. 3.

Erickson, K. P. (1977). *The Brazilian corporative state and working-class politics.* Berkeley: University of California Press.

Esteinou Madrid, J. (1988, October). The Morelos satellite system and its impact on Mexican society. *Media, Culture and Society, 10*(4), 419–446.

Eulau, H. H. F. (1942). Six great newspapers of South America. *Journalism Quarterly, 19*, 287–293.

Fagen, P. (1974, Winter). The media in Allende's Chile. *Journal of Communication, 24*(1), 59–70.

Faherty, R. (1965, August). Le journalisme n'est plus un sport d'amaterus mais une profession [Journalism is not any longer a sport of amateurs, but a profession]. *Informations UNESCO*, 463–464.

Fair, J. E. (1989). 29 years of theory and research on media and development: The dominant paradigm impact. *Gazette, 44*, 129–150.

Faraone, R., & Fox, E. (1988). Communication and politics in Uruguay. In E. Fox (Ed.), *Media and politics in Latin America: The struggle for democracy* (pp. 148–156). Newbury Park, CA: Sage.

Fejes, F. (1979). Public policy in the Venezuelan broadcasting industry. *Inter American Economic Affairs, 32*, 3–32.

Fejes, F. (1980). The growth of multinational advertising agencies in Latin America. *Journal of Communication, 30*(4), 36–49.

Fejes, F. (1983, November). The U.S. in Third World communications: Latin America, 1900–1945. *Journalism Monographs*, No. 86.

Fejes, F. (1986). *Imperialism, media, and the good neighbor: New Deal foreign policy and United States shortwave broadcasting to Latin America.* Norwood, NJ: Ablex.

Fenby, J. (1986). *The international news services: A twentieth century fund report.* New York: Schocken Books.

Fernandez, G. (1978). ACAN: A solution to the problem of news flow in the Third World. In P. C. Horton (Ed.), *The Third World and press freedom* (pp. 151–155). New York: Praeger.

Fernandez, J. (1966). Problems related to the training of journalists in Latin America. *Gazette, 12*, 45–51.

Ferreira, L., & Straubhaar, J. (1988). Radio and new Colombia. *Journal of Popular Culture, 22*, 131–144.

Flora, C. B. (1980). Fotonovelas: Message creation and reception. *Journal of Popular Culture, 14*, 524–534.

Fonseca, J. M. (1977). *Communication policies in Costa Rica.* Paris: UNESCO.

Foster, D. W. (1980, Winter). Mafalda: An Argentine comic strip. *Journal of Popular Culture, 14*, 497–508.

Fox, E. (1984). Mass communications in the Falklands/Malvinas war. *Media, Culture & Society, 6*, 45–51.

Fox, E. (1988a). Media policies in Latin America: An overview. In E. Fox (Ed.), *Media and politics in Latin America: The struggle for democracy* (pp. 6–35). Newbury Park, CA: Sage.

Fox, E. (Ed.). (1988b). *Media and politics in Latin America: The struggle for democracy.* Newbury Park, CA: Sage.

Fox, E. (1988c). Nationalism, censorship and transnational control. In E. Fox (Ed.), *Media and politics in Latin America: The struggle for democracy* (pp. 36–44). Newbury Park, CA: Sage.

Frank, A. G. (1979). *Latin America: Underdevelopment or revolution*. New York: Monthly Review Press.

Fraze, B. (1988, March 19). Guyana Catholic paper ordered to pay damages in libel suit. *Editor & Publisher*, pp. 22, 45.

Friedman, C. (1959, May 10). Unrest in Cuban TV studios. *The New York Times*, Sec. II, p. 10.

Furtado, R. (1989). Brazil's digital evolution of telecoms. *InterMedia, 17*(1), 30–34.

García Marquez, G. (1982). *One hundred years of solitude*. Madrid: Espasa-Calpe.

García Marquez, G. (1987). *Love in the times of cholera*. Madrid: Mondadori.

Gardner, M. A. (1963). The press of the Honduras: A portrait of five dailies. *Journalism Quarterly, 40*, 75–82.

Gardner, M. A. (1965). The Inter American Press Association: A brief history. *Journalism Quarterly, 42*(4), 75–82.

Gardner, M. A. (1980). Latin American journalism has great political heritage. *Community College Journalist*, pp. 11–13.

Gardner, M. A. (1985). Colegiacion: Another way to control the press? In W. C. Sodurlund & S. H. Surlin (Eds.), *Media in Latin America and the Caribbean: Domestic and international perspectives* (pp. 76–94). Ontario, Canada: Ontario Cooperative Program in Latin America and Caribbean Studies.

Garneau, G. (1988a, November 26). UPI has a strong Latin clientele. *Editor & Publisher*, p. 11.

Garneau, G. (1988b, November 26). UPI in Latin America. *Editor & Publisher*, pp. 9–10, 31.

Garrison, B. (1984, October). Estudio muestra nivel de modernizacion tecnica de los periodicos del continente [Technological adaptation and modernization in major Latin American newspapers]. *Centro Tecnico de la SIP: El Boletin* (217), 1–8.

Garrison, B. (1989). *Professional feature writing*. Hillsdale, NJ: Lawrence Erlbaum Associates.

Garrison, B., & Muñoz, J. E. (1986, Summer). Commentary: The free and not-so-free press of Latin America and the Caribbean (Report No. 3). *Newspaper Research Journal, 7*(4), 63–69.

Garrison, B., & Salwen, M. B. (1989). Newspaper sports journalists: A profile of the "profession." *Journal of Sport and Social Issues, 13*(2), 57–68.

Gerard, J. E. (1931). Aspects of journalism in South America. *Journalism Quarterly, 8*, 213–223.

Ghorpade, S. (1984). Foreign correspondents and the new world information order. *Gazette, 33*, 203–208.

Giffard, C. A. (1984). Inter Press Service: News from the Third World. *Journal of Communication, 34*(4), 41–59.

Giffard, C. A. (1985). The Inter Press Service: New information for a new order. *Journalism Quarterly, 62*(1), 17–23, 44.

Gilbert, D. (1979). Society, politics, and press: An interpretation of the Peruvian press reform of 1974. *Journal of Interamerican Studies and World Affairs, 21*(3), 369–393.

Gill, K., & Smith, D. L. (1989). *Gale international directory of publications*. Detroit: Gale Research Inc.

Glass, P. (1988, April 20). Haiti gets over 300,000 books. *The Times of the Americas*, p. 4.

Golden, T. (1989a, May 11). Argentine economy caves in as presidential vote nears. *The Miami Herald*, p. 11A.

Golden, T. (1989b, July 8). Alfonsin leaves office today with badly tarnished image. *The Miami Herald*, p. 1A.

Goldman, F. (1988, August). Sad tales of La Libertad De Prensa: Reading the newspapers of Central America. *Harper's Magazine*, pp. 56–62.

Gonzalez, H. (1978). The Latin American press and UNESCO maneuvers. *Inter-American Economic Affairs, 32*, 77–94.

Gonzalez-Manet, E. (1988). *The hidden war of information*. Norwood, NJ: Ablex.

Graff, R. D. (1983). *Communications for national development: Lessons from experience*. Cambridge, MA: Oelgeschlager, Gunn & Hain.

Graham, W. G. (1979, July 16). The piracy picture worldwide. *Publishers Weekly*, pp. 33-34.

Greenwood, E. (1957). Attributes of a profession. *Social Work, 2*(3), 45-55.

Guimaraes, C., & Amaral, R. (1988). Brazilian television: A rapid conversion to the new order. In E. Fox (Ed.), *Media and politics in Latin America: The struggle for democracy* (pp. 125-137). Newbury Park, CA: Sage.

Gupte, P. (1988, November 28). The marketing of a despot. *Forbes*, pp. 242, 244.

Habermann, P. (1985). Development in the Caribbean and media coverage of Grenada: A theoretic view. In W. C. Sodurlund & S. H. Surlin (Eds.), *Media in Latin America and the Caribbean* (pp. 208-229). Windsor, Ontario: Ontario Cooperative Program in Latin American and Caribbean Studies, University of Windsor.

Hachten, W. A. (1981). *The world news prism: Changing media, clashing ideology*. Ames, IA: The Iowa State University Press.

Hagstrom, J. (1990, March). How does one define Latin America exactly? *The Bulletin* (ASNE), pp. 4-5.

Hall, P. (1983, January-February). What's all the fuss about Inter Press? *Columbia Journalism Review*, pp. 53-57.

Harley, W. G. (1984). United States concerns with the UNESCO communication programs. In D. R. Shea & W. L. Jarret (Eds.), *Mass communication in the Americas: Focus on the New World Information and Communication order*. Milwaukee: The Center for Latin America, University of Wisconsin.

Harris, N. (1987). *The end of the Third World: Newly industrializing countries and the decline of ideology*. London: Penguin Books.

Harris, P. (1981). News dependence and structural change. In J. Richstad & M. H. Anderson (Eds.), *Crisis in international news: Policies and prospects* (pp. 356-368). New York: Columbia University Press.

Harrison, C. (1989, November 23). Reporter slain seeking his dream. *The Miami Herald*, p. 24A.

Hartlyn, J. (1988). Colombia: The politics of violence and accommodation. In L. Diamond, J. J. Linz, & S. M. Lipset (Eds.), *Democracy in developing countries* (Vol. 4). Boulder, CO: Lynne Rienner.

Hartung, B. W. (1985). *Newspaper publishing in Tijuana: A 50-year historical review*. Paper presented to the International Communication Association, Honolulu, HI.

Harvey, M. F. (1959). The IAPA. *American Editor, 3*(3), 5-15.

Head, S. W. (1963). Can a journalist be a "professional" in a developing country? *Journalism Quarterly, 40*, 594-598.

Head, S. W. (1985). *World broadcasting systems: A comparative analysis*. Belmont, CA: Wadsworth.

Hedman Marrero, H. (1969, January-March). Marti por Espana: incursion bibliografica [Marti in Spain: Bibliographic incursion]. *Vida Universitaria* (Havana), *22* (214), 2-6.

Heine, J. (1989, June). Countdown for Pinochet: A Chilean diary. *Political Science and Politics, 21*(2), 242-247.

Hereter, H. J. (1989, May 2). Hispanic publisher changes hands. *The Miami Herald*, p. 6B.

Hinds, H E., Jr. (1980, Winter). Latin American popular culture: A new research frontier: Achievements, problems and promise. *Journal of Popular Culture, 14*, 405-412.

Hinds, H.E., Jr., & Tatum, C. M. (1984). Images of women in Mexican comic books. *Journal of Popular Culture, 18*, 146-162.

Hispanic magazines growing. (1988, September 29). *The Miami Herald*, pp. 15-16.

Hochberger, S. (1957). IAPA and the search for freedom. *Journalism Quarterly, 34*, 80-85.

Hockstader, L. (1990, January 24). *Haitian leader bans TV, radio newscasts; Prominent businessman is arrested*. Washington Post Foreign News Service, CompuServe.

Hosein, E. N. (1975, April). The implications of expanded government ownership of mass media for freedom of the press in Guyana. *Caribbean Monthly Bulletin, 9*(4), 18-22.

Hosein, E. N. (1976). The problem of imported television in the Commonwealth Caribbean. *Caribbean Quarterly, 22*(4), 7-25.

Hoskins, C., Mirus, R., & Rozeboom, W. (1989). U.S. television programs in the international market: Unfair pricing. *Journal of Communication, 39*, 55-75.

Howell, W. J. (1986). *World broadcasting in the age of the satellite: Comparative systems, policies, and issues in mass telecommunication.* Norwood, NJ: Ablex.

Hurley, N. P. (1974). Chilean television: A case study of political communication. *Journalism Quarterly, 51*, 683-689, 725.

Irish, J. A. G. (1976). The revolutionary focus of Guillen's journalism. *Caribbean Quarterly, 22*, 68-78.

Jackson, S. F. (1989a, October 7). Killing of Mexican journalists. *Editor & Publisher*, pp. 14-15, 33.

Jackson, S. F. (1989b, October 14). Journalism in Mexico. *Editor & Publisher*, p. 14.

Janus, N. (1986). Transnational advertising: Some considerations on the impact of peripheral societies. In R. Atwood & E. G. McAnany (Eds.), *Communication and Latin American society: Trends in critical research, 1960-1985.* Madison: University of Wisconsin Press.

Jeffres, L. W. (1986). *Mass media: Process and effects.* Prospect Heights, IL: Waveland Press.

Jensen, L. R. (1988). Periodicos and political repression: The origins of the Cuban literary tradition. *Heritage, 2*(1), 4-12.

Jimenez, M. J. (1989). Update on press freedom. Argentina: economic earthquake. (Report). *IAPA at FIEJ: Focus on Latin America.* New Orleans.

Jobim, D. (1954). French and U.S. influences upon the Latin American press. *Journalism Quarterly, 31*, 61-67.

Johnson, J. D., Oliveira, O. S., & Barnett, G. A. (1989). Communication factors related to closer international ties: An extension of a model in Belize. *International Journal of Intercultural Relations, 13*, 1-18.

Johnson-Hill, J. (1976). Unheard voices: Jamaica's struggle and the multinational media. *Caribbean Quarterly, 27*(2-3), 1-20.

Jonassaint, J. (1981). Haitian writers in exile: A survey of North America. *Caribbean Quarterly, 27*(2-3), 13-20.

Jones, D. (1989). A panorama of Latin American communication periodicals. *International Communication Bulletin, 24*, 9-12.

Junco de la Vega, A. (1989, April). Publishing in Mexico is a perilous business. *IAPA News*, p. 6.

Katz, I. (1990, June 24). Argentina's first family feud. *The Miami Herald*, pp. 1A, 6A.

Kim, S. J. (1989). *EFE: Spain's news agency.* New York: Greenwood Press.

King, J. (1981). Visnews and UPITN: News film supermarkets in the sky. In J. Richstad & M. H. Anderson (Eds.), *Crisis in international news: Policies and prospects* (pp. 283-298). New York: Columbia University Press.

Knudson, J. W. (1969). The press and the Mexican revolution of 1910. *Journalism Quarterly, 46*, 760-766.

Knudson, J. W. (1978, February). Herbert L. Matthews and the Cuban story. *Journalism Monographs* (No. 54). Lexington, KY: Association for Education in Journalism.

Knudson, J. W. (1979). Licensing newsmen: The Bolivian experience. *Gazette, 25*, 163-175.

Knudson, J. W. (1981). The Chilean press since Allende. *Gazette, 27*, 5-20.

Knudson, J. W. (1987a). Introduction to special issue on the press and broadcasting in Latin America: Pebbles on the Pond. In H. E. Hinds, Jr. & C. M. Tatum (Eds.), *Studies in Latin American and popular culture* (pp. 1-9). Tucson, AZ: Department of Spanish and Portuguese, University of Arizona.

Knudson, J. W. (1987b). Journalism education's roots in Latin America are traced. *Journalism Educator, 41*(4), 22-24, 33.

Knudson, J. (1989, February 22). Self-censorship in the Venezuelan press. *Times of the Americas*, p. 10.

Koch, H. (1970). *The panic broadcast.* Boston: Little, Brown.

Kraiselburd, R. (1978). Establishing and maintaining a free press: A Latin American viewpoint. In P. C. Horton (Ed.), *The Third World and press freedom* (pp. 156-161). New York: Praeger.

Kurian, G. T. (Ed.). (1982). *World press encyclopedia.* London: Mansell Publishing.

Lall, S. (1983). *The new multinationals: The spread of Third world enterprises.* Chichester: Wiley.

Lealand, G. (1984). *American television programmes on British screens.* London: Broadcasting Research Unit.

Lee, J. S. (1990, February). *Transnational advertising and host culture: The Brazilian and Korean experience.* Paper presented to the Intercultural Communication Conference, Miami, FL.

Lemez, A. B. (1974). *La television en America Latina* [Television in Latin America]. Caracas: Universidad Central de Venezuela.

Lent, J. A. (1979). Recent political economic aspects of mass media in Trinidad, Barbados, Jamaica and Guyana. In J. H. Herd (Ed.), *Mass media in/on Cuba and the Caribbean area: The role of television, radio, and the press* (Latin American Monograph Series). Erie, PA: The Northwestern Pennsylvania Institute for Latin American Studies, Mercyhurst College.

Lent, J. A. (1985). Cuban mass media after 25 years of revolution. *Journalism Quarterly, 62*(3), 609–704.

Lent, J. A. (1987). Mass media in the Leeward Islands: Press freedom, media imperialism and popular culture. In H. E. Hinds, Jr. & C. E. Tatum (Eds.), *Studies in Latin American popular culture* (Vol. 6, pp. 245–258). Tucson: University of Arizona, Department of Spanish and Portuguese.

Lent, J. A. (1988). Cuba. In P. T. Rosen (Ed.), *International handbook of broadcasting systems* (pp. 79–89). New York: Greenwood Press.

Lent, J. A. (1989). Communication technology in the Caribbean: The ever-increasing dependency. *Caribbean Affairs, 2*(1), 155–179.

Lindstrom, N. (1980, Winter). Social commentary in Argentine cartooning: From description to questioning. *Journal of Popular Culture, 14*, 509–523.

Link, J. H. (1984). Test of the cultural dependency hypothesis. In R. L. Stevenson & D. L. Shaw (Eds.), *Foreign news and the new world Information Order* (pp. 186–199). Ames, IA: The Iowa State University Press.

Lobsenz, A. (1984). Representing a foreign government. *Public Relations Journal, 40*, 21–22.

Logan, R. A., & Kerns, R. L. (1985). Evolving mass and news media concepts: A Q study of Caribbean communicators. *Mass Comm Review, 12*(1–3), 2–10.

Lottman, H. R. (1990, February 16). Argentina: Climbing back. *Publishers Weekly*, pp. 33–43.

Lowery, S. A., & De Fleur, M. (1988). *Milestones in mass communication research* (2nd ed.). New York: Longman.

Lozano, E., & Rota, J. (1990). *Encounters and dissolutions: A critical reflection on Latin American communication research.* Paper presented to the International Communication Association, Dublin, Ireland.

Lusterman, S. (1985). *Managing international public affairs* (Report No. 861). New York: The Conference Board Inc.

Maeckle, M. (1983, June 15). Costa Rican court sparks debate over free press. *Christian Science Monitor*, p. 5.

Mahan, E. (1985). Mexican broadcasting: Reassessing the industry–state relationship. *Journal of Communication, 35*(1), 60–75.

Mahan, E. (1987). Broadcasting–state relationships in Latin America: Are generalizations valid? In H. E. Hinds, Jr. & C. M. Tatum (Eds.), *Studies in Latin American Popular Culture* (Vol. 6, pp. 135–147). Tucson: University of Arizona, Department of Spanish and Portuguese.

Manheim, J. B., & Albritton, R. B. (1984). Changing national images: International public relations and media agenda setting. *American Political Science Review, 78*, 641–657.

Marash, D. (1989a, July-August). A Chilean Cronkite awaits his country's liberation. *Washington Journalism Review*, pp. 24–26.

Marash, D. (1989b, July-August). Hot in Chile: Investigative reporting. *Washington Journalism Review*, p. 27.

Marash, D. (1990, January-March). Patricio Banados: Un chileno en lista negra espera regresar a la TV [Blacklisted Chilean waits to return to TV]. *Pulso*, pp. 57–59.

Mariaurelia. (1988, August). Publishing for pesos: Miami company forges links with Latin America. *South Florida*, p. 36, 39.

Marquis, C. (1989a, August 27). Violence shocks media into taking brave stance. *The Miami Herald* p. 16A.

Marquis, C. (1989b, August 29). Confiscated riches awe Colombians. *The Miami Herald*, p. 1A.

Marquis, C. (1989c, August 31). Medellin curfew aims to halt attacks. *The Miami Herald*, p. 7A.

Marquis, C. (1990a, March 7). Ortega urges overturning press law. *The Miami Herald*, p. 22A.

Marquis, C. (1990b, April 8). Novelist seeks chance to run chaos that is Peru. *The Miami Herald*, p. 20A.

Marquis, C., & McReynolds, M. (1990, January 31). For Nicaragua voters, there's a poll for every taste. *The Miami Herald*, p. 11A.

Marston, J. E. (1973). Isn't freedom of speech indivisible? *Public Relations Journal, 29*, 20–22.

Massing, M. (1979, November/December). Inside the wires' banana republics. *Columbia Journalism Review*, pp. 45–49.

Mattelart, A. (1976). El control de los medios: Una nueva batalla [Control of the media: A new battle]. *Nueva Politica, 1*(3), 55–62.

Mattos, S. (1982). *The impact of the 1964 revolution on Brazilian television.* San Antonio, TX: V. Klingensmith Independent Publisher.

Mattos, S. (1984). Advertising and government influences: The case of Brazilian television. *Communication Research, 11*, 203–220.

McCann, T. P. (1976). *An American company: The tragedy of United Fruit.* New York: Crown Publishers.

McClintock, C. (1988). Peru: Precarious regimes, authoritarian and democratic. In L. Diamond, J. J. Linz, & S. M. Lipset (Eds.). *Democracy in developing countries: Latin America.* Boulder, CO: Lynne Rienner.

McCullough, E. (1989, June 21). *Argentina—Newspapers.* Associated Press, CompuServe edition.

McGregor, L. (1984). Press freedom: The role of UNESCO. *International Journal of Advertising, 2*, 95–111.

McLeod, J. M., & Rush, R. R. (1969a). Professionalism of Latin American journalists: Part I. *Journalism Quarterly, 46*, 583–590.

McLeod, J. M., & Rush, R. R. (1969b). Professionalization of Latin American journalists: Part II. *Journalism Quarterly, 46*, 784–789.

McLeod, J. M., & Hawley, S. E., Jr. (1964). Professionalization among newsmen. *Journalism Quarterly, 41*, 529–538.

McNelly, J. T. (1966). Mass communication and the climate for modernization in Latin America. *Journal of Inter-American Studies, 8*(3), 345–357.

Menanteau-Horta, D. (1967). Professionalism of journalists in Santiago de Chile. *Journalism Quarterly, 44*, 715–724.

Merrill, J. C. (1968). *The elite press: Great newspapers of the world.* New York: Pitman.

Merrill, J. C. (1981). A growing controversy: The "free flow" of news among nations. In J. Richstad & M. H. Anderson (Eds.), *Crisis in international news* (pp. 151–160). New York: Columbia University Press.

Merrill, J. C. (1987). Governments and press control: Global attitudes on journalistic matters. *Political Communication and Persuasion, 4*, 223–262.

Merrill, J. C., Bryan, C. R., & Alisky, M. (1972). *The foreign press: A survey of the world's journalism.* Baton Rouge: Louisiana State University Press.

Michaels, J. (1987, April 13). Brazilian creative mix avante garde, sentiment. *Advertising Age*, p. 64.

Michaels, J., & Downee, S. (1986, September 8). Latin America feels sting. *Advertising Age*, p. 58.

Mitchell, R. E. (1965). Barriers to survey research in Asia and Latin America. *American Behavioral Science, 9*(3), 6–12.

Moffett, M. (1989, September 1). A challenger takes on the Mexican airwaves. *The Wall Street Journal*, p. A4.

Molina, G. (1987). Mexican television news. *Media, Culture and Society, 9*, 159–187.

Montalbano, W. L. (1987, May 22). New newspaper tests the limits of Chile regime. *The Miami Herald*, p. 21D.

Montgomery, L. F. (1985, Winter). Criticism of government officials in the Mexican press. *Journalism Quarterly, 62*(4), 763–769.

Moody, J. (1989, June 12). Don't call her comrade. *Time*, pp. 62–64.

Moreau, J. (1989, July). Brazil's "citizen Globo." *World Press Review*, p. 56.

Morris, J. A. (1957). *Deadline every minute.* Garden City, NY: Doubleday.

Mowlana, H. (1975, Summer). Who covers America? *Journal of Communication, 25*(3), 86–91.

Muñoz, J. E. (1983). *The new international information and communication order: A descriptive and content analysis with a proposal for its solution.* Unpublished doctoral dissertation, University of Minnesota, Minneapolis, MN.

Murray, W. (1989, July 31). To the left of zero. *The New Yorker*, pp. 57–66.

Neelankavil, J. P., & Stridsberg, A. B. (1980). *Advertising self-regulation: A global perspective.* New York: Hastings House.

Nichols, J. S. (1975). LATIN—Latin American regional news agency. *Gazette, 21*, 170–181.

Nichols, J. S. (1980). The Havana hustle: A new phase in Cuba's international communication activities. Studies in Third World societies, No. 10. In J. A. Lent (Ed.), *Case studies of mass media in the Third World.* Williamsburg, VA: Department of Anthropology, College of William and Mary.

Nichols, J. S. (1982, November). Cuban mass media; Organization, control and functions. *Journalism Monographs* (No. 78). Lexington, KY: Association for Education in Journalism.

Nixon, R. B. (1960). Factors related to freedom in national press systems. *Journalism Quarterly, 37*, 13–28.

Nixon, R. B. (1970). *Education for journalism in Latin America.* New York: Council on Higher Education in the Americas.

Noblet, K. (1989, August 1). Reporter broke taboo on "holy trinity." *The Miami Herald*, p. 2A.

Norton, M. (1989, August 1). Haitian publishers open new chapter. *The Miami Herald*, p. 2A.

Obermayer, H. J. (1989a, September 2). Why Belize's election is "too close to call". *Christian Science Monitor*, p. 8.

Obermayer, H. J. (1989b, November 25). Press independence is illusory in socialist Guyana. *Editor & Publisher*, pp. 25, 44.

O'Brien, R. C. (1980, July). The best news there is. *Journalism Studies Review*, 5, 6–9.

Ogan, C. L., Fair, J. E., & Shah, H. (1984). "A little good news": Development news in Third World newspapers. In R. N. Bostrom (Ed.), *Communication yearbook 8* (pp. 628–644). Beverly Hills: Sage.

Ogan, C., & Rush, R. (1985). Development news in CANA and Interlink. In W. C. Sodurlund & S. H. Surlin (Eds.), *Media in Latin America and the Caribbean: Domestic and international perspectives* (pp. 95–119). Windsor, Ontario: Ontario Cooperative Program in Latin American and Caribbean Studies, University of Windsor.

Ogilvie, J. W. G. (1945). The potentialities of Inter-American radio. *Public Opinion Quarterly, 9*, 19–28.

Oliveira, O. S. (1988a). Brazilian media usage as a test of dependency theory. *Canadian Journal of Communication, 13*, 16–27.

Oliveira, O. S. (1988b). Brazil. In P. T. Rosen (Ed.), *International handbook on broadcasting systems* (pp. 35–46). New York: Greenwood Press.

Oppenheimer, A. (1986, May 19). Mexican tycoon buying UPI is vexed by his critics' "lies." *The Miami Herald*, p. 1A.

Oppenheimer, A. (1989, April 9). Satellite TV dishes out Americana to hemisphere. *The Miami Herald*, p. 1A.

Oppenheimer, A. (1990a, February 4). Hot off the press: Newspapers booming after invasion. *The Miami Herald*, p. 21A.

Oppenheimer, A. (1990b, April 9). Cuba necesita reformas, afirma Garcia Marquez [Cuban reforms necessary, affirms Garcia Marquez]. *El Nuevo Herald*, p. 1.

Ortega, L., & Pierce, R. N. (1984). Venezuela. In G. T. Kurian (Ed.), *World press encyclopedia* (Vol. 2, pp. 1023–1036). New York: Facts on File.

Ostroff, R. (1986, January 25). From teacher to journalist to investment broker. *Editor & Publisher*, pp. 50, 61.

Otis, J. (1990, March 8). *Nicaraguan assembly abolishes media law.* United Press International, Com-puServe edition.

Paraschos, M. (1989). *Constitutional provisions on the press: A world view.* Paper presented to the Associa-tion for Education in Journalism and Mass Communication, Washington, DC.

Picard, R. G. (1988a) *The ravens of Odin: The press in Nordic nations.* Ames, IA: The Iowa State Univer-sity Press.

Picard, R. G. (1988b). State intervention in Latin American newspaper economics. *World Communi-cation, 17,* 35–47.

Pierce, R. N. (1979). *Keeping the flame: Media and government in Latin America.* New York: Hastings House.

Pierce, R. N. (1988, Summer). Fact or fiction? The developmental journalism of Gabriel Garcia Mar-quez. *Journal of Popular Culture, 22,* 63–71.

Read, W. H. (1976). *America's mass media merchants.* Baltimore: The Johns Hopkins University Press.

Reding, A. (1986, April). Unhidden agenda. *Channels,* 62–63.

Renaud, J. L. (1985). U.S. government assistance to AP's worldwide expansion. *Journalism Quarterly, 62,* 10–16.

Reyes Matta, F. (1977). La evolucion historica de las agencias transnacionales de noticias hacia la dominacion [The historical evolution of transnational news agencies towards domination]. In F. R. Matta (Ed.), *La informacion y el nuevo orden mundial.* Mexico City: ILET.

Reyes Matta, F. (1978). *El encandilamiento informativo de America Latina. La circulacion de noticias en Ameri-ca Latina.* [The understanding of information of Latin America: The circulation of news in Latin America]. Mexico, Federacion Latinoamericana de Periodistas.

Reyes Matta, F. (1979a). The information bedazzlement of Latin America: A study of world news in the region. *Development Dialogue, 2,* 29–42.

Reyes Matta, F. (1979b). The Latin American concept of news. *Journal of Communication, 29*(2), 164–171.

Reyes Matta, F. (1981). A social view of information. In G. G. Gerbner & M. Siefert (Eds.), *World communications: A handbook* (pp. 63–68). New York: Longman.

Reyes Matta, F. (1986). Alternative communication: Solidarity and development in the face of trans-national expansion. In R. A. Atwood & E. G. McAnany (Eds.), *Communication and Latin American society: Trends in critical research, 1960–1985.* Madison: University of Wisconsin Press.

Richeri, G., & Lasagni, C. (1987, May). Precocious broadcasting. *InterMedia, 15*(3), 22–33.

Robinson, L. (1989, October 3). *JAMPRESS: Serving a national need.* JAMPRESS News Feature, LTD. Kingston, Jamaica.

Rocha, J. (1988, October). Mino Carta: Sceptical crusader. *Index on Censorship,* pp. 15–17.

Rodriguez, E. J. (1985). An overview of Caribbean literary magazines: Their liberating function. *Caribbean Quarterly 31*(1), 83–92.

Rodriguez, J. V. R. (1989). The ethics of journalism in Peru. In T. W. Cooper (Ed.), *Communication ethics and global change* (pp. 219–224). New York: Longman.

Rogers, E. M. (1976). Communication and development: The passing of the dominant paradigm. *Communication Research, 3,* 213–240.

Rogers, E. M. (1980). The rise and fall of the dominant paradigm. In G. C. Wilhoit & H. de Bock (Eds.), *Mass communication review yearbook 1* (pp. 679–684). Beverly Hills: Sage.

Rohter, L. (1989a, June 15). Mexico arrests investigator in political journalist's murder. *The New York Times,* pp. A1, A13.

Rohter, L. (1989b, December 10). Mexico's newspapers resist offer of greater freedom. *The Miami Herald,* p. 35A.

Roncagliolo, R. (1986). New information order in Latin America: A taxonomy for national policies. In J. Becker, G. Hedebro & L. Paldan (Eds.), *Communication and cultural domination: Essays to honor Herbert I. Schiller* (pp. 168–176). Norwood, NJ: Ablex.

Ronfeldt, D., & Tuohy, W. S. (1969, June). Political control and recruitment of middle-level elites in Mexico: An example of agrarian politics. *Western Political Quarterly, 22*(2), 365–374.

Rosenblum, M. (1978). The Western wire services and the Third World. In P. C. Horton (Ed.), *The Third World and press freedom* (pp. 104-126). New York: Praeger.

Rota, J. (1985). *Training for communication in Latin America: Present state and future needs.* Paper presented to the International Communication Association, Honolulu, HI.

Rowe, S. (1989, July 26). Hispanic broadcaster files suit against satellite firm. *The Miami Herald,* p. 6B.

Ruofolo, A. C. (1987). Professional orientation among journalists in three Latin American nations. *Gazette, 40*(2), 131-142.

Ruth, M. (1985, August). A subtle method of censorship. *presstime,* pp. 12-13.

Salinas Bascar, R. (1986). Latin American communication policies: New battles around the world. In J. Becker, G. Hedebro, & L. Paldan (Eds.), *Communication and domination: Essays to honor Herbert I. Schiller* (pp. 207-214). Norwood, NJ: Ablex.

Salinas Quiroga, G. (1965, October 17). Influencia social de la radio y television. *Vida Universitaria* (Monterrey, Mexico), *25*(760), 3.

Salwen, M. B. (1990). *Political commentary in Cuban broadcasting, 1959-1960.* Paper presented to the Association for Education in Journalism and Mass Communication, Minneapolis, MN.

Salwen, M. B., & Garrison, B. (1989). Press freedom and development: U.S. and Latin American views. *Journalism Quarterly, 66,* 87-92, 168.

Salwen, M. B., Garrison, B., & Buckman, R. T. (1991). Latin America. In J. C. Merrill (Ed.), *Global journalism: A survey of the world's mass media* (2nd ed., pp. 267-310). New York: Longman.

Samper, D. (1982, Spring). The Latin American press in recent times. *Nieman Reports,* pp. 8-9.

Santa Cruz, A. (1988). Media images of Latin American women. *Media Information Australia, 47,* 50-55.

Schement, J. R., Gonzalez, I. N., Lum, P., & Valencia, R. (1984). The international flow of television programs. *Communication Research, 11,* 163-182.

Schiller, D. (1979). An historical approach to objectivity and professionalism in American news reporting. *Journal of Communication, 29,* 46-57.

Schiller, H. I., & Smythe, D. (1972, March). Chile: An end to cultural colonialism. *Society,* 35-61.

Schroeder, R. C. (1989, November 1). Privatization trend spreads in Latin America. *The Times of the Americas,* pp. 14-15.

Schudson, M. (1967). *Discovering the news.* New York: Basic Books.

Sciolino, E. (1989, January 17). Latin debt seen as threat to continent's new democracies. *The New York Times,* p. A3.

Segal, A. (1989, October 19). Latin America's book industry. *The Times of the Americas,* p. 14.

Servant, J., & Vissuzaine, L. (1985, January-March). Media au Paraguay: Privatisation et autocensure [Media of Paraguay: privatization and self-censorship]. *Amerique Latine, 21,* 23-26.

Sevcec, P. (1988b, December 4). Goar Mestre, 'padre de la TV Latinoamerican' [Goar Mestre: 'Father of Latin American TV']. *El Nuevo Herald* (Miami), pp. 1, 6.

Shakespeare, N. (1988). In pursuit of Guzman. *Granta, 23,* 149-195.

Shanks, L. C. (1988, December). Harold Hoyte: He's living on cloud 9 as a prominent Caribbean publisher. *presstime,* p. 36.

Shea, D. R. (1984). Introduction: Concepts and issues. In D. R. Shea & W. L. Jarrett (Eds.), *Mass communication in the Americas: Focus on the New World Information and Communication order.* Milwaukee: Center for Latin America, University of Wisconsin.

Sidel, M. K. (1984). New World Information Order in action in Guyana. *Journalism Quarterly, 61*(3), 493-498, 639.

Sidel, M. K. (1988). *Introduction of television to Guyana.* Paper presented to the Third World Studies Conference, Omaha, NE.

Sidel, M. K. (1989). *The Public Communications Agency as a method of information control: Guyana—A case study.* Paper presented at the International Conference on Professional Responsibilities in the Global Community, Carolina, Puerto Rico.

Skidmore, T. E., & Smith, P. H. (1989). *Modern Latin America* (2nd ed.). New York: Oxford University Press.

Skinner, J. (1987, September). Octopus of the airwaves. *Monthly Review, 39*(4), 44-49.

Smith, A. (1980). *The geopolitics of information: How western culture dominates the world*. New York: Oxford University Press.

Smith, M. (1988, May 23). Peru's Maoist rebels emerge from shadows. *The Times* (London), p. 10.

Sodurlund, W. C., & Schmitt, C. (1986). El Salvador's Civil War as seen in North and South American Press. *Journalism Quarterly, 63*, 268–274.

Steif, W. (1988). The crusade for an independent press in Guyana. *Nieman Reports, 17*(4), 22–24, 50.

Stein, M. L. (1986a, October 4). Many "so-called" democracies also restrict the press. *Editor & Publisher*, pp. 32–42.

Stein, M. L. (1986b, October 25). Press situation in Mexico called "one of the grimmest". *Editor & Publisher*, pp. 30, 54.

Stein, M. L. (1988, October 22). Wire services deny compromise charges. *Editor & Publisher*, pp. 28, 53.

Stern, A. L. (1985, September). The creative wave from Britain. *Dun's Business Month*, pp. 48–51.

Stevenson, R. L. (1984). Pseudo debate. *Journal of Communication, 33*(1), 134–138.

Stevenson, R. L. (1988). *Communication, development, and the Third World*. New York: Longman.

Straubhaar, J. D. (1989). Television and video in the transition from military to civilian rule in Brazil. *Latin American Research Review, 24*(1), 140–154.

Straubhaar, J. D. (1984). Brazilian television: The decline of American influence. *Communication Research, 11*(2), 221–240.

Sussman, L. R. (1990, March 5). It's time to rejoin UNESCO. *The Washington Post National Weekly Review*, p. 29.

Szulc, T. (1986). *Fidel: A critical portrait*. New York: Avon.

Tamayo, J. (1990, July 24). Newly free Nicaragua press is fighting dirty. *The Miami Herald*, p. 3A.

Tatum, C. (1980, Winter). Lagrimas, risas y amor: Mexico's most popular romance comic book. *Journal of Popular Culture, 14*, 413–423.

Tedlow, R. S., & Quelch, J. A. (1981, June). Communications for the nation-state. *Public Relations Journal, 37*, 22–25.

Terrell, R. L. (1990). *Revolutionary government control of mass communications and the press: Suriname, 1980–1988*. Paper presented to the Intercultural Communication Conference, Miami, FL.

Thomas, E. K. (1982). Mass media in Guyana: A critical appraisal. *Gazette, 29*, 173–178.

Thomas, E. K. (1987). British influence on radio broadcasting in British Guyana. In H. E. Hinds, Jr. (Ed.), *Studies in Latin American popular culture* (Vol. 6, pp. 343–351). Tucson, AZ: University of Arizona, Department of Spanish and Portuguese.

Treaster, J. B. (1989, February 7). On Castro's ship of state, is the ideology leaking? *The New York Times*, p. 4.

Tunstall, J. (1977). *The media are American*. New York: Columbia University Press.

Underwood, B. (1987). ALASEI: A new dimension in communications pluralism in Latin America. In H. E. Hinds, Jr. & C. E. Tatum (Eds.), *Studies in Latin American popular culture* (Vol. 6, pp. 289–300). Tucson: University of Arizona, Department of Spanish and Portuguese.

Valverde, J. L. (1989, July). Licensing and the IAPA. *IAPA News*, p. 8.

Vargas, A. (1976, September-October). The coup at Excelsior. *Columbia Journalism Review*, pp. 45–48.

Velez, O. (Ed.). (1990). *Editor & Publisher International Year Book*. New York: Editor & Publisher.

Volsky, G. (1989, February 11). Stations targeting Hispanic viewers. *The Miami Herald*, p. 7B.

Wagner, E. A. (1987, October). Cuban sports magazines. *Sociology and Social Research, 72*, 25–29.

Walsh, M. W. (1987, February 18). Amid dark-haired Mexicans, blonds really have more fun. *Wall Street Journal*, p. 30.

Weinstein, J. S. (1985). International satellite piracy: The unauthorized interception and retransmission of United States program-carrying satellite signals in the Caribbean, and legal protection for United States program owners. *Georgia Journal of International and Comparative Law, 15*, 1–28.

Wells, A. (1972). *Picture-tube imperialism? The impact of U.S. television on Latin America*. Maryknoll, NY: Orbis Books.

Wert, M. C., & Stevenson, R. L. (1988). Global television flow to Latin American countries. *Journalism Quarterly, 65*, 182–185.

Weschler, R. (1990, March-April). The media's one and only freedom story. *Columbia Journalism Review*, pp. 25–31.

White, D. (1976). Legal constraints and the role of the mass media in a Caribbean transition. *Caribbean Quarterly, 22*(4), 36–42.

White, D. (1977). *The press and the law in the Caribbean.* Barbados: Cedar Press.

White, D. M. (1969, Summer). Television in Argentina: An interview with Goar Mestre. *Television Quarterly, 8*(3), 23–34.

Whitefield, M. (1986a, September 10). Chilean editor slain, 60 detained under siege. *The Miami Herald*, p. 1A.

Whitefield, M. (1986b, September 11). Chileans bury editor, seek justice. *The Miami Herald*, p. 1A.

Whitefield, M. (1988, April 18). In marketing, Colombia is ahead of the herd. *Miami Herald*, p. A3.

Whitefield, M. (1989, December 17). Cubans watch reform in E. Europe, don't act. *The Miami Herald*, p. 31A.

Whitefield, M. (1990a, January 27). Cuba starts airing world news show produced by CNN. *The Miami Herald*, p. 8D.

Whitefield, M. (1990b, March 8). Arrecia critica de prensa sovietica a Cuba [Criticism by Soviet press of Cuba increases]. *El Nuevo Herald* (Miami), p. 1.

Wiarda, H. J. (Winter 1988–1989). Mexico: The unraveling of a corporatist regime? *Journal of Inter-American and World Affairs, 30*, 1–28.

Wiarda, H. J. (1980). The struggle for democracy and human rights in Latin America: Toward a conceptualization. In H. J. Wiarda (Ed.), *The continuing struggle for democracy in Latin America.* Boulder, CO: Westview.

Wilkie, J. W., & Ochoa, E. (Eds.). (1989). *Statistical abstract of Latin America* (Vol. 27). Los Angeles: UCLA Latin American Center Publications.

Wilkinson, K. T. (1990). *A forgotten factor in the sale of Spanish International Communications Corporation to Hallmark cards: The influence of Mexico's economy and politics.* Paper presented at the Intercultural Communication Conference, Miami, FL.

Williamson, W. (1989). *Board of directors directory 1989–90.* Miami: Inter American Press Association.

Windhausen, R. (1982). Argentina. In G. T. Kurian (Ed.), *World Press Encyclopedia* (Vol. 1, pp. 88–106). London: Mansell.

Work, C. B., & Bussey, J. (1989, October 16). Bienvenidos to a fire sale. *U.S. News & World Report*, pp. 96, 100.

Youm, Kyu H. (1989). *IACHR's ruling on licensing of journalists: Its impact on Latin America and the Caribbean.* Paper presented to the Intercultural Communication Conference on Latin America and the Caribbean, Miami, FL.

Youm, K. H. (in press-a). Fair report privilege as a libel defense: Status for foreign government statements. *University of Florida Journal of Law and Public Policy.*

Youm, K. H. (in press-b). Licensing of journalists under international law. *Gazette.*

ANONYMOUS SOURCES

Anon. (n.d.a). *Foundation, history, principles* (concise information). Montevideo, Uruguay: International Association of Broadcasting, Mimeo.

Anon. (n.d.b). *Telem: La agencia Argentina de noticias* [Telem: The news agency of Argentina]. Buenos Aires: Telem.

Anon. (1944, November 27). Those men from Mars. *Newsweek*, p. 89.

Anon. (1960, April 11). Poor man's conservative. *Time*, p. 42.

Anon. (1963). *Statistics on radio and television, 1950–1960.* Paris: UNESCO.

Anon. (1974, December). *Caribbean Contact*, p. 14.

Anon. (1975, February 20). U.S. still influences Cuban culture. *Christian Science Monitor*, Reuter report, p. 3A.

Anon. (1983, October-November). Pressures on the press. *Caribbean and West Indies Chronicle, 6*, 8.

Anon. (1984). Trends in total advertising expenditure in 29 countries, 1970-1982. A report by the JWT Unilever International Coordination Group for publication by International Journal of Advertising. *International Journal of Advertising, 2*, 63-93.

Anon. (1985a). *Report of the Attorney General to the Congress of the United States on the Foreign Agents Registration Act of 1938, as Amended for the Calendar Year 1983*. Washington, DC: U.S. Government Printing Office.

Anon. (1985b). *The world factbook 1985*. Washington, DC: The Central Intelligence Agency.

Anon. (1985, June). Latin publishers outline woes. *presstime*, pp. 40-41.

Anon. (1986). *Third world guide, 1986-1987*. Rio de Janeiro: Editora Terceiro Mundo.

Anon. (1986, June). Exit polls provide tallies. *Hispanic Business*, p. 12.

Anon. (1986, October). Mexico's first national newspaper. *Graphic Arts Monthly*, p. 156.

Anon. (1987). *World advertising expenditures*. Mamaroneck, NY: Starch INRA Hooper.

Anon. (1988a). *IPS Fact Sheet*. Rome: IPS.

Anon. (1988b). *Willings press guide 1989* (115th Ed.). West Sussex, England: British Media Publications.

Anon. (1988, February). Caracas rally claims press freedom hurt. *IAPA News*, p. 3.

Anon. (1988, March 28). Strong spending: Foreign ad budgets again beat U.S. *Advertising Age*, pp. 33, 57.

Anon. (1988, May 27). In the Americas: Journalist jailed. *The Miami Herald*, p. 8D.

Anon. (1988, June 4). In the Americas: Chile. *The Miami Herald*, p. 7A.

Anon. (1988, August). Mexican publisher espouses link to PC systems. *presstime*, p. 45.

Anon. (1988, December). *IPI Report*, p. 32.

Anon. (1989a). *IPS Fact Sheet*, Mimeo.

Anon. (1989b). *1989 Jamaica all-media survey*. Kingston, Jamaica: Market Research Services, Limited.

Anon. (1989c). *Willings press guide 1989*. (115th ed.). West Sussex, England: British Media Publications.

Anon. (1989, January). Controversy in Guyana. *Caribbean Insight*, p. 2.

Anon. (1989, May 17). FELAP and the new information order. *The Times of the Americas*, p. 12.

Anon. (1989, June). *El Comercio* marks 150th anniversary. *IAPA News*, p. 2.

Anon. (1989, July 24). Top advertising agencies in Latin America in 1988, *Advertising Age*, p. 45.

Anon. (1989, August 9). Two Soviet publications banned in Cuba. *The Times of the Americas*, p. 5.

Anon. (1989, September). *Constitutions of countries of the world*. Dobbs Ferry, NY: Oceana Publications.

Anon. (1989, October 8-12). *Report on Press Freedom in the Americas*. Inter American Press Association. XLV General Assembly, Monterrey, Mexico.

Anon. (1989, October 9). Barbados. Investors to begin weekly newspaper. *The Miami Herald*, p. 9A.

Anon. (1990, January). Freedom of the press. *IAPA News*, pp. 4-5.

Anon. (1990, January 24). Haiti imposes censorship but says vote will occur. *Miami Herald*, p. 8A.

Anon. (1990, February). *Country reports on human rights*. Report submitted to the Committee on Foreign Affairs House of Representatives and the Committee of Foreign Relations Department of State, 101st Congress, second session, Department of State. Washington, DC: U.S. Government Printing Office.

Anon. (1990, February 23).Will pistols at sunrise settle spat in Uruguay? *The Miami Herald*, p. 6A.

Anon. (1990, April 8). Chronicle loses Rashid Osman. *Catholic Standard*, p. 1.

Anon. (1990, May). Country notes (for Reuters in Latin America). Research document produced by Reuters.

Anon. (1990a, June). Embattled daily in drug war halts editorials. *IAPA News*, pp. 1, 5.

Anon. (1990b, June). Venezuelan agency going private? *IAPA News*, p. 7.

PERSONAL CORRESPONDENCE AND INTERVIEWS

Cano, L. A. (1990, January 25). U.S. representative, *El Espectador*, Bogota, Colombia. Personal interview with authors in Miami.

Castany, S. M. (1990, March 21). Editor, *Cosmopolitan en Espanol*. Personal interview with authors in Miami.

Castany, S. M. (1989, December 27). Editor, *Cosmopolitan en Espanol*. Personal interview with authors in Miami.

Clark, S. (1990, January 23). Administrative assistant, Corporate Communications, Associated Press, New York. Personal communication with authors.

Clarke, O. (1990, January 13). Chairman and managing director, *The Daily Gleaner*, Kingston, Jamaica. Personal interview with authors in Miami.

Conte Agüero, L. (1990, March 9). Former Cuban television commentator. Personal interview with authors in Miami.

Cousley, J. (1989, October 20). Executive director of JAMPRESS, Jamaica's national news agency. Personal communication with authors.

Delman, Dorothy L. (1990, June 19). Assistant manager of publicity, Reuters, New York. Personal communication with authors.

Haworth, S. (1990, February 5). Director of public relations at Cable News Network. Telephone interview with authors.

Hossie, L. (1990, February 15). Correspondent, *The Globe and Mail*, Toronto, based in Mexico City. Personal communication with authors.

Jimenez Borbon, M. (1990, February 15). Publisher, *La Nacion*, San Jose, Costa Rica. Personal communication with authors.

Knight-Ridder/Tribune News Graphics Network (1990). Nicaragua's divided Chamorros. Personal communication to authors.

Merrill, J. C. (1989b, December). Professor, Louisiana State University, Baton Rouge. Personal communication with authors.

Mestre, A. (1990, March 12). Former station co-owner of CMQ-TV, Havana, Cuba. Personal interview with authors in Miami.

Mestre, G. (1990, May 10). Former station co-owner of CMQ-TV, Havana, Cuba. Personal interview with authors in Miami.

Muñoz, J. (1989, June 19). Assistant Director, Inter American Press Association. Personal interview with authors in Miami.

Muñoz, J. (1990, January 26). Assistant Director, Inter American Press Association. Personal interview with authors in Miami.

Rivas, M. (1989, December 11). President of the Public Relations Association of Trinidad & Tobago (PRATT). Personal communication with authors.

Solomon, J. (1990, May 14). Committee to Protect Journalists Latin America specialist. Personal communication with authors.

The Miami Herald (1990). Central and South America and the Caribbean elections, 1989–90. Personal communication to authors.

Van Bennekom, P. (1990, January 31). Senior vice president, International Operations, United Press International, Washington. Personal communication with authors.

Index

208